Birth Control Battles

Birth Control Battles

HOW RACE AND CLASS DIVIDED
AMERICAN RELIGION

Melissa J. Wilde

UNIVERSITY OF CALIFORNIA PRESS

University of California Press
Oakland, California

Library of Congress Cataloging-in-Publication Data

Names: Wilde, Melissa J., 1974- author.
Title: Birth control battles : how race and class divided American religion
/ Melissa J. Wilde.
Description: Oakland, California : The University of California Press,
[2020] | Includes bibliographical references and index.
Identifiers: LCCN 2019023215 (print) | LCCN 2019023216 (ebook) |
ISBN 9780520303201 (cloth) | ISBN 9780520303218 (paperback) |
ISBN 9780520972681 (ebook)
Subjects: LCSH: Birth control—Religious aspects—History. | Birth
control—United States—History. | Social classes—United States. |
Eugenics—United States—History. | Race relations—Religious aspects.
Classification: LCC HQ766.5.U5 W534 2020 (print) | LCC HQ766.5.U5
(ebook) | DDC 261.8/36—dc23
LC record available at https://lccn.loc.gov/2019023215
LC ebook record available at https://lccn.loc.gov/2019023216

Manufactured in the United States of America

28 27 26 25 24 23 22 21 20
10 9 8 7 6 5 4 3 2 1

Contents

*Methodological appendix is available on the UC Press website at
www.ucpress.edu/book/9780520303218/birth-control-battles.*

Illustrations and Tables

Acknowledgments

The data-gathering tasks associated with this book were immense. This project would not have come to fruition without the help of more than sixty research assistants who worked for me over the years. As my coauthor for the first half of this research, Sabrina Danielsen deserves thanks and credit for all kinds of tasks organizational and creative. She helped to get this project off the ground, develop the "manuals" and directions for assistants that I used throughout the rest of the project, figured out the complicated denominational histories that we needed to nail down, and worked through the emerging sociological story with me, over and over and over again. It was a pleasure and a privilege to work with her.

At the Graduate Theological Union in Berkeley, California, Fareen Parvez directed Katheryn Castagna, Sharmeen Morrison, and Lauren Springer in their use of the resources at the Flora Lamson Hewlett Library, where I accessed many periodicals that were either not available or noncirculating everywhere else in the United States.

The majority of periodicals were circulating, however, and these generally found their way to me and my research assistants via the Interlibrary Loan Department at the Van Pelt-Dietrich Library at the University of

Pennsylvania. It is possible that the folks at the Interlibrary Loan Department are as happy as I am to have this project come to fruition. I am very grateful for the myriad ways they helped me over the years, with special gratitude to Peter Collins and Lapis.

I also benefited from much research assistance from many students from the University of Pennsylvania, most of whom I recruited after teaching them in my Introduction to Research Methods undergraduate class. At the risk of leaving someone out, my thanks go to Jenna Ackerman, Fjora Arapi, Hadley Assail, Rebecca Batchelder, Iyassu Berhanu, Margaret Borden, Luis Bravo, Rebecca Brown, Nicole Cabanez, Kathyrn Coneybear, Bernadette D'Alonzo, Solomon David, Nora Donovan, Rachel Eisenberg, Shayna Fader, Olivia Graham, Siqing He, Laura Herring, Julia Hintlian, Kajaiyaiu Hopkins, David Jackson, Erica Janko, Yasmeen Kaboud, Doga Kerestecioglu, Sarahjean Kerolle, Julia Kinzey, Janice Kong, Ian Lachow, Jeewoong Lee, David Li, Nicole Malick, Kelsey Matevish, Alexis Mayer, Michael McCarthy, Talia Moss, Samantha Myers-Dineen, Allison Mygas, Charlotte Noren, Andrea Giovanna Pineda, Gillian Reny, Melissa Retkwa, Jasmine Riodin, Sarah Russo, Anna Sabo, Rachel Schonwetter, Samantha Simon, David Sorge, Alex Standen, Alba Tuninetti, Kyra Williams, Sarah Wilson, Kalikolehuaakanealii Zabala-Moore, and Iris Zhang.

Nicole Malik and Kajaiyaiu Hopkins deserve special recognition here. Both worked for me for almost their entire time as undergraduates at Penn, beginning by doing key word searches of periodicals and graduating to many more complex tasks over the years. Thank you both. And, although she began working for me as this book was going to press, I am grateful for Eliza Becker's steadfast and cheerful help throughout the copyediting phase.

I was able to hire many of these assistants because of generous support from the University of Pennsylvania—including a University Research Foundation Grant as well as continued financial support from the Department of Sociology. Later in this research, I was blessed to meet and receive the unwavering support of John DiUlio and the financial and other resources available through Penn's Program for Research on Religion and Urban Civil Society (PRUCCS). It is through PRUCCS that I have gotten to know political scientists with whom I share many intellectual interests and whose colleagueship has enhanced life at Penn—especially John Lapinski and Michele Margolis.

The project was conceived and birthed while I was a member of the Department of Sociology at the University of Pennsylvania. During that time I have benefited from the support or comments of almost all of my colleagues but especially: Chenoa Flippen, Pilar Gonalons-Pons, Annette Lareau, and Emilio Parrado. Special thanks to Camille Charles for her support both big and small and to Amada Amenta for friendship too strong and workouts too numerous to count. Katee Dougherty and Aline Rowens have made so many aspects of my work easier and more enjoyable at Penn that I cannot sufficiently name them all. I have also been fortunate to have graduate students who are wonderful intellectual colleagues. Thanks go to Rachel Ellis, Lindsay Glassman, Peter Harvey, Tessa Huttenlocher, Haley Pilgrim, and Patricia Tevington. I also have great colleagues at Penn outside of sociology who have provided feedback and friendship over the years. Special thanks to John Jackson and Deb Thomas in anthropology and Julie Lynch and Dawne Teele in political science.

I have benefited from presenting this research at Baylor University, Princeton University, the University of California, Berkeley, the University of Chicago, the University of Notre Dame, the University of Wisconsin, and Yale University.

Although their connection to this project is more distant than it was to my other work, I remain grateful for the intellectual generosity of Mike Hout, Ann Swidler, and Kim Voss. Their influence is indelibly etched on my sociological imagination. Thanks also to Mark Chaves, Michele Dillon, Robert Robinson, Chris Smith, and Robert Wuthnow, who have provided encouragement over the years.

Deep thanks, also, to Naomi Schneider for understanding and believing in this book.

Finally, I am beyond fortunate to have the family that I do. Let me begin with my incredible partner in life, Steve Viscelli, who understands the myriad ways that research and writing need to be protected from the chaos and joy of having a family. Thanks to him for helping me to do that for the past two decades, especially the most recent one as our brood has grown. My children, Armando, Stella, and Sonny Viscelli, deserve thanks for the few times they actually listened to me and left me alone to work when I requested it. Despite that, I love all three of you dearly. To my parents, Adele and Paul Wilde, thank you for everything!

Introduction

Why do the politics of sex and gender divide American religion? For many, this question might seem almost rhetorical—how could sex and gender *not* divide progressives and conservatives, religious or not? This book is an attempt to problematize such taken-for-granted assumptions. It does so by examining the moment that American religious groups first diverged over an issue of sex and gender—and by tracing the paths those groups took for the next three decades. Many will likely find the argument put forward in this book surprising, if not shocking. This is because American religious groups first became divided over sex and gender when they began to take sides on the issue of contraception around 1930. While that in and of itself might not be surprising, the key takeaway for this book is: the sides they took had almost nothing to do with gender—at least not in the way we typically think about it—at all (and this book will show that this remained the case well into the 1960s). By this I mean that whether a particular religious group supported legalizing access to contraception circa 1930 had nothing to do with whether they were feminist or concerned about women's rights. Instead, whether a religious group supported legalizing access to contraception depended on whether they were believers in the white supremacist eugenics movement and thus

1

deeply concerned about reducing some (undesirable) people's fertility rates.

This explanation comes from my analysis of one key watershed moment, the factors that led to it, and the consequences of that watershed for American religious groups over the decades that followed. That moment occurred between 1929 and 1931, when nine of America's most prominent religious groups rather suddenly proclaimed that birth control, rather than being a sin, as was commonly understood, was actually a *duty*—for some people. These groups' proclamations were met by consternation by some, support by others, and silence by still others. *Birth Control Battles* explains why these groups took this path of activist liberalization, while most others did not, and traces the implications of that decision until contraceptives gained acceptance among all but the most stalwart of religious groups by the mid-1960s.

The story this book tells is not a pretty one. The early promoters of birth control were concerned about curtailing some people's fertility rates because they deeply believed that *race suicide* was imminent. The *suicide* part of *race suicide* was intentional. The term was promoted by eugenicists— believers in the same pseudoscience that would motivate Hitler during the Holocaust a few years later—who wanted to emphasize that white Anglo-Saxon Protestants were voluntarily allowing themselves to be outbred. In article after article, speech after speech, eugenicists trumpeted calls for desirables to bear more children, printing facts such as these with great alarm:

> The Anglo-Saxon Protestant element, which has all along formed the core of American civilization, is now a diminishing quantity . . . the number of children per marriage in Massachusetts in the years 1870, 1880, 1890, was: native stock—2.2, 2.2, and 2.4 respectively; foreign stock—4.4., 5.0, 4.3 respectively.[1]

By the mid-1920s, *almost half* of America's most prominent religious denominations professed support for such white supremacist principles and a deep concern about race suicide.

Although concern about race suicide was customary among many (indeed, virtually all elite, northeastern white) religious groups—not all of them officially liberalized. In analytical terms a concern about race suicide was necessary but not sufficient to explain who supported legalizing birth control. The religious groups that liberalized on birth control all had one other similarity—they were all believers in the social gospel movement.

The social gospel movement was a major progressive social movement within American religion from the late nineteenth century through the mid-twentieth century. Emerging in the wake of several major labor strikes, a key focus of the movement was on minimizing the negative effects of industrial capitalism. As postmillennialists, social gospelers believed that Christ would not return until society and its institutions had been redeemed.[2] As a result, social gospelers were active social reformers, believing it was their religious duty to combat poverty, inequality, war, and other social ills. Belief in the social gospel movement often coincided with a concern about race suicide. When it did, religious leaders became convinced that legalizing birth control was not only a wise racial move but also a religious duty.

The groups that liberalized early for eugenicist reasons continued to promote contraception well into the 1960s. As they did so, many particularities about their activism, especially whose fertility they specifically focused on reducing, changed. What began as a concern about being outbred by Catholic and Jewish immigrants in the United States shifted over the next few decades to alarm about the fertility rates in the poorest countries of the world and blacks in the inner cities. However, as this happened one thing remained constant—these groups' promotion of birth control was always concerned with other people's fertility rates and never, not even in the mid-1960s, about their own members' right to use it.

In a nutshell, *Birth Control Battles* demonstrates that it is only possible to understand how and why some groups liberalized before others and continued to promote contraception for the next several decades if we acknowledge that religion intersects with inequality in important, complex ways. I call this argument *complex religion*.

COMPLEX RELIGION: RACE, CLASS, RELIGION, AND INTERSECTIONALITY

Scholars of inequality recognize that inequality is complex and constituted via many social structures.[3] The argument and analysis throughout this book are deeply influenced by these theories—which are often referred to as *intersectionality*. However, while these theories have been crucial to the argument developed in this book, it is also true that religion has not typically been a part of the research and writing that constitutes this conversation.[4] Thus, while we have many good studies of religion and race, or religion and immigration or ethnicity, most of these studies are not in dialogue with intersectionality. Furthermore, unlike the study of religion and race or religion and immigration, which has remained strong, the study of religion and class, or religious inequality, had largely fallen out of popularity in the subfield until very recently.[5] This is despite the fact that it also used to be a core part of the sociology of religion, with the class differences between American religious groups considered so germane that many early sociologists took them as a given.[6]

Complex religion argues that religion is part and parcel of racial, ethnic, class, and gender inequality. Its key takeaway is that research that focuses on inequality or religion would be better off taking those intersections into account more explicitly.[7] In many ways, then, complex religion simply brings the field back to where it started—to a place where we acknowledge and try to operationalize, as best we can, the ways in which religion intersects with inequality.

Of course, in doing so, complex religion theory benefits from advances in the study of inequality since the sociology of religion took such intersections for granted, as well as from a myriad of studies of American religion that do not place race and class in a central analytical position.[8] The most important of these influences, perhaps even more than intersectionality, comes from theories of race, especially theories of racialization.[9] My use of the term *race* follows that of racialization theorists who view race "as a concept which signifies and symbolizes social conflicts and interests by referring to different types of human bodies."[10] When I use the term *racialization*, I mean the process of ascribing racial or ethnic identities to a group that did not necessarily have that identity before the process. Racialization theorists acknowledge the important role of religion in racialization processes historically. However, despite this, and as with studies of intersectionality more generally, few analyses of race or racialization processes treat religion as a central analytical category.[11]

Throughout the book I emphasize that religion was a core part of the racialization process that Irish and Italian (Catholic) and Eastern European (Jewish) immigrants went through in the first part of the twentieth century. Even more importantly, religion was a key part of why their greater fertility was seen as problematic and undesirable. This book demonstrates that religion was not just correlated with a "desirable" or "undesirable" status. It was an essential piece of that status. Religion was a critical dimension on which race was "culturally figured and represented, the manner in which race [came] to be meaningful as a descriptor of group or individual identity, social issues, and experience."[12]

At its most basic level, then, complex religion helps us to understand that one cannot explain early birth control reform within the American religious field without understanding how race was seen at the time.[13] And, one cannot understand the racial categories at the time (particularly in the Northeast) without understanding how they were influenced, and even determined, by religion. This is true not only in terms of whose fertility was to be controlled but also in terms of explaining who was attempting to do the controlling.

Theorists who study race describe a racial project as "an effort to reorganize and redistribute resources along particular racial lines."[14] In no uncertain terms, birth control reform became a "racial project," the focus of America's most prominent religious denominations by the late 1920s and one that lasted, as this book will demonstrate, well into the 1960s.

DATA AND METHODS

This book employs research methods that have come to be called *comparative-historical sociology*. In my view these methods entail trying to examine history as systematically as possible—by thinking through issues of generalizability, bias, and comparison—and by identifying and, ideally, falsifying, alternative explanations in the process of making one.[15] It is these methods, and the macrosociological questions they entail, that most clearly differentiate *Birth Control Battles* from other related studies, especially the rich and varied body of research on American religion.[16] This is because these methods, particularly the effort to compare similar groups that varied on different dimensions, led me to see the enduring importance of inequality, especially when associated with race and class, for American religion.

In order to conduct a comparative-historical study of American religious groups' views of contraception, I had to make a number of important decisions. These decisions have implications for the claims I make in this book and, most importantly, of course, for whether the reader will believe those claims. Below I detail what I see as the most important of these.

Timing—1926 as a Baseline

Because this book covers almost fifty years of American history in great depth (1918–65), the denominations that form the basis of this analysis are in some sense a moving target. Early ruptures often resulted in two new denominations (one in the North and one in the South) because of abolition prior to the American Civil War, just as movements for reconciliation often resulted in those groups reuniting and even merging with other like-minded denominations by the mid-1960s. Thus, the point at which I chose and introduce the reader to my sample needs explication.

Table 1 introduces you to the American religious field as it was circa 1926. As the story in *Birth Control Battles* unfolds, these denominations change significantly. Their modern-day names are presented in table 9, in part III of the book.

The year 1926 proved to be the best baseline for this study for three reasons: First, it represents the year of the last census of religious bodies conducted by the US government. This incredible historical resource allows me to examine and present a significant amount of data that would otherwise be unavailable. Second, 1926 was just a few years before the peak of the first wave of birth control reform. Thus, it represents the American religious field as it was on the eve of that first wave. Finally, 1926 was midway between the schisms that rocked American religious groups around the time of the Civil War and the mergers that sought to reconcile those divisions in the later part of the twentieth century. It thus provides a useful starting point to get to know the American religious field, both in terms of what it had been and what it would become.

The Sample

In many ways the comprehensive sample of American religious groups in *Birth Control Battles* is its greatest asset.[17] To answer my questions, I needed a sample that reflected the diversity of American religious groups. But within that diversity, I also needed enough similarities to make comparisons between denominations possible. From Mormons to Methodists, from Southern Baptists to Seventh-day Adventists to the Society of Friends, from Reform Jews to the Reformed Church in America, and to historically black groups like the African Methodist Episcopal Zion Church and every major denomination in between, this book tells a story that only a comprehensive sample capturing the diversity of religion in the United States can. Creating this sample, however, involved a great many decisions—more, perhaps, than any other aspect of the research reported here.

SIZE CONSIDERATIONS

The first decision I made regarding the sampling frame had to do with size. Given the likelihood that many smaller denominations would not have had the resources—for example, a periodical or archive—to leave much of a trace of their views and deliberations, using the 1926 census I decided to include any denomination that had more than four hundred thousand members.[18] The majority of the denominations listed in table 1 ($n = 17$) were included simply because they met this basic threshold.

A few denominations smaller than this threshold in 1926 became much more prominent over the next decades. I did not want my sample to overlook these fast-growing denominations, particularly if their growth was partly demographic and thus connected to less use of contraceptives, as research suggests.[19] I thus also included any denomination that was too small to be included in the 1926 sample but had more than one million members by 2017. There were three of these: the Assemblies of God, the Jehovah's Witnesses, and the Seventh-day Adventists, bringing my initial sample to twenty denominations.

INCLUDING ALL LIBERALIZERS

It turned out that liberalizing early on birth control was actually quite rare, in terms of the overall proportion of denominations in the American religious

Table 1 Sample of Religious Denominations

Denominations	Members in 1926[a]	Periodical	Liberalized on Birth Control
		Early Liberalizers	
Society of Friends (Orthodox)	91,326	Friend; American Friend; Friends Intelligencer	1929[b]
Reform Judaism	—	Yearbook of the Central Conference of American Rabbis; Union Tidings[c]	1929[d]
Universalist Church	54,957	Universalist/Christian Leader	1929[e]
American Unitarian Association[f]	60,152	Christian Register	1930[g]
Methodist Episcopal Church	4,080,777	Christian Advocate	1931[h]
Congregational Churches	881,696	Congregationalist*	1931[i]
Christian Church	112,795	Herald of Gospel Liberty*	1931[j]
Presbyterian Church in the United States of America	1,894,030	New Era and Presbyterian Magazine	1931[k]
Protestant Episcopal Church	1,859,086	Living Church	1934[l]
		Unofficial Supporters	
Evangelical Synod of North America	314,518[m]	Evangelical Herald	1947[n]
Northern Baptist Convention	1,289,966	Baptist	1959[o]
United Presbyterian Church of North America	171,571	United Presbyterian	1959[p]
Norwegian Lutheran Church in America	496,707	Lutheran Church Herald	1966[q]

		Critics	
Presbyterian Church in the United States	451,043	Presbyterian Survey	1960[r]
Southern Baptist Convention	3,524,378	Christian Index	1977[s]
Church of Jesus Christ of Latter-day Saints	542,194	Improvement Era	1998[t]
Lutheran Church–Missouri Synod	1,040,275	Lutheran Witness	1981[u]
Orthodox Judaism	—	Jewish Forum	Never
Roman Catholic Church	18,605,003	America; Commonweal	Never

		Silent	
Reformed Church in the United States	361,286	Reformed Church Messenger	1947[v]
Methodist Episcopal Church, South	2,487,694	Methodist Quarterly Review	1956[w]
Conservative Judaism	—	S.A.J. Review[x]	1960[y]
Reformed Church in America	153,739	Christian Intelligencer[z]	1962[aa]
United Lutheran Church in America	1,214,340	Lutheran	1966[ab]
Disciples of Christ	1,377,595	World Call	1972[ac]
African Methodist Episcopal Zion Church	456,813	A.M.E.Z. Quarterly Review	Silent
Churches of Christ	433,714	Gospel Advocate	Silent
National Baptist Convention, USA, Inc.[ad]	3,196,623	National Baptist Union Review	Silent

* The Congregationalist and Herald of Gospel Liberty after 1930.

a. Data is from and names are based on those in US Bureau of the Census, Census of Religious Bodies, 1926. If the group did not exist in 1926, the name on the table reflects its first known name.

b. Women's Problems Group of the Social Order Committee of the Philadelphia Yearly Meeting, "A Statement on Birth Control," Friends Historical Library of Swarthmore College, Yearly Meeting of the Religious Society of Friends (Orthodox) Archive, Collection on the Social Order Committee: PG1.

c. Reform Jews' official publication, The Yearbook of the Central Conference of American Rabbis, was not popularly oriented. Union Tidings, the "official" periodical of the Union of American Hebrew Congregations,

(note c continued)

was only available until 1930 and focused mainly on the Reform Movement, not national news in general.

d. Israel, "Report of the Commission of Social Justice."

e. Universalist General Convention, 1929.

f. Unitarians in the 1926 census.

g. American Unitarian Association, 1930.

h. Committee on Marriage and the Home of the Federal Council of the Churches of Christ in America, 1934.

i. General Council of the Congregational and Christian Churches, 1931.

j. General Council of the Congregational and Christian Churches, 1931.

k. Presbyterian Church in the United States of America (PCUSA), 1931. The pronouncement was ratified by "the special commission on marriage divorce and remarriage" of the PCUSA, April 27, 1931, but tabled at the General Assembly meeting one month later because of merger talks with the Southern PCUS. "Birth Control Out as Issue of Presbyterians."

l. Episcopal Church, 1935 (liberalized in November 1934, published in 1935).

m. Does not include those under age thirteen.

n. "Christian Social Action: Report of the Committee: Future Program: The Family," 1947.

o. American Baptist Convention, 1959.

p. United Presbyterian Church in the United States of America, 1959.

q. American Lutheran Church, 1966.

r. Presbyterian Church in the United States, 1960.

s. Southern Baptist Convention, 1977.

t. Church of Jesus Christ of Latter-day Saints, "Birth Control."

u. Lutheran Church–Missouri Synod, Commission on Theology and Church Relations, Social Concerns Committee, 1981.

v. "Christian Social Action: Report of the Committee: Future Program: The Family," 1947.

w. Methodist Church, 1956.

x. Unfortunately, the *S.A.J. Review* was not a popularly oriented periodical and folded on May 31, 1929, just as the birth control liberalizations were taking off.

y. Bokser, "Statement on Birth Control."

z. In 1922 the *Christian Intelligencer* merged with the *Mission Field* and became the *Christian Intelligencer and Mission Field.* In 1930 it returned to the *Christian Intelligencer.*

aa. Reformed Church in America, 1962.

ab. American Lutheran Church, 1966.

ac. "Concerning World Population Growth," 167–168.

ad. *Negro Baptists* in the 1926 census

field that did so. It also turned out that quite a few of the early liberalizers, while very prominent, were indeed smaller religious groups. Given that the focus of the study was to explain why certain groups liberalized before others on birth control, I needed to make sure my sample included any religious group that made an early pronouncement in support of it.

Fortunately, denominations' stances on birth control were closely watched by a number of organizations at the time of the first wave. By examining lists from the American Eugenics Society (AES) and the Federal Council of Churches, I was able to determine that there were five of these: Reform Jews, the American Unitarian Association, the Society of Friends, the Universalist Church, and the Christian Church, which merged with the larger Congregationalist Church in 1930, one year before the new denomination made its official pronouncement liberalizing on birth control. With the addition of these five groups, my sample grew to twenty-five religious denominations.

Given the centrality of the eugenics movement to my emerging argument, I also looked for any denomination that was prominent in the AES archives and thus likely a strong eugenicist, but not an early liberalizer, to make sure any additional factors associated with liberalization were not overlooked. Only one denomination fit this category: the Reformed Church in America, which turned out not to be a strong supporter of eugenics. Including the Reformed Church in America brought my sample to twenty-six religious denominations.

Beyond making sure that I included all groups that liberalized early or were connected to the AES in my sample, I wanted to examine many other factors connected to groups' openness to birth control. As my argument emerged and it became clear that various structures of inequality connected to race, ethnicity, class, and geography were crucial to explaining groups' stances, the issue of theology became an ever more important alternative to my more structural explanation. Surely, openness to the issue of birth control might be related to groups' theological views? I needed to be sure that I had enough variation theologically to examine that possibility.

THEOLOGICAL VARIATION AND COMPARABILITY

So that I did not end up with only the early liberalizing denominations among some smaller theological families (thereby, in effect, biasing my sample theologically), I also added any major denomination that was not an early liberalizer but would later merge with one. There were three of these: the Evangelical Synod of North America, the Reformed Church in the United States, and the United Presbyterian Church in North America. Along similar lines, I added any denomination that would provide an important comparison group for an early liberalizer, which Conservative and Orthodox Jews did for the early liberalizing Reform Jews.

After ensuring theological variation and comparability, I was left with a sample of thirty-one religious denominations from 1926, which because of mergers represent twenty-two religious denominations today. These denominations represent more than 90 percent of the Americans who claimed membership in a religious group in 1926.[20]

In the end the theological diversity of my sample proved to be an incredible resource. Having it allowed me to see that groups' theological histories—in the strict sense of whether they were Calvinists, Reformed, other types of Protestants, or even not Christian at all, such as Jews—had almost no relationship to whether they were early liberalizers on, or even critics of, contraception.

Take, for example, the Presbyterian Church in the United States of America and its Southern sister denomination, the Presbyterian Church in the United States (both of which were initially included in the sample simply because each had more than 400,000 members). Their similarities were not in name or history only. They ultimately merged to form the Presbyterian Church in the United States of America in 1983. Despite their theological similarities, however, they were diametrically opposed on the issue of birth control. A similar tale emerged about Methodists, Lutherans, and many other denominations whose theologies were so similar that they would also merge within the next fifty years but ended up with different views on contraception circa 1930.

This is not to say that theology plays no role in the explanation that follows. In many ways the social gospel movement was about theology and whether groups believed their primary duty as Christians was to save society or souls. Given the explanatory weight this factor ended up playing in *Birth Control Battles*, I explore the social gospel movement, and the factors behind groups' embrace or rejection of it, in much greater detail in the next chapter.

The fact that theology, in the strict sense of the word, could not explain groups' early views on birth control allowed me to explore the social factors that differentiated the groups in my sample. It was this exploration that led me to conclude that many of the structures that connect to inequality, especially race, class, and ethnicity, are more crucial to religious change than theology. Demonstrating this systematically proved to be more difficult than I expected—and thus the measures of class, race, and ethnicity that I refer to throughout the book also need more explanation.

Class, Race, and Ethnic Variation among American Religious Denominations

Liston Pope, who wrote one of the first and most thorough sociological studies that presented clear measures of socioeconomic differences between American denominations, summarized the relationship between religion and the class structure in his article with that title in 1948:

> There remains a significant difference between the Catholic constituency and all others except the Baptist, which parallels it almost precisely in stratification. . . . a majority of [Episcopalians] . . . still come from the middle and upper classes, and this is even more largely the case for the Presbyterians and the Congregationalists. . . . Significant differences within Protestantism [exist], ranging from the least-educated Baptists to the most-educated Congregationalists. Measured against the Protestant scale in this respect, the Catholics are above the Baptists and almost on a par with the Lutherans; the Jews are near the top, almost precisely on the same level as the Presbyterians.[21]

Unfortunately, only one concrete measure of class was available from the censuses: ministers' mean salaries from 1916. While certainly not as good as a measure of members' incomes or educational levels, this measure is generally consistent with the picture that Pope painted above and with what is known of denominations' class positions in the earliest American surveys, the first of which was conducted by Gallup in 1939.[22] In general, as indicated in table 2, the Protestant "establishment," Episcopalians, Unitarians, Universalists, Presbyterians, and Congregationalists, were the oldest American denominations and constituted the wealthiest and most educated of Americans. Methodists and Baptists were more solidly middle

Table 2   Demographics of American Religious Denominations circa 1926

Denominations	Date Founded[a]	Mean Ministers' Salary in 1916[b]	Percent Growth 1916–26[c]	Percent Urban[d]	Percent Northeast[e]
Early Liberalizers					
Society of Friends	1900[f]	$681	-1	39	12
Reform Judaism	1873	—	—	—	—
Universalist Church	1866	$1,641	-6	75	68
American Unitarian Association[g]	1825	$2,080	-27	92	69
Methodist Episcopal Church	1844	$1,223	10	54	28
Congregational Churches	1620	$1,343	9[h]	69	47
Christian Church	1792	$776	-5	25	15
Presbyterian Church in the United States of America	1789	$1,474	17[i]	71	40
Protestant Episcopal Church	1789	$1,632	25[j]	83	52
Mean	**1811**	**$1,356**	**3**	**64**	**41**
Unofficial Supporters					
Evangelical Synod of North America	1872	$890	-8	65	10
Northern Baptist Convention	1814[k]	$1,166	8[l]	69	42
United Presbyterian Church of North America	1858	$1,351	7	66	57
Norwegian Lutheran Church in America	1917	$1,081	8[m]	25	2
Mean	**1856**	**$1,122**	**4**	**56**	**28**

	Critics				
Presbyterian Church in the United States	1861	$1,351	26	60	0
Southern Baptist Convention	1845	$1,072	30[n]	28	0
Church of Jesus Christ of Latter-day Saints	1830	—	34	52	1
Lutheran Church–Missouri Synod[o]	1847	$755	68[p]	55	10
Orthodox Judaism	1898	—	—	—	—
Roman Catholic Church	1565	$838	18	80	50
Mean	**1866[q]**	**$1,004**	**35**	**57**	**12**

	Silent Groups				
Reformed Church in the United States	1747	$1,085	2[r]	56	63
Methodist Episcopal Church, South	1844	$1,037	18	36	0
Conservative Judaism	1913	—	—	—	—
Reformed Church in America	1792	$1,368	6	62	68
United Lutheran Church in America	1918	$1,205	18[s]	67	62
Disciples of Christ	1832	$1,251	12	55	4
African Methodist Episcopal Zion Church	1821	$502	78	42	11
Churches of Christ	1906	—	36	24	1
National Baptist Convention, USA, Inc.[t]	1895	$572	7[u]	39	6
Mean	**1856**	**$1,189[v]**	**22**	**48**	**27**

a. Altwood et al. 2005; Melton 2009.

b. Data from US Bureau of the Census, *Census of Religious Bodies*, 1926.

c. Calculated by 1916–1926 membership. US Bureau of the Census, *Census of Religious Bodies*, 1926, 46–51.

d. Percent urban is the percent of all members of a denomination that belong to a congregation located in an incorporated center with at least 2,500 inhabitants in 1920. US Bureau of the Census, *Census of Religious Bodies*, 1926, 15.

e. Maine, New Hampshire, Vermont, Rhode Island, Connecticut, Massachusetts, New York, New Jersey, and Pennsylvania.

f. Friends General Conference.

g. *Unitarians* in the 1926 census.

h. The Evangelical Protestant Church of North America merged with the Congregational Churches in 1925. The year 1916 membership numbers include both denominations so percent growth is not falsely inflated. US Bureau of the Census, *Census of Religious Bodies, 1926*, 49.

i. The Welsh Calvinistic Methodist Church merged with the Presbyterian Church in the United States of America in 1920. US Bureau of the Census, *Census of Religious Bodies, 1926*, 49.

j. We suspect that the Protestant Episcopal Church's growth rate is inflated by two factors: (1) Between 1916 and 1926, the church began counting members under the age of thirteen in its membership statistics. While the 1926 census reportedly adjusts for this change by increasing the 1916 figures by the proportions found to be under the age of thirteen in 1926, it is impossible to ascertain how accurately this was done. US Bureau of the Census, *Census of Religious Bodies, 1926*, 48; (2) The Protestant Episcopal Church benefited more than any other churches, except German denominations (which were also growing at this time), from the Immigrant Restriction Act of 1924. By my estimates, more than 10 percent of the growth reported between 1916 and 1926 (or almost half of the overall growth) was a result of the new quotas.

k. The denomination traces its origins to 1814 but split into separate Northern and Southern groups in 1845.

l. Free Baptists merged with the Northern Baptist Convention in 1911, but the 1916 census still presented their data separately. The 1926 census adjusted the 1916 numbers to include both denominations, so percent growth is not falsely inflated. US Bureau of the Census, *Census of Religious Bodies, 1926*, 49.

m. Hauge's Synod and the United Norwegian Church merged with the Norwegian Lutheran Church in 1917. The membership numbers for 1916 include all three denominations, so percent growth is not falsely inflated. Between 1916 and 1926, Lutheran churches began counting members under the age of thirteen in their membership statistics. The census increased 1916 figures by the proportion found to be under the age of thirteen in 1926 for all Lutheran denominations. US Bureau of the Census, *Census of Religious Bodies, 1926*, 49.

n. The American Baptist Association splintered off of the Southern Baptist Convention in 1924 and became a denomination itself, totaling 117,858, in 1926. Thus, the percent growth of the Southern Baptist Convention is slightly suppressed. US Bureau of the Census, *Census of Religious Bodies, 1926*, 49.

o. Named the Evangelical Lutheran Synod of Missouri, Ohio and Other States in the 1926 census and until 1947.

p. Because all Lutheran churches began counting members under the age of thirteen in their membership statistics between the 1916 and 1926 census, the US Census Bureau increased the 1916 figures by the proportion found to be under the age of thirteen in 1926 for all Lutheran denominations. US Bureau of the Census, *Census of Religious Bodies, 1926*, 49.

q. Excludes the Roman Catholic Church because its extremely early founding date skews the results.

r. The Hungarian Reformed Church merged with the Reformed Church in the United States in 1921. The 1916 membership numbers include both denominations, so percent growth is not falsely inflated. US Bureau of the Census, *Census of Religious Bodies, 1926*, 49.

s. The United Lutheran Church in America was formed in 1918 out of a merger between the General Synod, the United Synod in the South, and the General Council. Percent growth is calculated using the sum of these three denominations in 1916. Between 1916 and 1926, Lutheran churches began counting members under the age of thirteen in their membership statistics. The census increased 1916 figures by the proportion found to be under the age of thirteen in 1926 for all Lutheran denominations. US Bureau of the Census, *Census of Religious Bodies, 1926*, 49.

t. *Negro Baptists* in the 1926 census.

u. To calculate percent growth of the National Baptist Convention, USA, Inc, "Negro churches" formerly reported with the Northern Baptist Convention were included in the 1916 membership for the National Baptist Convention and excluded from the Northern Baptist Convention 1916 membership. US Bureau of the Census, *Census of Religious Bodies, 1926*, 49.

v. This average excludes African American denominations because their salaries were so much lower than white denominations.

class, especially in the Northeast. Catholics were generally working class and poor.

As may be obvious in terms of what is missing from table 2, unfortunately, the censuses did not provide any information on the racial or ethnic composition of denominations. While identifying historically black religious denominations was relatively straightforward, there is no doubt that a measure of the percent of each denomination who were foreign-born (as well as other measures of racial and ethnic diversity) would have been most useful for this analysis. That said, I was able to glean much information about groups' ethnic and racial identities from the periodical research that I describe below. Thus, while this study lacks quantitative measures of groups' experiences with immigration, a plethora of data presented in the chapters that follow demonstrate what many groups were well aware of at the time—some American religious groups were undoubtedly seen as, and felt, more "American" than others.

The Geography of Reform

Of course, immigration, economic development, class, and systems of racial stratification are also strongly correlated with geography. Although not an intentional sampling decision on my part, a quick glance at table 2 indicates that my sample also incorporates significant geographic diversity, including denominations that were predominantly located in almost every area of the country.

This geographic diversity is illustrated by maps for various types of denominations (i.e. the early liberalizers, critics and so forth) throughout the book. Please see the methodological appendix on the UC Press webpage for this book for maps of each individual denomination. All maps were made with ArcGIS 10. Data on the number of members of each religious denomination were gathered from the *Census of Religious Bodies* (1926), and county borders were determined by the County Shape file from the National Historical Geographic Information System (1930). When discrepancies between the 1926 and 1930 borders arose, I used the 1930 borders.

In the end, I found that geography, by which I mean the corresponding economic, ethnic, and racial systems reflected in different regions of the country, was essential to understanding groups' views on contraception.

For example, the Southern Baptists, who openly espoused segregation and white supremacy but were relatively friendly to immigrants, allowed me to see just how crucial the racial context was for groups' views of contraception. The same Catholic and Jewish immigrants whose whiteness was deeply threatening in the North were seen as white enough to help diversify the white gene pool in the South. The only thing that needed to be changed about them (according to white Southern groups) was their religion.

Of course, drawing these conclusions required more than just a systematic sample. It also required a systematic data source that would allow me to examine all of the denominations in my sample.

The Data

Once I had my sample, my search began for the data I needed to figure out why nine of America's most prominent religious groups rather suddenly liberalized on the issue of contraception between 1929–31 and the effect of that liberalization in the years that followed. I began with the archives, visiting about a dozen and ultimately relying on the long-distance help of archivists from many more places.[23]

THE ARCHIVES

The most interesting and useful archival materials came from a series of competitions for the best sermon on eugenics held by the AES, which provided valuable data on the denominations reached by the AES as well as the context and content of pro-eugenics religious leaders' messages to their congregations.[24] However, while the connections I could see in the archives were ultimately very important in terms of helping me understand the mechanism that lead to liberalization, I quickly found that I could not answer my research questions with archival materials alone. While there was, for example, a great deal of information about the religious groups closely connected to the eugenics movement, there was nothing about those that were not.

The same was true in relation to the issue of birth control. As I ultimately found, most of the religious groups in my sample said nothing official about birth control during the first wave—and a good proportion of those actually said nothing at all. I needed a data source that would allow me to examine this diverse sample systemically. Ultimately, I realized that the best source came from what American religious groups wrote about, and for, themselves.

THE PERIODICALS

More than ten thousand articles from more than seventy secular and religious periodicals form the basis of the argument put forward in this book. That said, to be clear, when presenting the data from the periodicals, I do not claim nor assume that every member who was reading these periodicals agreed with the views expressed in them (or indeed, with the official stances of the denomination, which are the focus of this analysis). Instead, I treat these periodicals and the articles in them as representative of the general beliefs and opinions of each denomination. This assumption is justified by the fact that many of the periodicals seemed to take great pains to represent both sides of the story if there was any conflict or disagreement on an issue. However, such disagreements were surprisingly rare. By and large, what was striking about the periodicals was the authoritative tone they took relative to their readership and the lack of conflict reported, especially regarding issues such as eugenics or birth control, about which I expected more controversy.

Determining what periodical was the official, or even the best, representation of a particular group was not an easy or straightforward process, especially as groups and periodicals changed over time. While I instinctively sought out circulation statistics as an aid in this process, I found that they were surprisingly elusive. None of the more than seventy religious periodicals I ultimately examined reported their circulation statistics in even a superficially systematic manner. In the end, to determine which periodical was the "primary" or official periodical for a denomination, I often had to rely on the kindness of archivists, who had to go to the shelves in their libraries. When I could not determine which periodical was the best reflection of a particular denomination, I analyzed all of the periodicals affiliated with that group. Please see tables 1 and 9 for the specific periodicals I analyzed for each denomination and how they changed over time.

Once I determined what periodical(s) was the best representative of a particular denomination, I found that although they contained some unavoidable variation, in general, they were remarkably comparable.

Table 3 Key Words Searched

Any Focus Year	First and Second Wave	Historical Context
BIRTH CONTROL Contraceptives Family planning Margaret Sanger The pill Malthus Population explosion Food insecurity Voluntary parenthood Responsible parenthood	**SEX AND GENDER** **Feminism** Women's issues Women's rights **Abortion** **Sexuality** Sexual education Sexual revolution Summer of Love Homosexuality **Marriage** Divorce **RACE** **Eugenics** Juvenile delinquency Anglo-Saxon Superior/inferior Racial stock/bloodline Genetics/genes/heredity Un/desirable **Race suicide** Differential birth rates	**FIRST WAVE (1918–19, 1924–25, 1929–32)** **Woman suffrage** **Temperance** Prohibition **The Depression** Capitalism Socialism New Deal Social Security **Science** Evolution Darwin Scopes Trial **Labor** Labor unions Labor movement **SECOND WAVE (1935, 1945, 1955, 1965)** **World War II** Nazis Hitler Germany Religious persecution

Immigration
Race (black/white)
Negro/es
Lynching
Racial justice
Brown v. B of Education
Segregation
Civil rights
THEOLOGY/DENOMINATION
Fundamental/modernists
Federal Council of Churches
Social gospel
Catholicism
Rome
Ecumenism
Vatican II
Religious growth/decline
Internal division/strife
Revivals/evangelism
Billy Graham
Evangelicals/ism
Missions

Jews
Roma or Gypsies
Fascists/ism
Conscientious objection
United Nations
COMMUNISM
Cold War
Russia
USSR
China
Korean War
Vietnam War
McCarthyism
Higher education
College

Two-thirds of the periodicals were weeklies, and all but two of the periodicals were popularly oriented and written for a general lay audience.

With the rare exception of those that were electronically searchable, I or my assistants examined each of the periodicals by hand and gathered all the articles that mentioned anything having to do with birth control, eugenics, immigration, and a host of other issues. Although the specific key words often changed over time, the basic concepts and factors they illuminated did not. For the exact key word search terms used over the course of the analysis, please see table 3.

YEARS SEARCHED

I searched for the topics crucial to this analysis (including any mention of birth control, eugenics, and the social gospel movement) in all nine years that I call "focus" years: 1919, 1925, 1929–31, 1935, 1945, 1955, and 1965. All denominations had key word searches conducted in these focus years or in the closest year available (no more than two years before or after a particular focus year) when a specific year of a periodical proved unavailable after extensive searching.

I quickly found, not surprisingly, that certain years yielded a great deal more information about certain issues. I thus ended up relying more on some years than others for different issues. To distill groups' views on suffrage and prohibition, I relied on what was said in 1919 (because that year saw the passage of the Eighteenth and Nineteenth Amendments). For evolution and science, as well as immigration, 1925 was particularly helpful because it marked the Scopes Monkey Trial and immigration restriction. The years 1929–31 proved to be the most useful for determining groups' views on birth control.

As I sought to understand the effects of liberalization (or the lack thereof) on American religious groups' views of birth control after the first wave, I focused on gathering data from ten-year intervals, beginning with 1935, including 1945 and 1955, and concluding in 1965. It will be apparent to the reader that 1935 and 1945 were years of relative quiescence on the topic of birth control but that by 1955 and 1965 the topic was thrust back into the public, and religious, spotlight.

Finally, I found that if a denomination merged with another, the year that merger occurred was often very fruitful for data. Because of their need to be clear about certain positions, groups were, in a sense, moved to take positions on issues they might not have held publicly prior to a merger. Thus, I conducted searches for all merger years for any denomination in my sample that was involved in a merger, even if that year was not included in the list of years searched above.

In the end, almost all denominations in my sample have data from at least ten focus years. Many, because they went through multiple mergers, have more than that. On average the key word searches over the ten focus years resulted in about three hundred articles being "found" for each of the thirty-one denominations in my sample, resulting in a data set of about ten thousand articles.

CODING AND ANALYSIS

All found articles went through at least one initial coding pass. Approximately 10 percent of those went through a much more detailed process of transcription, coding, and analysis. The articles chosen for more detailed analysis were typically longer articles that touched on a variety of key words at the same time, a strategy that allowed me to see how issues—for example, immigration, concerns about urban political machines, and fears of race suicide—were interconnected with support for birth control. The codes for all of my measures capture both the frequency and fervor with which issues were mentioned in the denominations' periodicals.

Beginning first with the issue of early views of birth control, denominations coded as *early liberalizers* had an official statement in support of birth control promulgated by an important committee or the official denominational leadership (all also promoted legalization in their periodicals) during this time. *Unofficial supporters* did not make an official statement in favor of legalization for at least another twenty years but published at least one supportive article per year. Groups coded as *critics* either officially condemned contraception or published numerous articles criticizing it, and often the early liberalizers, during peak years.

Denominations coded as *silent* on birth control said nothing on the subject during the peak years of discussion (1929–32). It is important to note that the periodicals for most of the denominations coded as silent were not more likely to simply be silent on all issues and were not published less often. The majority of the periodicals from the denominations that were silent on birth control were in fact published weekly.

Two silent denominations, the African Methodist Episcopal Zion Church and the Methodist Episcopal Church, South, are the exception to this rule. Both groups did have periodicals that were published less often and thus presented fewer opportunities to register opinions. The African Methodist Episcopal Zion Church's periodical, *A.M.E.Z. Quarterly Review*, however, did not refrain from commenting on other social issues, such as eugenics, in the pages that it did print—a factor consistent with my findings about the other groups that were silent on birth control at the time. In contrast, the collapse of the *Methodist Quarterly Review* in 1930, just as many groups were making their pronouncements on birth control, made conclusively coding the Methodist Episcopal Church, South's position on birth control next to impossible. Their silence was consistent with the positions of other silent denominations and with the overall argument presented in the book, but given the limited evidence, I do not focus on the Methodist Episcopal Church, South, as evidence for any of my claims.

In terms of my codes for the other factors and reform movements analyzed in this book, in general, *strong supporters* of eugenics, race suicide, immigration restriction, the social gospel, or most of the other movements discussed in the chapters to come published one or two supportive articles per year during the peak years of discussion. Groups coded as *weak* supporters of an issue did not discuss it often, but when they did, their support was clear. Groups opposed to eugenics, race suicide, the social gospel or other reform movements published very few articles on these subjects (with the exception of the Roman Catholic Church, whose opposition to eugenics and race suicide was vehemently and frequently expressed). They produced, on average, one article roughly every five years, but those they did publish were very strong in their criticism.

In the end, and in combination with each other, the data I gathered and coded allow me to explain why America's most prominent religious denominations took certain sides at a crucial moment in history and to trace the effects of that decision over the next three decades. Given the relatively long historical period covered in this book, some explanation of how this book is structured is in order.

STRUCTURE OF THE BOOK

Over the course of the twentieth century, the issue of birth control waxed and waned. This, coupled with the fact that the data that contributed to the argument came just as much from the decades leading up to that reform as from the decades after, has given this book a unique structure. The book is divided into three parts: Part I examines the historical movement precursors that might have created a greater openness (or opposition) to birth control reform. Part II examines the movement for birth control reform itself, explaining the stances taken by thirty-one of the largest and most prominent religious groups in America at the time. Part III examines the legacy of those stances over the next three decades.

Beginning with abolition and ending with eugenics, part I of *Birth Control Battles* examines American religious groups' activism over almost one hundred years of social movement activism. Crucial to any analysis that hopes to be comparative-historical, chapter 1 examines eight movement precursors that could be, in any way, connected to later activism on the issue of birth control. These include three secular social movements (by which I mean that the focus of the movement was the state)—abolition, temperance, and suffrage—and five issues connected to two religious movements (by which I mean that the focus of these movements was mostly other religious institutions)—the social gospel movement and its organizational home of the Federal Council of Churches, the modernist/fundamentalist divide, and connections between those beliefs and views of evolution and science.

While chapter 1 demonstrates that the religious groups that liberalized on birth control did have one strong movement similarity—they all believed in the social gospel movement—it makes another point that is perhaps even more important: American religious activism did not follow the neat path that many might expect. It is simply not true that the most ardent abolitionists were also the biggest advocates of prohibition, the groups with modernist religious identities, the most passionate advocates of the social gospel movement, the founders of the Federal Council of Churches, and, ultimately, the early promoters of birth control. While there are some prominent groups who undoubtedly took this activist path and remained on it throughout the twentieth century, there are others that did not but ended up with similar stances on birth control by 1930. These findings suggest that other factors, along with the social gospel movement, are more important when it comes to understanding groups' early views on birth control, and it is this point that undergirds the data presented in chapter 1.

Of course, birth control entered the public imagination because of the actions of particular individuals and the organizations and movements they led. Chapter 2 examines the connections between American religious groups and the two movements central to birth control reform during the 1920s: Margaret Sanger's American Birth Control League (ABCL) and its close organizational collaborator, the AES. Beginning with the obvious, chapter 2 demonstrates that although the ABCL's focus on broadening access to contraceptives was certainly necessary, it alone cannot explain which groups supported legalizing contraceptives. Very few of the early liberalizers had much contact with her or her organization.

Chapter 2 then goes on to demonstrate that in contrast to the weak connections most groups had to the ABCL, the AES developed strong, intentional, and long-lasting relationships with many religious leaders, particularly those whose denominations were located in the Northeast. Through their Committee on Cooperating with Clergymen, the AES convinced many religious groups that legalizing birth control was crucial to the racial health of the nation.

With these first two chapters, part I of the book thus establishes that connections with the social gospel movement and the eugenics movement seem to have been crucial to explaining which groups ultimately embraced early birth control reform and which groups did not. However, it is not until part II that the reader will find details about how any particular religious group approached and understood the debates about contraception that invigorated the field between 1929–31. Even though the debates about birth control reform between American religious groups took place largely over the course of only three years, telling this story takes up the bulk of the pages in this book, with four chapters—each dedicated to one of the four cells in table 4.

Chapter 3 examines the early liberalizers—those for whom belief in the social gospel movement coincided with a concern about race suicide and ultimately created religious leaders who believed that legalizing birth control

Table 4 Stances on Birth Control by Belief in Race Suicide and the Social Gospel

	Did Not Believe in the Social Gospel	Believed in the Social Gospel
Concerned about Race Suicide	**Unofficial Supporters** • Evangelical Synod of North America • Northern Baptist Convention • United Presbyterian Church of North America • Norwegian Lutheran Church in America	**Early Liberalizers** • Reform Judaism • Universalist Church • American Unitarian Association • Protestant Episcopal Church • Christian Church • Congregational Churches • Methodist Episcopal Church • Society of Friends (Orthodox) • Presbyterian Church in the United States of America
Not Concerned about Race Suicide	**Critics** • Presbyterian Church in the United States • Southern Baptist Convention • Church of Jesus Christ of Latter-day Saints • Lutheran Church–Missouri Synod • Orthodox Judaism • Roman Catholic Church	**Silent** • Reformed Church in the United States • Methodist Episcopal Church, South • Conservative Judaism • Reformed Church in America • United Lutheran Church in America • Disciples of Christ • African Methodist Episcopal Zion Church • Churches of Christ • National Baptist Convention, USA, Inc.

was not only a wise approach for the racial health of the nation but that lobbying for it was a religious duty. The certitude and impatience with which these nine denominations approached the issue of birth control is captured well by the following quote from the *Congregationalist and Herald of Gospel Liberty*, which asked readers:

> How long are we going to allow the unreflective and helpless mass production of the weakest and least fit of our population to continue without attempting to shift the emphasis from quantity to quality? . . . When and how are . . . ministers and physicians going to be allowed to give this priceless information to these unfortunate people who need it most?[25]

Of course, the explanation put forth in chapter 3 would not be convincing unless it could also explain the stances that other groups took on birth control at this time. As table 4 demonstrates, the denominations that were concerned about race suicide but did not believe in the social gospel became unofficial supporters of legalizing birth control. Chapter 4 examines these denominations and demonstrates that the unofficial supporters were even more openly white supremacist than the early liberalizers chronicled in chapter 3. Because they were more rural and thus distanced from the urban problems that sparked the social gospel movement, these four denominations eschewed the more activist role that social gospelers embraced and gave only unofficial support. As an article titled "Birth Control" in the Norwegian Lutheran Church's *Lutheran Church Herald* put plainly in 1931: "It is the part of wisdom, at times to be silent rather than to write and talk about certain questions. We have no authority to make any *ex cathedra* pronouncement for the Lutheran Church [but] we can give some information."[26] Such unofficial support was the solution for the religious denominations that were deeply concerned about race suicide but rejected the religious activism encouraged by the social gospel movement.

Of course, many other religious groups rejected the social gospel at this time as well. When those groups also rejected race suicide concerns, either because they lived in a different geographical context, such as the South, or because they were themselves the target of those concerns, they openly criticized birth control reform and the religious groups that supported it. Chapter 5 presents these critics and the factors that resulted in such unlikely bedfellows as the Roman Catholic Church agreeing with the vehemently anti-Catholic Southern Baptist Convention when it said the following in 1934:

> The Southern Baptist Convention hereby expresses its disapproval of the Hastings Bill, now pending in the Congress of the United States, the purpose of which is to make possible and provide for the dissemination of information concerning contraceptives and birth control; whatever the intent and motive of such proposal we cannot but believe that such legislation would be vicious in character and would prove seriously detrimental to the morals of our nation.[27]

Chapter 6 tells the stories of the *silent denominations*. Although largely overlooked at the time, these denominations are crucial analytically because they believed in the social gospel movement but not race suicide. For the most part middle class but racially or ethnically marginalized in America more generally, the denominations examined in this chapter openly questioned eugenic beliefs. While they questioned their fellow religious activists' eugenics beliefs, they tended to remain silent on the issue of birth control. These denominations demonstrate that at this time in American history, even silence was a statement.

The story of the American religious field being divided by contraception does not end in 1930. Part III of *Birth Control Battles* follows all of the religious groups in my sample over the next thirty years with the same rigorous analysis of their religious periodicals that formed the basis of the data in parts I and II. Given the longer time period and the more dispersed liberalization that occurred during it among the later liberalizers, part II focuses on what the thirty religious groups in my sample said in 1935, 1945, 1955, and, most importantly, 1965, by which time the pill had received US Food and Drug Administration approval. It does so over the course of two chapters.

Chapter 7 focuses on "America's religious promoters" of contraception, a group that includes all of the early liberalizers in addition to, because of mergers, all of the former unofficial liberalizers, for a total of eight denominations. Chapter 7 demonstrates that these groups continued to focus on promoting contraception, with motivations that remained focused on decreasing other people's fertility rates—although the particular focus of their concern shifted from the whitening Catholic and Jewish immigrants and their descendants to the poor in the "Third World" and America's inner cities.

Chapter 8 tells the story of the former critics and silent groups, the vast majority of whom eventually liberalized on birth control. When they did so, they did so reluctantly and in a much more limited fashion than the religious promoters. In total, twelve (which would soon become eleven) of the groups in my sample of America's most prominent religious denominations fall into the category of *reluctant converts* to contraception. Although diverse theologically, geographically, and historically, these groups have one crucial factor in common: all of them either openly rejected birth control or were completely disconnected from the movement during the first wave of liberalization.

In the end, *Birth Control Battles* tells a story of the enduring importance of race and class in the American religious field and how those intersections complicate our understandings what it meant to be progressive and conservative in America. But before we can get to that conclusion, we must start where it all began—or at least where many argue that American religious activism began—with the fight to end slavery and the subsequent movements, both religious and secular, that would engage the American religious field over the next century.

PART I From Abolition to Eugenics

1 American Religious Activism in the Twentieth Century

American religious groups have been roiled by conflict since before the American Civil War. From abolition, to prohibition, to suffrage, from the social gospel movement to modernism and fundamentalism, to debates about evolution and science, American religious groups have had to choose their battles and the sides on which they would fight, or not, many times over. While the historical research on these movements and various religious groups' roles in them is rich, no researcher has systematically examined which religious groups have supported American movements for social and religious reform throughout the past century and a half and which have not. Thus, until now, the connections between early religious activism and groups' current religious identities have been sketchy at best.

Given the potential importance of this history not only for America's religious groups but for the popular imagination as well, any study that seeks to understand how American religious groups ended up divided so dramatically by birth control had to examine these precursor movements.[1] Thus, I coded all of my religious groups by their views on more than ten other issues that could, in any way, be connected to later activism on the issue of birth control. Eight of these are investigated in this chapter. These include three secular social movements (by which I mean that the focus of the movement was the state)—abolition, temperance, and suffrage—and five issues connected to two religious movements—the social gospel movement and its organizational home of the Federal Council of Churches (FCC), views of the modernist/fundamentalist divide, and connections between those views and views of evolution and science. The remaining two movements I investigated are examined in the next chapter, which examines the connections between American religious groups and the secular movements and organizations that were most directly focused on promoting contraception—the American Birth Control League and the American Eugenics Society.

While this chapter demonstrates that the religious groups that liberalized on birth control did have one strong movement similarity—they were all believers in the social gospel movement—it makes another point that is perhaps even more important: The story this chapter tells is not one that follows the neat path that many might expect. It is simply not true that the most ardent abolitionists were also the biggest advocates of prohibition, the groups with modernist religious identities, the most passionate advocates of the social gospel movement, the founders of the FCC, and, ultimately, the early promoters of birth control. While some prominent groups undoubtedly took this activist path and remained on it throughout the course of the twentieth century, others did not but ended up with similar stances on birth control by 1930. These findings suggest that other factors are more important when it comes to understanding groups' early views on birth control, and it is this point that undergirds the data presented in this chapter.

ABOLITION

American religious groups were highly visible in the fight to abolish slavery. It is thus not surprising that some scholars see the "possibility of drawing a line from antislavery, through emancipation and Reconstruction, to the social gospel," as does Molly Oshatz in *Slavery and Sin: The Fight against Slavery and the Rise of Liberal Protestantism*.[2] Such impressions are not rare. The leading historian of progressive Protestantism, Henry May, argued that "the growth and eventual triumph of the antislavery crusade stirred churchmen more than any prewar reform movement and led them into more fundamental criticism of existing society."[3]

Given how early agitation against slavery began among American religious groups, I could not rely on groups' religious periodicals to assess their support for abolition, as almost no periodicals from the mid-nineteenth century have survived (and many denominations did not yet have one). As a result, abolition is the only issue for which I relied on secondary historical sources exclusively—thus, more information about how I coded these sources is in order.

My coding of abolition erred on the side of inclusivity, rather than exclusivity. This was a conservative decision given that May found that "churches later tended to exaggerate the part they had played in early abolition struggles."[4] Groups were coded as abolitionists if either denominational histories or prominent histories of abolition mentioned their activism against slavery. Groups were coded as not being abolitionists if they were not mentioned in any histories of the movement and if their denominational histories also did not mention abolition activism.[5] My results of this research are presented in table 5, which also provides my findings about groups' engagement with the two other important secular social reform movements—prohibition and suffrage—examined below.

Table 5 suggests that abolition is only weakly correlated with support for early birth control reform. Starting with the early liberalizers, it is apparent that a history of abolitionist activism cannot be either a direct or indirect cause of groups' later support for early birth control reform. While most were indeed abolitionists, there are two important exceptions. The Christian Church falls into this category. No histories of abolition mention this denomination. Likewise, no histories of abolition mention the Christian Church, even in passing. However, it is possible that the data missed an overall abolitionist sentiment on the part of the Christian Church because it was smaller and more rural. Thus, if the Christian Church were the only early liberalizer to not be coded as an abolitionist, I would be more likely to conclude that abolition may have played an important role in predicting later activism in the American religious field.

The Protestant Episcopal Church suggests otherwise, however, and further calls into question the idea that early activism on abolition sowed the seeds for support for contraception. In contrast to the Baptists, Methodists,

Table 5 Early Religious Activism in the American Religious Field[a]

BY STANCES ON EARLY BIRTH CONTROL REFORM

Denominations	Abolition	Prohibition	Woman Suffrage
Early Liberalizers			
Society of Friends (Orthodox)	Mixed[b]	Strong	Weak
Reform Judaism	Yes	No[c]	Strong[d]
Universalist Church	Yes[e]	Strong	Weak
American Unitarian Association	Yes[f]	Strong	Strong
Methodist Episcopal Church	Yes[g]	Strong	Strong
Congregational Churches	Yes[h]	Strong	Strong
Christian Church	No[i]	Strong	Weak
Presbyterian Church in the United States of America	Yes[j]	Strong	Weak
Protestant Episcopal Church	No[k]	Strong	Strong
Unofficial Supporters			
Evangelical Synod of North America	No	Opposed	Weak
Northern Baptist Convention	Yes[l]	Strong	Strong
United Presbyterian Church of North America	Silent	Strong	Strong
Norwegian Lutheran Church in America	Silent[m]	Strong	Silent

Presbyterian Church in the United States	Opposed[n]	No	Silent
Southern Baptist Convention	Opposed[o]	Strong	Silent
Church of Jesus Christ of Latter-day Saints	Yes[p]	No[q]	Weak[r]
Lutheran Church–Missouri Synod	No	No	Opposed[s]
Orthodox Judaism	No	Silent	Strong[t]
Roman Catholic Church	No	No	Opposed

Reformed Church in the United States	No	Strong	Weak
Methodist Episcopal Church, South	Opposed[u]	No	Opposed[v]
Conservative Judaism	No	Silent[w]	Silent[x]
Reformed Church in America	No	Strong	Opposed
United Lutheran Church in America	No	Opposed[y]	Weak
Disciples of Christ	No	Strong	Silent
African Methodist Episcopal Zion Church	Yes	Unavailable[z]	Unavailable
Churches of Christ	No	Weak	Opposed
National Baptist Convention, USA, Inc.	Yes	Weak	Strong

a. Unless otherwise noted, the sources for all data on this table come from the periodicals listed in table 1.

b. The Society of Friends (Quakers) were abolitionists long before other denominations became so and were actively involved in many abolitionist activities. During the schism between Hicksite and Orthodox Quakers, Orthodox Quakers distanced themselves more from abolitionist causes, although individual Orthodox Quakers were still actively involved in the movement. Hinks and McKivigan, "Quakers and Antislavery," 549–554.

c. Reform Jews said little on temperance or prohibition except in regard to abuses of the loopholes that allowed religious groups to use wine. A total of four articles to this effect were found in the *Yearbook of the Central Conference of American Rabbis* between 1918 and 1921. No articles were found in *Union Tidings* between 1919 and 1922 that mentioned temperance.

d. Four articles mentioning women's suffrage were found in the *Yearbook of the Central Conference of American Rabbis* between 1913 and 1921, all

(note d continued)

supportive of women's suffrage—for example: "*Resolved*, That this Central Conference of American Rabbis, by common recognition the largest and most representative organization of progressive Judaism today in the entire world, places itself on record as a body in sympathy with and in support of the latest appeal for the extension of liberty . . . and recommends that its members individually in their pulpits, and through their ministry, advocate and advance the cause of women's equal political suffrage with man's." Jacobson et al., 1913, p. 120.

e. Universalists made the first official denominational pronouncement against slavery in 1790. Despite this early denominational activism and the fact that Universalists were generally antislavery, they were less likely to be part of mainstream antislavery movements, mostly due to a belief that religion and politics should not mix. Harris, "Abolition of Slavery," 2–5.

f. Unitarians were abolitionists, although there were still debates in the denomination about if there should be gradual or immediate emancipation and how disruptive of tactics to use in the movement. There were some antiabolitionist Unitarian leaders in the 1830s and 1840s, but by the 1850s, the denomination had moved in a solidly abolitionist direction. Hinks and McKivigan, "Unitarianism and Antislavery," 695–697.

g. In 1845, Southern proslavery Methodists broke off from the Methodist Episcopal Church because of its abolitionist views. Hinks and McKivigan, "Methodism and Antislavery," 468–470.

h. Congregationalist laypeople and clergy disapproved of slavery, and many abolitionist leaders were Congregationalists. However, due to the decentralized nature of the denomination, the denomination never took an official position on the issue. Hinks and McKivigan, "Congregationalists and Antislavery," 182–185; Youngs, *Congregationalists*, 135–136.

i. Groups were coded as silent on abolition if they were not mentioned in official histories of the movement, and abolition was not mentioned in official denominational histories.

j. The Presbyterian Church General Assembly argued that slavery was inconsistent with Christianity in 1818, with Southern Presbyterians disagreeing. The Presbyterian Church started breaking apart in 1837 into a New School and an Old School, with slavery being one issue in this schism. The Presbyterian Church fully broke apart into Northern and Southern denominations in 1861 over the issue of slavery. Hart, *Dictionary of the Presbyterian and Reformed Tradition*.

k. While Baptists, Methodists, and Presbyterians split into Northern and Southern wings over the issue of slavery, the Protestant Episcopal Church generally remained distant from abolitionist politics and remained largely intact as a denomination as a result. Hein and Shattuck, *Episcopalians*.

l. Hillerbrand, "Abolition of Slavery," 1744.

m. Lutheran denominations were largely silent about abolitionism. The only synods of Lutherans that spoke out against slavery were the Frankean Synod of upstate New York, which excluded membership of any tavern-keeper and slave holder, and the Augustana Synod, which criticized slavery in the 1850s. Gassmann, "Slavery," 309.

n. Hart, Dictionary of the Presbyterian and Reformed Tradition.

o. Hillerbrand, "Abolition of Slavery," 1744.

p. The Church of Jesus Christ of Latter-day Saints was antislavery from its founding in 1830, which resulted in much persecution for the church. In 1844, Joseph Smith, the founder of the church, ran as a third-party candidate for president, largely on an abolitionist platform. Hinks and McKivigan, "Church of Jesus Christ of Latter-Day Saints and Antislavery," 158–160.

q. The Church of Jesus Christ of Latter-day Saints was very much against the use of alcohol but was not a strong advocate for prohibition.

r. The three articles found in the Mormon periodical the *Improvement Era* in 1919 that mentioned women's suffrage were entirely factual in tone.

s. All four articles found in the *Lutheran Witness* between 1919 and 1920 that mentioned women's suffrage were against the movement—for example: "We find, then, that the woman occupies an equal position with man in the Church in the offers of God's grace in the Gospel, equal privilege of service, the right to meet with the Church, the right quietly and unostentatiously to express her opinion, but that she is not granted suffrage nor leadership in the congregation and is barred from public ministry." Sieck, "Attitude Lutherans Should Take towards Women's Suffrage," 162.

t. The one article found in the *Jewish Forum* between 1919 and 1920 that mentioned women's suffrage suggests that Orthodox Jews were supportive of the movement. The author writes about the lives of women in Palestine, discussing their right to vote: "Without exaggeration, here in our Palestinian colonies, woman secured the 'vote' and 'equal rights' before anywhere else." Trager, "Jewish Women in Palestine," 1305.

u. "Methodists and Antislavery," Hinks and McKivigan, "Methodists and Antislavery,". 2007, 468–470.

v. The Methodist Episcopal Church, South was silent in 1919 and 1920 on the issue of women's suffrage. I coded them as opposed to suffrage because the one statement they made on the issue, in 1929, was still quite conservative, asserting that the author of this article wrote, for example: "No education for woman that forgets that she is woman above all things else is good. It should have something in it to prepare her for life supremely as woman—for her womanly destiny. Nothing can atone for the loss of the distinctively womanly in woman." Steadman, "Male and Female," 451; "The new ideas advocated for woman should be tested by God's creative purpose for her. . . . While God created them male and female, there is a tendency to-day to make them both males in many particulars. . . . We should have no sympathy for the woman who wishes that she were a man. . . . Woman is becoming mans' business and professional rival. . . . She is driving him more and more from business positions." Steadman, "Male and Female," 454.

w. The American Jewish Committee argued that the loophole allowing religious groups to use wine for ritual purposes should be eliminated because of "widespread abuse." Ginzberg, "Response to the Question Whether Unfermented Wine May Be Used in Jewish Ceremonies," 401. However, I have coded Conservative Jews as not supportive of temperance because there was no mention of temperance in the *S.A.J Review* in 1921 (its first year of publication) or in the United Synagogue of America or the Women's League annual report in 1919 or 1920.!

x. The *S.A.J. Review* began publication in 1921, two years after the peak years of discussion on women's suffrage, but there were no mentions of women's suffrage in the United Synagogue of America and the Women's League annual report between 1919 and 1920.

y. Although there was a significant amount of discussion of temperance in the *Lutheran* between 1919 and 1920, most of the articles took a neutral tone, reporting on the passage of the Nineteenth Amendment but critical of people who thought that prohibition would change "human nature itself." "Expecting Too Much of Prohibition," 71.

z. I could not locate any copies of the *American Methodist Episcopal Zion Quarterly Review* from 1919 to 1920 for analysis of their views on temperance and women's suffrage.

and Presbyterians, which split into Northern and Southern wings over the issue of slavery, the Protestant Episcopal Church generally tried to keep its distance from abolitionist politics and stayed largely intact as a denomination as a result. One Southern Episcopalian group, the Protestant Episcopal Church in the Confederate States of America, did splinter off in 1862, but it remerged with the general Protestant Episcopal Church just three years later.[6] Despite its lack of abolitionist agitation, the Protestant Episcopal Church was a central early supporter of birth control legalization. Thus, it does not seem that abolitionist activism was an early precursor to reform.

This conclusion is further supported by other findings in table 5, which demonstrates that there were abolitionists, although not that many, among each of the other categories of stances on birth control. Thus, it does not appear that a history of abolitionist activism was necessary or sufficient to explain early support for contraception among American religious groups. Of course, there were many other relevant religious and social movements between the time of abolition activism and birth control reform, any of which could have intervened to explain the outliers I examine below.

Unlike abolition, the remainder of the movements that this chapter examines occurred at a time when American religious periodicals were accessible. Thus, the evidence I present throughout the rest of this chapter relies on the same firsthand examination of primary sources as the remainder of this book.

DATA AND METHODS FOR RESEARCH
ON OTHER SOCIAL MOVEMENTS

As it did for eugenics, my coding of groups' views of American social and religious movements captures both the frequency and fervor with which they commented on a particular issue. The frequency with which an issue was discussed proved to be very informative in and of itself. For example, I found that prohibition received a great deal more attention, often as many as ten times the number of articles, than suffrage. Most groups coded as a strong advocate of prohibition published between 15 and 16 articles strongly in favor of the movement per year. In comparison, even the strongest suffragist groups published only one or two articles a year advocating giving women the right to vote. As I discuss below, this proved crucial to my conclusion that suffrage simply was not an issue that galvanized or divided the American religious field and that birth control really was the first issue connected to sex and gender to do so.

Of course, as I mention above, the coding that I use throughout this book reflects far more than just frequency of discussion. The fervor with which views were expressed was just as important to my coding of groups' views—especially for those opposed to a particular issue, who tended to discuss it less often, but in no uncertain terms, when they did so. For example, the groups opposed to prohibition only published around three articles a year on the topic—less than a quarter of the ink the advocates of prohibition spent on the issue. But their criticism of the movement was clear in the relatively smaller amount of space devoted to it. The strength of groups' views is often best communicated in the words used by the groups themselves. Therefore, in the sections that follow I also give a qualitative sense of how views varied, both from group to group and from issue to issue, as I discuss the possible relationships between those views and stances on birth control.

Finally, as with abolition, the historical literature on each of the other movements examined—both religious and secular—in this chapter is vast. However, many of the existing studies on these movements focus only on connections between a movement and a particular religious group (or groups) or leaders. As a sociologist I am concerned with whether those connections were causal, which means needing to be able to systematically assess whether such connections hold up across all similar groups—and if they do not, whether there is another plausible explanation. Thus, when making claims about any such relationship, I rely strictly on my original primary research because it is only by doing so that I can ensure the same systematic examination of data and sources across groups. I cite the historical research that supports, and sometimes refutes, my findings as they arise.

PROHIBITION

Although movements to reform America's "wet" nature began almost contemporaneously with abolition, prohibition took longer to secure and, of course, was much more impermanent than the abolition of slavery.[7] The Eighteenth Amendment, or Volstead Act, which officially prohibited the production, transport, and sale of alcoholic beverages in the United States, passed in 1917 and was ratified by enough states to become law the next year.

Many scholars have identified the fight for the prohibition of alcohol as a potentially significant precursor to later religious activism—in particular, the social gospel. For example, historian Paul A. Carter observed that "with the exception of the Protestant Episcopal, all the churches which had been permeated by the social gospel were also officially committed to Prohibition."[8] Similarly, Phillips writes that the temperance movement "served . . . a midwife function between the womb of the evangelical world of self-improvement and the world of societal regeneration."[9] Historian Ferenc Morton Szasz saw glimmers of the nascent social gospel movement in the way that religious supporters of prohibition thought about the world: "The prohibition movement at this time extended beyond the desire to regulate the consumption of alcohol by the individual to include a view of the ideal social order. The advocates of prohibition saw it as the chief cure for poverty, crime, and prostitution."[10]

However, contrary to these claims, this examination of the American religious field's beliefs about prohibition demonstrates that, in fact, even less than abolition, prohibition cannot be credited with being the foundation of the divisions between conservative and progressive religious groups today. The reason for that is quite simple—support for prohibition was too common to explain the more varied views on birth control that would become apparent only a decade later.

This wider support for prohibition is indicated clearly in table 5. It demonstrates that while almost all of the early liberalizers were strong prohibitionists (with the exception of Reform Jews), so, too, were many other denominations that did not share the early liberalizers' belief in the importance of legalizing birth control. This is because prohibition was popular among Protestants in both the North and the South, with more than half of the groups in my sample expressing so much support for the movement that I coded them as strong supporters at the time the Eighteenth Amendment was being ratified.

Perhaps the best example of groups that were strong prohibitionists but highly critical of birth control (and the other religious movements examined below) is the Southern Baptist Convention. In 1919 the Southern Baptist periodical the *Christian Index* noted "great rejoicing throughout the United States on January 16th, when the wires flashed the news to all parts of the country that the National Constitutional Prohibition Amendment had been ratified by the legislatures of two-thirds of the States." The article claimed the victory as "a vindication of the efforts of evangelical Christianity" and went on as follows:

> The liquor traffic has been one of the most deadly enemies of the American republic throughout all the years. It has impoverished its millions, it has filled our ever-enlarging sanitariums with its victims, and sent thousands upon thousands to untimely graves. Our American people have been blind to their best and highest interests by allowing the continued existence of the liquor traffic. . . . Municipalities and communities in general should co-operate most heartily in the continued effort to suppress vice, whether legalized or not. Of all people in the world, our American people ought to be sober and clean.[11]

Support for prohibition was wide—so wide that groups generally known as conservatives who would later openly criticize birth control reform, such as the Southern Baptist Convention, strongly supported it.

Furthermore, support for moderating America's wet nature went even further than indicated by table 5. Many of the groups opposed to prohibition took great pains to explain that even though they were critical of the potential for prohibition to save the country, they remained supportive of temperance. For example, in 1919 the Evangelical Synod of North America's periodical the *Evangelical Herald* asserted that "with a vast number of honest and intelligent citizens we have consistently opposed intemperance, but have advocated voluntary total abstinence from intoxicating liquor rather than state-wide or national prohibition."[12] That same year the *Lutheran* published an article skeptically titled "Is National Temperance a Cure for All Human Ills?" However, even this article asserted that "the weakness of mankind for strong drink has caused untold misery. Drunkenness is one of the greatest of evils, and it facilitates sin." The article went on to clarify that their concerns about prohibition lay in the fact that "human frailty is not confined to a single outlet. If one is stopped up, it seeks, and readily finds, many others."[13]

Thus, prohibition, and its less legalistic cousin of temperance, enjoyed quite wide support within the American religious field. The support was so wide that one would be hard-pressed to argue that prohibition activism explains groups' views on birth control a decade later.

WOMEN'S SUFFRAGE

While it has been well known that abolition and prohibition enjoyed strong support from some of America's most prominent religious groups, much less ink has been spilled examining religious groups' support for the other contemporaneous secular movement of the day—the movement to give women the franchise. This is perhaps because, in contrast to the strong support for abolition among some groups and the wide support prohibition enjoyed among most American religious groups, woman suffrage gained almost no traction among American religious groups.

This is not to say that there were no differences among American religious groups' views of women's suffrage. Certainly, there were. And, of course, predictably, some of its staunchest supporters were indeed the early liberalizers on birth control. For example, the *Congregationalist* reported with pride:

> The *Congregationalist* declared for woman suffrage in advance of many of its religious contemporaries. Now that it has come, it congratulates the more than twenty million women voters who next week will stand shoulder to shoulder with the men at the place of power. . . . American politics ought to be cleaner, American life purer, America's influence in the world greater, because of what the women will do at the polls.[14]

However, even those who were strong supporters of women's suffrage (relative to other denominations at the time) paid it relatively little attention. For example, the Christian Church's *Herald of Gospel Liberty* published twenty-five articles on prohibition in 1918 alone but only four on women's suffrage. This is similar to the coverage each issue received among all of the groups coded as strong supporters of both issues.

Furthermore, along with more lackluster coverage, there was no vehement opposition to the issue of suffrage, even among groups known to be conservative on most issues, such as Orthodox Jews, who expressed relatively supportive views of women's rights and suffrage (although not often). For example, an article that expressed many feminist sentiments in the *Jewish Forum* in 1919 titled "The Jewish Woman in Palestine" asserted, "Without exaggeration, here in our Palestinian colonies, woman secured the 'vote' and 'equal rights' before anywhere else."[15]

Of course, this is not to say that none of America's most prominent religious groups were opposed to suffrage. As table 5 demonstrates, five of the more than thirty groups in my sample expressed distaste for the movement—often by emphasizing the importance of women's role at home. For example, in 1919 the periodical for the Reformed Church in America, the *Christian Intelligencer*, argued that the home "was her special field . . . 'wherein her great strength lieth'":

> The fact of women having the suffrage is only one element of her power in the Republic. She can vote and register on paper or on the dial of a machine her verdict on candidates and policies. She is now able to count one when the polls are open. It is her blessed privilege too to educate her children in paths of virtue and to cultivate their ideals and thus count from two to ten every day in the year. Here is her special field. May she never forget "wherein her great strength lieth." In the home she may make drinking, gambling, sensuality and irreverence absolutely loathsome by her own behavior.[16]

Finally, as table 5 indicates, even taking into account the overall more lackluster attention given to the issue in general, it does not seem that support for women's right to vote was an early precursor of support for women's right to access contraception. While a few of the religious groups that liberalized early on birth control expressed only weak support for suffrage, some groups that expressed relatively strong support for woman suffrage were not supportive of birth control reform a decade later. This was especially the case for the National Baptist Convention, U.S.A Inc., a historically black denomination—whose support for widening the franchise but rejection of birth control as a movement tinged by eugenic undertones a decade later should be expected from a complex religion standpoint. Two articles mentioning women's suffrage were found in the

National Baptist Union Review in 1919. Both were very supportive, describing the passage of the resolution submitting the amendment as a "splendid victory for the women and for democracy" and as something that has "brought to light the latent powers which have hitherto lain dormant in women."[17] A decade later, however, the National Baptist Convention had nothing to say about the movement to legalize contraception—but it did publish the following ominous warning for its fellow "white Baptists": "God will not, God cannot, with reverence we say it, bless in full measure a people whose selfishness, prejudice substitute Christian affection."[18]

In sum, none of the secular movements examined so far seem to be key precursors for later support for birth control reform. Although there certainly was a history of abolitionist activity among some of the early liberalizers, this was not the case for all. Furthermore, many abolitionist groups were not supportive of birth control reform when it arose nearly a century after abolitionist agitation. In contrast, almost all of the early liberalizers on birth control *were* strong supporters of prohibition. But so were many of the groups that would adamantly criticize birth control just a decade later.

Finally, even though its related focus on women's issues make suffrage an interesting precursor movement to examine in terms of seemingly predicting groups' support for birth control reform just a decade later, the periodical research indicates that this is just too much of a stretch. Groups gave it barely passing attention, especially for an issue that had captured national attention at the time. And when they did pay attention to suffrage, groups made it clear that they did not see it as a *religious issue*. The best indication of this? The fact that I found no articles referencing other religious groups' stances on suffrage in any of the religious periodicals I examined. Such was not the case with the religious movements that divided the American religious field at the time. It is to them that we now turn, beginning in chronological order with the organizational center of American Protestantism at the time, the FCC. We then shift to the more divisive fundamentalist/modernist divide and the ensuing differences over views of evolution and science and, finally, to the movement that seems to have held the greatest explanatory leverage over the greatest number of religious groups examined here: the social gospel movement.

THE FEDERAL COUNCIL OF CHURCHES

The preeminent organization in the American religious field was, without a doubt, the Federal Council of Churches (FCC). Founded in 1908 with the express intent of enacting ecumenism and the social gospel movement (which will be discussed below), the FCC chronicled which religious denominations made pronouncements in favor of birth control.[19] In 1931 it even made its own pronouncement on birth control. These facts initially led me to suspect that the FCC was crucial to birth control reform.

However, I soon found that the FCC's support for birth control reform seemed to be one of effect (on the part of some of its powerful members), rather than cause (in terms of being the catalyst promoting those views). This was because, as with prohibition, membership in the FCC was broader than support for birth control. Thus, as table 6 indicates, many members of the FCC were not early supporters of reform, and some of these groups were extremely displeased that the FCC made its own statement in 1931, with one even severing its relationship with the FCC as a result. These views were chronicled by the *Lutheran Witness*, the periodical for the Lutheran Church–Missouri Synod, that same year:

> When birth control and contraceptives were discussed, the Federal Council of Churches, which purports to speak authoritatively for all Protestants, issued a statement which virtually approved of birth control and contraception. That action aroused a number of Protestant bodies to express their disapproval. Indeed, this procedure of the Federal Council has so exercised a number of denominations that they are now asking whether they should not leave the Council and separate from these men who pretend to represent them.[20]

Thus, the FCC's support for the legalization of contraception was not without controversy. This fact, however, does not mean that it was not a crucial organizational center of the movement for support of contraception among American religious groups. Put another way, perhaps the FCC actually weeded out those groups that could not support their pro-birth control views? However, this also does not seem to have been the case. While membership in the FCC was broad, it also had its limits. The most important of these limits was the fact that groups had to be a "church," by which the FCC meant Protestant, and exclusively so. This means that important early liberalizers such as the Unitarians and the Universalists were refused membership, on the grounds that their beliefs were too broad to be considered doctrinally Christian. Likewise, note that no Jewish groups were members—leaving us with the conclusion that membership in the FCC can explain neither groups' support for nor resistance to birth control reform.

MODERNISM AND FUNDAMENTALISM

Of all the religious movements that have divided the American religious field over the years, by far the most studied, referenced, and possibly maligned is the modernist/fundamentalist divide. Beginning almost contemporaneously with the eugenics movement and thus the movement to legalize birth control, the fundamentalist/modernist divide has had long-standing consequences for American religion.

Modernists "de-emphasized literal reading of the Bible, particularly its reports of miracles," and instead stressed a "broader interpretation that emphasized the Bible's general moral and ethical teachings."[21] In contrast, fundamentalists stressed the infallibility of the Bible. This divide became readily apparent to the American public in 1925, during the Scopes Monkey Trial on whether evolution should be taught in public schools. In that trial the key difference between the sides, which would become inseparable from the movement, were the two groups' disparate views of science.

Several scholars have suggested that modernist denominations became social gospelers, while fundamentalist denominations did not. For instance, in his history of the Progressive Era, Chambers conflates religious modernism with support for the social gospel, writing that modernists "emphasized liberal theological views including social activism on behalf of the poor and the downtrodden, a greater toleration of other faiths, and a belief that human society was making progress on earth and moving toward the realization of the Kingdom of God."[22] Similarly, Hutchinson argues that although contemporary journalists tended to define religious modernism simply as the "conscious, intended adaptation of religious ideas to modern culture" or "the direct opposite and negation of biblical literalism," in practice, modernism merged with social gospel beliefs:

> For the Protestant theologians, preachers, and teachers . . . two further and deeper notions were important. One was the idea that God is immanent in human cultural development and revealed through it. The other was a belief that human society is moving toward realization . . . of the Kingdom of God.[23]

It was clear from the periodical research that the fundamentalist/modernist divide was alive and well during the early part of birth control reform. Most groups knew where they stood and, perhaps just as importantly, seemed to have a sense of who stood there with them and who did not. Even more importantly, perhaps, as an indication of the centrality of the issue for American religious groups, even those groups that were not compelled to identify as either modernist or fundamentalist were forced to be clear about the fact that they were not taking a side. A few even discussed their refusal to do so at great lengths.

Beginning with the most obvious relationship, and one supported by the data presented in table 6, it is clear that there was a strong correlation between having a religious identity as a modernist and supporting birth control reform.

The following quote from the Universalist periodical *Christian Leader* gives a good sense of the careful but clear support for modernism apparent among those that professed their identities as religious groups open to change: "Modernism recognizes the great natural law of change, the universal flux both in the world of matter and of mind, and in order to accommodate itself to newly-discovered facts and newly-established positions pulls up its stakes, though with caution, and, obedient to the spirit of Protestantism, moves its tents."[24] Also indicated in table 6 is that modernists saw science as the greatest driver of, and legitimator of, that change. Perhaps not surprisingly, then, modernist groups were much more likely to discuss and advocate for the theory of evolution or a general belief in science than they were to discuss modernism or fundamentalism themselves. For example, the Universalist Church published only about one article a year on modernism or fundamentalism between 1925 and 1934

Table 6 Religious Identity and Membership in the American Religious Field circa 1930

Denominations	Federal Council of Churches[a]	Religious Identity	Belief in Evolution	Social Gospel
Early Liberalizers				
Society of Friends (Orthodox)	Yes	Modernist	Strong	Strong
Reform Judaism	No	Modernist	Strong	Strong
Universalist Church	No	Modernist	Strong	Strong
American Unitarian Association	No	Modernist	Strong	Strong
Methodist Episcopal Church	Yes	Modernist	Strong	Strong
Congregational Churches	Yes	Modernist	Strong	Strong
Christian Church	Yes	Modernist	Strong	Strong
Presbyterian Church in the United States of America	Yes	Silent	Weak[b]	Strong
Protestant Episcopal Church	Cooperating	Modernist	Strong	Strong
Unofficial Supporters				
Evangelical Synod of North America	Yes	Neutral	Weak	Opposed
Northern Baptist Convention	Yes	Neutral	Strong	Conflicted
United Presbyterian Church of North America	Yes	Neutral	Strong	Opposed
Norwegian Lutheran Church in America	No	Fundamentalist	Opposed[c]	Opposed
Critics				
Presbyterian Church in the United States	No	Silent	Strong	Silent
Southern Baptist Convention	No	Fundamentalist	Opposed	Opposed

Church of Jesus Christ of Latter-day Saints	No	Fundamentalist	Weak	Silent
Lutheran Church–Missouri Synod	No	Fundamentalist	Opposed	Opposed
Orthodox Judaism	No	Silent	Strong	Silent
Roman Catholic Church	No	Silent	Strong	Silent
	Silent			
Reformed Church in the United States	Yes	Modernist	Strong	Strong
Methodist Episcopal Church, South	Yes	Modernist	Strong	Strong
Conservative Judaism	No	Silent	Strong	Weak
Reformed Church in America	Yes	Fundamentalist	Silent	Weak
United Lutheran Church in America	Consultative	Fundamentalist	Weak	Weak
Disciples of Christ	Yes	Silent	Silent	Strong
African Methodist Episcopal Zion Church	Yes	Modernist	Strong	Strong
Churches of Christ	No	Fundamentalist	No	Silent
National Baptist Convention, USA, Inc.	Yes	Fundamentalist	No	Silent

a. As of 1932.

b. Groups that were coded as weak believers of evolution generally had very few articles published on the theory that were also not especially supportive. For example, the Presbyterian Church, USA, had three articles mentioning science and/or evolution. Two of these articles were not supportive of the theory, while the third article urged the church to apply psychology to religion, indicating some support for science. Thus, this group was coded as a weak supporter of science/evolution.

c. Groups coded as opposed to evolution actively criticized the theory and its supporters in statements such as: "No doubt we have been too slow in aggressive efforts to counteract the destructive influence of the evolutionary speculations posing as science." Vigness, "Educational Notes," 934.

yet published twice that many on science or evolution during those same years.[25]

However, the key purpose of this chapter is to examine possible explanations for groups' early stances on birth control. Here, the issue of religious identity becomes much stickier, suggesting that identifying as a modernist was neither necessary nor sufficient to explain reform.

Beginning first with the issue of whether a modernist identity was necessary, we must examine the case of the Presbyterian Church in the United States of America (PCUSA), the only early liberalizer that did not trumpet a modernist identity, in more detail. *Presbyterian Magazine* said nothing about the fundamentalist/modernist controversy between 1924 and 1925 and 1929 and 1932. However, the PCUSA tended to self-censor on issues with which its more conservative Southern "brethren," the Presbyterian Church in the United States (PCUS), with whom it was actively trying to merge, had difficulty. And it is certainly true that its silence on the issue mirrored the PCUS's at this time—thus leaving us with the possibility that perhaps the periodical research, for this one group, did not actually pick up that group's operational religious identity. Although I reject this argument for other reasons (if a group does not discuss its religious identity in its periodical, then where might one expect such discussions to occur—not to mention, how strong can that identity really be?), there are other reasons to question whether being a modernist was crucial to supporting birth control reform. Note that a number of strongly identified modernist groups remained silent on the issue of birth control—and that when they did so they were joined by other groups with fundamentalist identities as well as by groups that held neither identity strongly.

Thus, while there was clearly a strong correlation between being a modernist religious group and being an early liberalizer on birth control the modernism/fundamentalism divide does not seem to neatly explain the other possible stances groups took on birth control. In particular, both modernist and fundamentalist groups decided to stay silent on the issue of birth control. This suggests that while the issue of contraception certainly touched on groups' religious identities, it did more than that. It forced them to examine whether they believed that making pronouncements in favor of such secular—indeed, such profane—things as contraception could actually be understood as a religious duty. One crucial movement in the American religious field worked tirelessly for decades to convince American religious groups that yes, fixing society was not only a religious good but a religious duty. That movement was the social gospel movement.

THE SOCIAL GOSPEL MOVEMENT

First emerging in the United States in the late 1880s, social gospelers believed that Christ would return only after humans had finished preparing the earth for his arrival and that doing so required eradicating a number of social ills, especially poverty and war.[26] As a result of their beliefs, social gospelers were active social reformers.[27]

Belief in the social gospel was linked to major social disruptions, particularly "a series of large-scale, violent labor conflicts" (the railroad strikes of 1877, the Haymarket disaster of 1886, and the steel, coal, and other strikes between 1892 and 1894).[28] May argues that these three crises

> forced clerical observers to admit ... [that] despite free government and free religion, class gulfs had somehow grown up. . . . Already a major influence on American thought in 1895, [the social gospel] owed its existence to the impact of labor conflict than to any other cause.[29]

Although the term *social gospel* was not coined until later, by 1892 groups such as the Brotherhood of the Kingdom, which emphasized the importance of "the realization of Christ's Kingdom on earth" via the elimination of inequality, poverty, and misery, had been formed.[30] This progressive religious movement was first embraced by those with the most direct experience of life in the slums of industrialized cities.[31]

Although a systematic study of the movement that examines both its supporters and critics has been lacking, researchers agree that the Northern branches of "Presbyterian, Baptist, Methodist, and Episcopalian" and the Unitarians and Universalists were very active in the movement.[32] Despite the fact that these were all progressive Protestants working to bring about the second coming of the Messiah, Reform Jews had a deep belief in the holiness of social justice work and were also involved in the social gospel movement.[33] As historian of the social gospel movement

Paul Carter noted, the social gospel movement's emphasis on "social reform" appeared "among Jews in certain of the doctrines of Reform Judaism."[34]

Finally, although most studies of the movement argue that it was in decline by the 1920s, Carter found that it was revitalized by the Great Depression, with groups who had begun to be "lukewarm" about it by 1929 blazing "forth with all the old vigor."[35]

Given the lack of systematic information about the movement and the powerful effects of the Depression that were indeed often directly mentioned by many religious groups, particularly in relation to concerns about poverty, the only way to accurately measure belief in the social gospel at the time of birth control reform was to gather data on each denomination's views.[36] Doing so demonstrated that belief in the social gospel was a distinct theology that was still very much alive when American religious groups were making pronouncements on birth control circa 1930–31. More than one-third of the denominations in my sample (eleven out of twenty-seven) expressed a strong belief in the social gospel at this time, saying things similar to the Congregationalist Christian Church, which in 1931 railed against "the attempt within the church to silence the pulpit on vital questions, and to penalize those ministers who voice a protest against social and economic injustice and oppression."[37]

Coding the groups according to their actual statements on the social gospel proved crucial. This was especially the case for denominations like the Northern Baptist Convention, which claimed key social gospel theologian Walter Rauschenbusch as a member but which was quite ambivalent about the movement.[38] The details of their ambivalence and how it lead to their unofficial support for birth control reform despite their deep concerns about race suicide are explored more fully in chapter 4. For the purposes of this chapter, it is simply necessary to note that the ambivalence expressed by the Northern Baptists is consistent with other factors that differentiated them from strong social gospelers, especially their geographic location. Whereas most of the stronger social gospelers lived in urban areas, the Northern Baptists had "a large rural membership."[39]

That the movement was focused on urban and industrial concerns is apparent in many statements by the religious groups who were strong supporters. For example, the *Congregationalist* published the following quote by prominent theologian Reinhold Niebuhr, which directly connects industrialization and class inequality to the theology:

> The people who bear the burdens of modern industry and suffer from its moral limitations are, on the whole, not in the churches. The people in the churches are the higher middle classes who reap whatever advantages modern machine industry brings to the few and the lower middle classes who enjoy the comforts and conveniences which are the real blessings of modern industry with its high mechanical efficiency and tremendous productivity.... We can, therefore, if we want to, remain gloriously oblivious to the task of humanizing industry.... [This increases the burden for] every prophet of social righteousness who insists on applying Christ's gospel to industrial relationships.[40]

Concerns about the unfairness of industrial relationships were clearly connected to concerns about the awful reality of life in the urban slums. As one author in the *Herald of Gospel Liberty* aptly stated, "No man who opposes the social gospel ever has spent much time in the receiving ward of a great city hospital, where the bruised and maimed and dying are carried in from the shops and the streets."[41]

All of the early liberalizers expressed such beliefs in the social gospel movement, as did the groups who remained silent on birth control. It is the central argument of this book that denominations' views of the social gospel movement combined with their concerns about race suicide (or the lack thereof) to explain their views on birth control. But the point of this chapter has been to establish that, with the exception of belief in the social gospel, the divisions that most take for granted between America's progressive and conservative religious groups do not seem to have been the result of a progressive or conservative path as it relates to religious activism.[42] I argue that this is because a key, but largely overlooked, factor about the American religious field and American religion in general is the way American religious groups intersect with inequalities of race and class. As a result of these intersections, views and even doctrine on things regarding sex and gender reflect groups' racial and class positions rather than support for reform movements, such as abolition or temperance—however important to the modern-day identities these movements remain for some groups.

The next chapter examines the relationship between American religious groups and the key place where their racial and class positions were made apparent—the eugenics movement. In doing so, it explains why and how although most of the early liberalizers had no strong connections to Margaret Sanger's American Birth Control League (ABCL), they ultimately threw their weight behind her reform efforts because of the ABCL's strong connections to the eugenics movement.

2 Mobilizing America's Religious Elite in the Service of Eugenics

How and why did some religious groups come to see promoting birth control as their religious duty, while others did not? Although the American Birth Control League (ABCL), and the activism of its leader, Margaret Sanger, was certainly a necessary precondition, they alone cannot explain which groups supported reform. Sanger was largely disconnected from religious groups, and this chapter demonstrates that many of the early liberalizers had no discernible contact with her or her organization. In comparison, archival documents from the American Eugenics Society (AES) demonstrate strong, intentional, and long-lasting relationships with many religious leaders, particularly those whose denominations expressed the greatest concern about race suicide.

THE AMERICAN BIRTH CONTROL LEAGUE: OUTSIDE OF THE RELIGIOUS FIELD

The movement to legalize contraceptives was spearheaded by feminist activist Margaret Sanger. Sanger promoted her cause through public lectures, the publication of the *Birth Control Review*, beginning in 1917, and the formation of the ABCL in 1921. An outspoken and tireless feminist, Sanger frequently made arguments such as the following, published in 1919 in the *Birth Control Review*:

> When laws are passed that men (or some men) don't like, they have so many wonderful ways of evading them. . . . When women want medical information, safe, sane, decent contraceptive information to protect their health and their homes and their children—they are hounded, villified, jailed, fined, trapped.[1]

About religion, Sanger said little, save to gather data on the religion of the women who visited her clinic (and, in the case of Protestants, whether their husbands were Catholic) and to report, happily, that Catholics were using the clinic's services. Both eugenicists and their religious allies seemed to have eagerly awaited this data, reporting on it in their own periodicals— something that I explore more below. In terms of other religious groups, however, particularly those that supported Sanger's efforts, there seem to have been surprisingly few connections. As the second column of table 7 demonstrates, there was no discernible connection visible in the archives between the ABCL and nearly half of the denominations that made early pronouncements.

And formal contacts between denominational supporters and the ABCL were not the only missing connections. There were no standing committees dedicated to mobilizing friendly religious leaders, few relevant articles in the *Birth Control Review*, and no other evidence of interest in or attempts to communicate with friendly religious leaders in general.[2] This is not to say that involvement with the ABCL was not an important indication of other qualities, particularly feminism. The religious groups with formal involvement with the ABCL were among the first to make pronouncements on birth control, and their periodicals suggest that they were more feminist in their orientation than the other early liberalizers and more strongly supported women's suffrage and rights than those who had no relationships with the ABCL).[3] However, these more feminist groups were far from the only early liberalizers—a fact that suggests that neither involvement in the ABCL nor even openness to feminism can explain early stances on birth control.[4]

In actuality the story is a bit more complicated and much darker than many, especially religious progressives, might expect. Religious leaders—

even those more feminist groups that seemed more open to working with Sanger—were, in effect, brought into the birth control movement not by Sanger and the ABCL but by her crucial organizational and ideological ally: the AES.

THE AMERICAN EUGENICS SOCIETY AND THE RACIALIZATION OF RELIGION

Considering itself the "leader in its field" dedicated to "education," the AES sought to advance "the self-direction of human evolution" by curtailing the fertility of "undesirables."[5] Believers in the movement, which provided justification for involuntary sterilization in the United States and the Holocaust in Germany, believed that humans could engineer a better race by harnessing natural selection, encouraging desirable parents to have more children, and limiting the number of children born to undesirables.

Although eugenicists were concerned about poor whites' fertility, by and large the groups who most concerned eugenicists were the ethnic groups not considered "white" at the time—especially Irish and Italian Catholics and Jews.[6] The increase of the Catholic and Jewish populations (and the corresponding decrease of Protestants) was well documented in both the popular press and religious periodicals. For example, an article in the popular *American Magazine* reported that "thousands of Roman Catholics and Jews . . . [were] pouring into the city every year and settling districts formerly occupied by Protestants" in 1909.[7] The article was accompanied by the following figure, which powerfully illustrated how these changes had affected New York City.[8]

Catholic and Jewish immigrants were not considered part of the same "stock" as the immigrants who had founded the country, were generally poor, and were seen as racially and religiously inferior. As an example of just how deeply connected race, religion, and fertility concerns were at the time, take a 1915 article from the periodical *Current Opinion* that argued:

> Because of a greater Roman Catholic birth-rate, the United States is becoming a great stronghold of the Roman Catholic Church. . . . Present-day Protestantism, which in practices stands for a declining birth-rate, is thus

Table 7 Measures of Feminism among American Religious Groups circa 1930

Denominations	American Birth Control League	Autonomous Women's Groups[a]	Ordained Women, 1930[b]
Early Liberalizers			
Society of Friends (Orthodox)	0	Semi	Yes
Reform Judaism	3		No
Universalist Church	1	Semi	Yes
American Unitarian Association	2	Fully	Yes
Methodist Episcopal Church	2	Fully	No[c]
Congregational Churches	0	Semi	Yes
Christian Church	0	Semi	Yes
Presbyterian Church in the United States of America	0	Fully	No
Protestant Episcopal Church	3	No	No
Unofficial Supporters			
Evangelical Synod of North America	0	No	No
Northern Baptist Convention	0	Fully	Yes
United Presbyterian Church of North America	0	Semi	No
Norwegian Lutheran Church in America	0	No	No
Critics			
Presbyterian Church in the United States	0	No	No
Southern Baptist Convention	0	No	No

Church of Jesus Christ of Latter-day Saints		0	No
Lutheran Church–Missouri Synod	No	0	No
Orthodox Judaism		0	No
Roman Catholic Church	No	0	No

Silent

Reformed Church in the United States	No	0	No
Methodist Episcopal Church, South	No	0	No
Conservative Judaism		0	No
Reformed Church in America	No	0	No
United Lutheran Church in America	No	0	No
Christian Church (Disciples of Christ)	Fully	0	Yes
African Methodist Episcopal Zion Church	Semi	0	Yes
Churches of Christ	No	0	No
National Baptist Convention, USA, Inc.	Fully	0	Yes

a. Courtesy of Mark Chaves. *Fully* means that the denomination had a fully autonomous national board at some point in history. *Semi* means it had an independent board that cooperated with the denomination board. *No* means that women's groups were subsidiary to the denomination or that it did not differentiate by gender.

b. Chaves, *Ordaining Women*, 16–17.

c. The Methodist Episcopal Church "ordained women as local preachers in the early 1920s" but did not grant "full clergy rights" until 1956 (www .umc.org/what-we-believe/ask-the-umc-when-did-the-church-first -ordain-women) being driven back in all the great centers of civilization. . . . The situation in the United States is attributed to the influx of large masses of European Catholics who cling tenaciously to their religion, and to the much greater profitability of these stocks as compared with the native population.[9]

The article went on to quote a number of facts about differential birth rates between Protestants and Catholics in various US states, all of which, the article concluded, "indicate a remarkable increase of the foreign and non-Protestant section of the American people as compared with the Anglo-Saxon and Protestant."[10]

Not only were these groups considered inferior, however, they were also numerically and politically threatening to Anglo-Saxon Protestants.[11] Since the 1880s, the northeastern United States had been inundated with these immigrants, whose political machines soon "controlled one-half of the nation's twenty largest cities."[12] By the 1920s, native-born Americans found themselves outnumbered nearly three to one in New York City, with some estimating that up to 75 percent of urban adults were foreign-born.[13]

The AES was initially skeptical of birth control reform, believing that it would only exacerbate the "dysgenic" reality that better educated, wealthier white women were having far fewer babies than their poorer immigrant counterparts. Thus, for years eugenicists had steadfastly (but futilely) condemned birth control and promoted *positive eugenics*, the idea that "desirable" people should have more children, often emphasizing that at least "four children [were] requisite for maintenance of the stock."[14]

Although they never gave up their efforts to encourage more desirable people to have more children, by the mid-1920s there was a growing realization that the situation was only going to get worse (from the perspective of the Anglo ruling classes). Even after immigration restrictions drastically cut the number of new immigrants from these countries, it was well known that the foreign-born were reproducing at almost twice the rate of native-born whites. This situation created deep concern about race suicide—the idea that white Anglo-Saxon Protestants were *voluntarily* allowing themselves to be overtaken by these nonwhite Southern and Eastern European immigrants and their (more numerous) offspring.

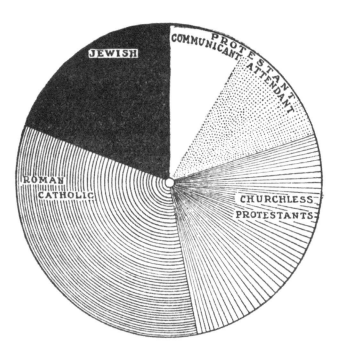

Figure 1. "Roman Catholics, Jews, and Protestants in New York
City," 1909.

As their concerns about race suicide grew, eugenicists also began to
promote *negative eugenics*, or the idea that undesirables (i.e., the poor and
immigrants) should be encouraged (or forced, if necessary) to have fewer
children. A 1930 article in the AES periodical *Eugenics: A Journal of Race
Betterment* illustrates these concerns clearly:

> Foreign born mothers averaged 3.8 children compared with 2.9 for the
> native . . . Italian and Irish mothers showed the greatest predominance in
> the large family groups. [Should] . . . these people . . . be allowed to perpetu-
> ate their pauper breed . . . society should protect itself from such burdens by
> sterilization of defectives and instruction about birth control methods.[15]

The AES began focusing on legalizing birth control after eugenicists won
a series of legislative victories that began with the passage of the Immigration
Restriction Act of 1924 and ended with involuntary sterilization legislation

in eleven states between 1927 and 1929.[16] Although immigration restriction had "stemmed the tide" of "inferior stock" coming into the United States and involuntary sterilization laws would prevent the "unfit" and "feeble-minded" from reproducing, eugenicists were still troubled by the immigrants who had entered prior to 1924 and were still living and reproducing in the United States.

Up until this point, the only legal way individuals could obtain contraceptives or contraceptive information was to consult a doctor. In no small part because of Sanger's tireless arguments on the matter, it gradually became clear that in order for the great masses of undesirables to be taught the "methods of birth control," contraceptive information needed to be taken out of doctors' hands and its distribution via other methods legalized. Although debate remains among historians as to whether Sanger's work with the AES was sincere or merely expedient, there is no doubt that connections ran deep.

CONNECTIONS BETWEEN THE AMERICAN BIRTH CONTROL LEAGUE AND THE AMERICAN EUGENICS SOCIETY

Key eugenicists had been publishing in the *Birth Control Review* and advising Sanger for some time. For example, Rev. W. R. Inge's article "Some Moral Aspects of Eugenics," first published in *Eugenics Review* in 1909, was reprinted in the *Birth Control Review* in 1920.[17] One year later a subtitle of the November 1921 issue of the *Birth Control Review* was *To Create a Race of Thoroughbreds*.[18] On the flip side, eugenicists had been listening to Sanger and using the data she gathered at her clinics—so much so that in 1929, the AES considered consolidating their periodical *Eugenics* with the *Birth Control Review*.[19]

In fact, the data that Sanger gathered was crucial for one of the key questions that bothered eugenicists in their campaign to curtail immigrant fertility: Given that the vast majority of undesirables who concerned eugenicists were Catholic and their church prohibited the use of contraceptives, would legalizing birth control do any good? Indeed, might it not make the problem even bigger if Catholics still eschewed contraceptives but contraceptives became more widely available to desirable populations? The following article from *Eugenics* attempted to reassure readers:

> Birth control will undoubtedly make many women healthier and their families happier, but who knows whether it alone, will be an effective factor in permanent racial improvement? One may predict with a reasonable degree of assurance that the more general use of contraceptives will at least reduce the extent to which the less efficient strata of society outbreed the upper social levels.[20]

In efforts to provide more ammunition to combat these fears, both Sanger and her supporters reported findings from her clinics that underprivileged *Catholic* and Jewish women would use birth control if it was made available.[21] For example, the *Birth Control Review* reported:

> Clinics are very largely used by the under-privileged. Impressive evidence of this is furnished by a careful analysis . . . of the first 500 cases at the Clinic on Maternal Health in Cincinnati. In 444 cases, or 89 per cent, the weekly family income was below $6.25 per member of the family. Fifty-six per cent already had four or more living children—nearly double that of the privileged classes—with a weekly per capita income of but $2.11. . . . Evidence could be multiplied. During the first two years of the Bronx House Clinic, in a *Jewish* neighborhood in New York, 403 women applied. Of these 231 had husbands without regular employment. . . . Eighty-two of the women were *Catholics*, and six of the 29 Protestant women had *Catholic husbands*.[22]

These efforts paid off. By 1930, articles in *Eugenics: A Journal of Race Betterment* were clear that the AES "should like to see contraceptive information extended so widely that everybody will know about it and then we believe that we shall see a new evolution."[23] By 1931, as the wave of religious pronouncements on birth control peaked, the AES distributed a promotional pamphlet that listed birth control, alongside standard eugenics programs such as immigration restriction and compulsory sterilization, as one of its principle legislative concerns.[24] It is worth mentioning, of course, that this timing almost exactly coincides with the peak years of pronouncements among America's most prominent religious groups, which will be examined in detail in the next chapter. When connections between the AES and these religious groups are examined, it becomes clear that this was no coincidence.

MOBILIZING AMERICA'S RELIGIOUS ELITE: A CORE STRATEGY OF THE AMERICAN EUGENICS SOCIETY

Although researchers acknowledge that many prominent American religious groups were involved in the eugenics movement, most studies of birth control or eugenics say nothing about religion, other than in reference to the infamous opposition of the Roman Catholic Church to birth control.[25] Likewise, most studies of American religion, even those that have examined the social gospel movement through the 1930s, say nothing about the wave of birth control pronouncements that took place among American religious groups in the early 1930s.[26] When these connections are examined systematically, it becomes clear that the AES saw America's most "nationally prominent ministers" as key allies in the fight to breed better humans.[27]

Knowing that it lent legitimacy and visibility to the movement, the AES worked hard to gain religious leaders' public support and made sure to catalog and reference that support often. Take, for example, the AES pamphlet titled "What I Think about Eugenics," which highlighted the American religious leaders and other important persons, such as university presidents, who backed its agenda.[28] In general, far beyond such advertisements, working with religious leaders was a key strategy for the AES and something into which it put a surprising amount of energy and resources.

The primary place where the AES collaborated with religious leaders was within its Committee for Cooperation with Clergymen (CCC), which was such a key organization for the AES that it received almost a quarter of its operating budget for committee work in 1927.[29]

Much of this money was spent on advertising, publicizing, and paying for a series of contests for the best sermon on eugenics.[30] The announcement of the 1926 contest in *Eugenical News* provides a nice picture of both how actively the AES worked to reach ministers, whom it called its "eugenic apostles," and how doing so was part of the plan to get its message to "good people" of the "intelligent classes":[31]

> Prizes of $500 for the best, $300 for the second, and $200 for the third
> best sermon are the rewards. Since the churches are in a measure a natural
> selective agency and since a large percentage of the intelligent classes are

church members, it is hoped that the message of eugenics will be received by thousands of people in the United States who otherwise would not hear it. The award should stimulate ministers to a deeper study of this subject, which has such an important bearing on the welfare of America. It has been said that good people make the churches and that the churches seldom make people good. Even if this is so, the American Eugenics Society hopes that this award will be a help toward the increase of good people in America.[32]

Table 8 presents the results of these and the other efforts the AES made to mobilize America's religious elite.

It indicates that the AES had much more thorough contact with all of the religious denominations that made early pronouncements on or expressed unofficial support for birth control than the ABCL. Two-thirds of the early liberalizers had representatives on the CCC, and all but one of the early liberalizers (the Quakers, who do not write sermons) had ministers submit sermons to the AES's competitions in 1926, 1928, and 1930.[33] In sum, almost all of the groups that provided either official or unofficial support for birth control in the early 1930s had either a representative on the CCC or at least one clergy who submitted a sermon. Most had both.

Admittedly, both of these measures could merely represent the views of the most extreme members of these denominations and not necessarily the mainstream. However, the next column of table 8 demonstrates that this is not the case. All of the denominations with strong connections to the AES via archival measures also expressed strong support for eugenics in their periodicals. And, except for two Southern denominations that will be examined in greater detail below, all of them also expressed deep concern about race suicide.

As the exception of the Southern denominations suggests, there is no doubt that geographic location was key to these patterns. In order to get a clear picture of the way in which geography was related to views of race and thus birth control, I created maps of the geographic concentration of all of the denominations.[34]

Map 1 demonstrates that Roman Catholics were fast becoming close to the majority of inhabitants in many areas of the country. Thus, when *Eugenics* informed readers that "the population which is Protestant by

Table 8 Support for Eugenics in the American Religious Field circa 1930

	Clergy on AES[a]	Sermons to AES	Eugenics in Periodical	Race Suicide in Periodical
Early Liberalizers				
Society of Friends (Orthodox)	1	0	Strong	Strong[b]
Reform Judaism	2	2	Strong	Strong
Universalist Church	0	1	Strong	Strong
American Unitarian Association	0	3	Strong	Strong
Methodist Episcopal Church	4	11	Strong	Strong
Congregational Churches	3	14[c]	Strong	Strong
Christian Church	0	2	Strong	Strong
Presbyterian Church in the United States of America	3	10	Strong	Strong
Protestant Episcopal Church	4	5	Strong	Strong
Percent of early liberalizers	**66%**	**100%[d]**	**100%**	**100%**
Unofficial Supporters				
Evangelical Synod of North America	0	0	Weak	Weak[e]
Northern Baptist Convention	5	5	Strong	Strong
United Presbyterian Church of North America	0	2	Strong	Strong
Norwegian Lutheran Church in America	0	1	Strong	Strong
Percent of unofficial supporters	**25%**	**75%**	**100%**	**100%**

Critics				
Presbyterian Church in the United States	1	1	Strong	Silent
Southern Baptist Convention	0	0	Strong	Opposed[f]
Church of Jesus Christ of Latter-day Saints	0	0	Silent	Silent
Lutheran Church–Missouri Synod	0	0	Opposed	Silent
Orthodox Judaism	0	0	Opposed	Silent
Roman Catholic Church	2	0	Opposed	Opposed
Percent of critics	**35%**	**17%**	**33%**	**0%**

Silent				
Reformed Church in the United States	0	0	Opposed	Silent
Methodist Episcopal Church, South	1	2	Opposed	Silent
Conservative Judaism	0	0	Silent	Silent
Reformed Church in America	1	2	Weak[g]	Silent
United Lutheran Church in America	0	1	Silent	Silent
Disciples of Christ	1	0	Silent	Silent
African Methodist Episcopal Zion Church	0	0	Opposed	Silent
Churches of Christ	0	0	Silent	Silent
National Baptist Convention, USA, Inc.	0	0	Silent	Silent
Percent of silent groups	**33%**	**33%**	**0%**	**0%**

a. Committee on Cooperating with Clergymen.

b. The *Yearbook's* "Resolution on Social Betterment" voiced concerns about the "disproportionate number of children born within those classes of society where destitution, unhygienic condition or irresponsibility prevail" and recommended, because "these circumstances" yield "comparatively poor progeny, to the detriment of the families concerned as well as of the nation," that "citizenship material ought to be more carefully and eugenically selected." Frisch, "Report of the Commission on Social Justice," 103.

c. Three of these were submitted by pastors at *Federated Churches*, a loose affiliation of Congregationalist, Northern Baptist, and/or Methodist Episcopal Churches.

d. This percentage excludes Quakers, who do not give sermons.

e. One article in the *Evangelical Herald* between 1929 and 1932 indicated concern about race suicide: "Historians ascribe the rudeness and coarseness of people and clergy in the Middle Ages to a large extent to the race suicide forced upon the priests and nuns. . . . Our cultured classes—for it is they which are in greatest danger—should be taught that the practice of birth control in such a way as to lead to permanent birth prevention is a *sin*—a sin against nature, against one's better instincts, against one's life-partner, and that it is also unpatriotic." "Is Birth Control Hostile to Race Culture?," 638.

f. Though there were three articles found in the *Christian Index* in 1919, 1924–25, and 1931 vaguely suggesting the existence of differential birth rates, the one article that explicitly mentioned race suicide was completely dismissive: "We note with pleasurable satisfaction that Atlanta does not believe in race suicide. Recently we had nineteen babies in the hospital at one time." "With the Hospital Family," 28.

g. Only two articles found in the *Christian Intelligencer* during the peak years of discussion (1929–32) mentioned eugenics, both of which focused on fitness for marriage, the most popular part of the movement. For example, "only a small percentage of married couples are fit physically, intellectually or morally, to bring up children." Studens, "The Point of View: An Obfuscated Rip Van Winkle," 56.

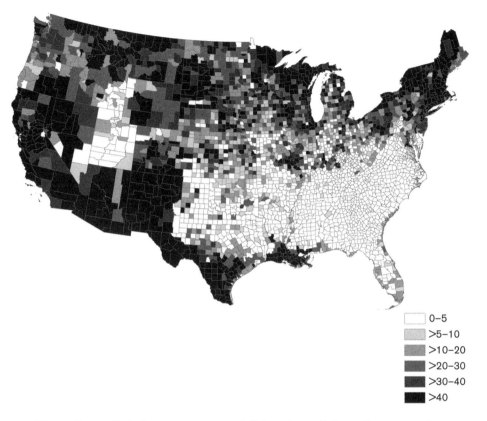

Map 1. Roman Catholics as a percentage of all American religious adherents, 1926.

heritage must be tending to decrease in proportion," it was right, particularly in the heavily industrialized areas of the Northeast, where the greatest proportion of Roman Catholics in the country lived.[35] As the sociologist Pope argued in 1948, most "new immigrants after 1880 were Roman Catholics, and their arrival greatly increased the strength of the Catholic Church in the United States, and also gave that church close connections with the growing mass of urban industrial workers."[36]

Of course, Roman Catholics were not the only immigrants whose fertility troubled eugenicists. Recent Jewish immigrants were also of concern. However, as table 8 indicates, Reform Jews (as well as two Catholic priests, but in a more limited way) were active in the AES. Given the fact that it will likely surprise many—indeed, it was initially quite surprising to me—Reform Jews' connections to the eugenics movement deserve some special attention.

JEWISH INVOLVEMENT IN THE AMERICAN EUGENICS SOCIETY

As an ethnic and religious group well known for suffering at the hands of eugenicists just a few years later in World War II and given the well-known anti-Semitism of leading eugenicists such as Charles Davenport and Madison Grant, how is it possible that Jews could have been involved with the AES? It is certainly not because Jewish fertility was of no concern. For example, the *Current Opinion* article quoted above "graded the different religious bodies in [New York] city with respect to the number of children per marriage in the following order: Jews (highest number), Roman Catholics, Protestant (orthodox), Protestant (liberal), Agnostic."[37]

However, not all Jewish fertility was high. Like Catholics, the Jews who had most recently immigrated had the highest birth rates. Unlike Roman Catholics, however, these newer immigrants did not belong to the same religious denomination as those who had come earlier.[38] Reform Jews were the earliest Jewish immigrants and thus the most assimilated, wealthiest, and educated of American Jews, with much lower birth rates than the newer cohorts of Jewish immigrants. Research by Rachel Ellis demonstrates that Reform Jews did not see recent Jewish immigrants as desirable members of their congregations.[39] In many ways, Reform Jews were closer to Mainline Protestants in their views toward immigrants than they were to Conservative and Orthodox Jews.

Given their views on immigrants, Reform Jews found common cause with the Protestant establishment that worked so closely with the AES to attempt to reduce immigrant birthrates. Like Mainline Protestant leaders, prominent Reform rabbis were involved in the AES.[40] Two Reform rabbis were closely affiliated with the CCC, and in fact, Jewish participation in the eugenics movement was so normal that a few rabbis even submitted sermons to the 1926 contest (although, perhaps not surprisingly, none of them won).[41]

Jewish involvement in the eugenics movement was facilitated in part by the fact that not all eugenicists were anti-Semitic—at least, not as openly as one would think prior to World War II, especially in the United States. In fact, a significant portion of the eugenics movement glorified Jews as the quintessential example of successful eugenics.[42] This is evident in the sermons submitted to the AES competition, of which fully one-third lauded Jews as great eugenicists. For example, according to Rev. John Archibald MacCullum from Walnut Street Presbyterian Church in Philadelphia, "many Jews rejoice in pedigrees that for length and detail throw those of oldest Nordic families far into the shade." He went on to argue that these pedigrees and way in "which [Jews] have always guarded the institution of marriage" provided "a partial explanation of the survival, ability and position of the Jewish people."[43]

Almost all of the pastors who lauded Jewish eugenics did so by relating Jewish genealogical practices to the advantages they conferred upon Jesus. For example, Rev. Arndt insisted that Jesus "was the climax of all that went before—eugenically."[44] The sermons that did not mention Jews positively simply said nothing at all. Jews were never spoken about in a negative way in the sermons.

Positive beliefs about Jewish eugenics were not limited to the sermons. Other archival documents from the AES suggest that most of the leadership was quite welcoming to Jews. For example, Henry S. Huntington Jr., chair of the CCC, stated unequivocally that "the verdict of history is that in a very real way [Jews] were superior."[45]

These sentiments were echoed, although in a much smaller proportion and counterbalanced with more negative statements about Jews, in the early liberalizers' periodicals. For example, a *Presbyterian Magazine* article noted "the presence of more than four million Jews in America . . . [who] boast a splendid past and possess natural endowments which insure to them a leading part in our nation's future."[46]

Thus, rather than posing a problem for this analysis, Reform Jews seem to be the exception that proves the rule—a group whose early support for birth control might not, initially, plausibly seem to be linked to a concern about race suicide or a belief in eugenics. Despite the anti-Semitism of many eugenicists, Reform Jews' support for eugenics is consistent with the way in which their immigration histories, class and ethnic backgrounds, and overall identities as part of the United States' upper class intersected. The next chapter will demonstrate that Reform Jews' statements on birth control clearly conveyed their eugenic concerns. We now turn to them and the other eight denominations that most wholeheartedly took part in America's project to prevent race suicide—and read, in their own words, why and how they became America's early liberalizers on contraception.

PART II Liberalization, 1929–1931

3 The Early Liberalizers

"THE CHURCH HAS A RESPONSIBILITY
FOR THE IMPROVEMENT OF THE HUMAN STOCK"

In his weekly column "Eugenics and the Church," the Reverend MacArthur wrote:

> The social ideal of the Kingdom of God on earth has been rediscovered by church leaders who are emphasizing an ideal humanity, a just and friendly world, a redeemed mankind. . . . Eugenics offers a way, consistent with Christian principles, of freeing the race in a few generations of a large proportion of the feeble-minded, the criminal, the licentious, by seeing to it . . . that persons carrying these anti-social traits shall leave behind them no tainted offspring.[1]

With this language, MacArthur was calling upon other religious leaders who believed they could and should work to bring about the "kingdom of God on earth" so the Messiah would return (or, as was the case with Reform Jews, finally come) to support their eugenic activities.

More than a quarter of the largest and most prominent American religious groups liberalized on birth control in the mere two years between 1929 and 1931. As map 2 demonstrates, these groups predominated on the coasts, especially the Northeast, where, where the biggest proportions of Roman Catholics (see map 1) and Jews lived.[2]

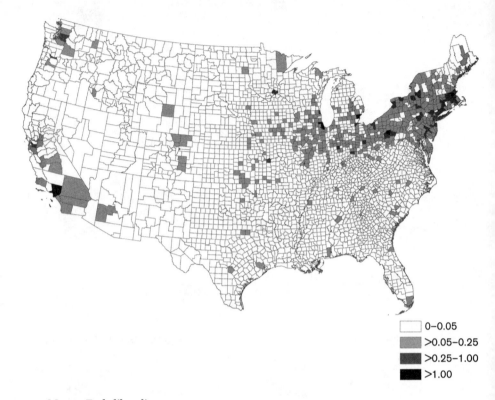

☐	0–0.05
▨	>0.05–0.25
▩	>0.25–1.00
■	>1.00

Map 2. Early liberalizers.

One after another, these nine religious groups (listed in the order of their official pronouncement)—Reform Judaism, the Universalist Church, the American Unitarian Association, the Protestant Episcopal Church, the Christian Church, the Congregational Churches, the Methodist Episcopal Church, the Society of Friends, and the Presbyterian Church in the United States of America—came out with public calls for the government to legalize the information and methods necessary to prevent unwanted pregnancies.

As the list indicates, these groups were mostly Mainline Protestants but were joined by Reform Jews, as well as Unitarians and Universalists, whose religious beliefs were too heterodox to be considered Christian in many circles. Furthermore, while the early liberalizers were mostly Mainline Protestants, there were many other Mainline Protestant denominations that did not liberalize.

The early liberalizers had two things in common that differentiated them from the groups that did not liberalize: they were extremely concerned that race suicide was threatening the future of the United States, and they believed deeply in the social gospel movement.

These cultural factors were dependent upon structural factors that this chapter will also explore. Key among them was their position as elites concentrated in the major urban centers of the Northeast whose political power was threatened by urban political machines adept at mobilizing immigrants and their offspring.

Until very recently, birth control had been virtually an untouchable topic. Despite the fact that it was almost universally condemned by religious groups and not discussed in polite company, it quickly became an "natural" solution to the early liberalizers' concerns. Such concerns were obvious in the Reverend Olin Stockwell's sermon that won third place in the 1926 American Eugenics Society (AES) competition. In it, Stockwell argued forcefully that "to relegate this subject of birth control to the limbo of the unspeakable is to invite further disaster and suffering upon both ourselves and our children."[3] Within a few years, religious groups began going officially on the record in agreement with such sentiments.

OFFICIAL SUPPORT FOR BIRTH CONTROL

By 1929 the denominations chronicled in this chapter had begun to take formal stances in favor of contraception. Their statements make it clear that these early liberalizers were not interested in simply pronouncing birth control acceptable; they wanted the laws that prevented the dissemination of contraceptive information changed. As the *Christian Leader*, the periodical for the Universalist Church, told its members in 1929, "We are stupid to allow such laws [against the distribution of contraceptive information] to remain on statute books and to be enforced. We are stupid unless we effectively organize and work against them."[4] One week later, joining the Society of Friends and Reform Jews, who had already made official statements earlier in the year, the Universalist Church formally called for "the immediate repeal of such Federal and State Laws as interfere with the prescription of contraception by physicians."[5]

The American Unitarian Association, the Presbyterian Church in the United States of America, the Methodist Episcopal Church, and the newly merged Congregational Christian Church followed suit the next year. The year 1930 also saw the Anglican Church liberalize at the Lambeth Conference. Although not an American religious body, the Anglican Church's statement was seen as the first major mainstream Christian denomination to officially make a pronouncement. The American wing of the Anglican Church, the Protestant Episcopal Church, liberalized a few years later.[6]

The eugenic influence on these statements is easily discernible. Take, for example, the Protestant Episcopal Church's statement:

> We endorse the efforts now being made to secure for licensed physicians, hospitals and medical clinics freedom to convey such information as is in accord with the highest principles of eugenics and a more wholesome family life, wherein parenthood may be undertaken with due respect for the health of mothers and the welfare of their children.[7]

Lest anyone doubt the true reasons behind reform, that statement was indexed not under *birth control* or *contraception* but under *eugenics*.

Even the Quakers, who generally shied away from openly promoting eugenics in their periodicals, clearly referenced it in their statement promoting birth control:

> Sociology and eugenics emphasize birth control continually as an important means of basically improving the quality of the human race. Obviously there should be a relatively large number of children from those parents who can support and educate them, and a relatively smaller number from less quali-fied parents.[8]

Eugenicists were delighted by the official and unofficial support they received from America's most prominent religious groups. Their periodi-cal, *Eugenics: A Journal of Race Betterment*, reported precisely and almost immediately about exactly which groups had made official pronounce-ments. By July 1930, *Eugenics* listed the "Universalist General Convention," "New York East Conference of the Methodist Church," "Connecticut Congregationalists," "American Unitarian Association," and "Rabbi Goldstein of the New York Free Synagogue" as religious leaders who had come out in favor of birth control.[9] As their religious supporters stood up to be counted one after the other, there was a palpable feeling of optimism among eugenicists. For example, that same year the executive secretary of the AES, Leon Whitney, wrote:

> I have said before that I felt that some day the twentieth century would be known as the eugenic century. Every indication points toward that fact, and I believe that a new century will find fewer hereditary unfortunates and in general a higher and a finer type of men and women with a greater capacity for happiness.[10]

However, while eugenicists were happy, where is the evidence that the religious leaders who were throwing their support behind the AES campaigns actually believed in eugenics? Maybe their support was simply expedient and does not indicate a true belief in eugenics? Their periodicals suggest differently.

BELIEF IN EUGENICS

The early liberalizers were not shy about discussing and promoting their belief in eugenics. All nine (which became eight in 1930) of the denominations that liberalized on birth control during this time period published at least one article per year promoting eugenics in their periodicals between 1929 and 1932, the peak years birth control was discussed. Most published twice that many. For example, the American Unitarian Association's periodical the *Christian Register* published seven articles between 1929 and 1932, an average of more than two per year, that promoted eugenic principles.[11] These articles were far from subtle. Take, as an example, the one titled "Religion and Eugenics," which argued simply that "the church has a responsibility for the improvement of the human stock."[12] Later, the same article asked readers, "Shall we harness heredity to produce better types of cattle, dogs, and horses, and do nothing with it to produce better types of men?" The answer, clearly, was no: "Surely as human beings we are as much entitled to the benefits of good breeding as are the brutes. If eugenics were to accomplish nothing more than the giving to the members of society a sound physical birthright, would not that in itself be a stupendous achievement?"[13]

In its least racialized, most general incarnation, their periodicals often mentioned the "difficult problem" of heredity. One article in the Universalist's *Christian Leader*, which published more than two articles per year during the peak years of discussion, asserted that such problems could be "corrected by the intelligent observation of the laws of eugenics."[14] It almost went without saying that a "sound physical birthright" would exclude any mental or physical illnesses that were seen as hereditary, which was made clear by articles in *Presbyterian Magazine*.[15] *Presbyterian Magazine* published five articles supportive of eugenics between 1929 and 1932. One of these was a two-part article. It marveled:

> What a complex personality the little child is! The scientists tell us that we can no longer attribute the child's heredity to his immediate parents and grandparents, but rather that he inherits from the entire blood-stream back of him. . . . "If one goes back to the days of Jesus, the number of calculated ancestors becomes some 18,000,000,000."[16]

The second installment continued:

> Marked individual differences, therefore, manifest among children along several lines. First of all there are the obvious physical differences, anatomical and glandular, which pre-dispose the child to a deficiency, abundance or super-abundance of vitality and activity. Complex racial strains filter down through the ancestry and strongly mark this child as vivacious, that one as phlegmatic.[17]

These groups deeply believed in the *science* of eugenics, seeing it as just an extension of the biological engineering humans had done for centuries. Thus, one finds calls for selective breeding like this article from the Methodist Episcopal Church's *Christian Advocate*:[18]

> Studying His attitude to sickness one finds it hard to believe that it is the will of God that men should be other than well. We question whether it is in accord with His will that we breed other than healthy human beings. . . . If we seek to purify a river, dry up the swamp that we may get rid of malarial fever, why not use the same sense in cleaning up the stream of life. . . . If we let nature alone she will fill up the swamp very slowly; she will breed the good fig but take a long time to do it. If we do a little selecting with figs and pigs and mice why not use the same common sense with men?[19]

The article closed by posing "Questions for Discussion" for Sunday school students, one of which was "Is 'breeding the race' compatible with the spirit of Jesus?"[20] The Methodists' answer? Yes.

Sterilization was the most radical method the early liberalizers promoted to achieve their eugenic hopes. For example, an article rather ironically titled "Prejudices" in the *Christian Register* intoned ominously that "nature keeps her human orchard healthy by pruning."[21] But even articles milder in tone promoted sterilization. For example, the Christian Church's *Herald of Gospel Liberty*, which averaged between two and three articles promoting eugenics per year, published an article that argued for the importance of "environment and training" (the most common phrases used to counter eugenic arguments) in attempts to reduce juvenile delinquency.[22] But even it advocated the sterilization of "sub-normals":

> There are those unfortunate individuals who have been endowed with such inferior physical or mental equipment that their misdeeds are easily misunderstood, and the treatment is not difficult to find. . . . Society will yet have to face frankly the situation that arises by reason of the propagation of sub-normal children by sub-normal parents. As yet, we have not passed beyond the stage where "sterilization" can be spoken above a whisper; but, until we are willing to think straight and act courageously, the agencies will be forced to continue to treat unnumbered individuals while prospective delinquents are propagated without restraint.[23]

These groups were also well aware that involuntary sterilization would only occur if eugenicists lobbied for legislation supporting it.

In his award-winning sermon on eugenics, reprinted in the *Congregationalist*, Rev. Edwin Bishop argued that "if marriage is entered into by those notoriously unfit . . . the state has a right to insist on sterilization." Clearly, however, the pastor recognized that involuntary sterilization, however ideal, was not likely to fix the problem. That sermon concluded: "Knowledge of birth control should be widely and freely disseminated, so that among certain groups in our civilization there may be not more, but fewer and better children."[24]

While these calls for sterilization, "pruning," or legal action in general were often intentionally vague, closer examination makes it apparent that those whose fertility was to be controlled were of a lower class. Often, this was implied via adjectives such as *superior* or *inferior* or *desirable* or *undesirable.* But often these discussions mentioned education or class, specifically. Discussions of class were especially common in relation to what these groups saw as the key issue facing America's eugenic legacy— differential birth rates between desirable and undesirable parents—as the mention of "fewer and better children" above implies.

Race Suicide

In article after article, these groups' concerns about birth-rate differentials were abundantly clear. The *Christian Register* warned that "the general mass of human wreckage" was "producing twice as fast" as the best stock:

> Insane, feeble-minded, criminals, paupers, and the general mass of human wreckage . . . are on the increase . . . reproducing itself twice as fast as the normal family. . . . What is to become of the race if we breed twice as fast from our poorest as from our best stock? It can only mean physical, mental, and moral decay.[25]

Likewise, an article in the Universalist's *Christian Leader* argued:

> The most alarming tendency of our time is found in the low birth-rate among the superior breeds and the high birth-rate among the inferior. Without much question we are breeding twice as fast from the worst as from the best. No observing and thinking person can overlook this problem.[26]

These religious leaders were often explicit about what qualities defined the "desirable." In a quote that equated desirability with education, the Unitarian *Christian Register* warned:

> The self-evident fact that the desirable classes are not reproducing themselves, and that the weaklings are, is ominous for the future. The average women American college graduate has only one and a half children when she ought to have four, if the members of her class are to be kept up.[27]

Reform Jews, who did not have a consistent, popularly oriented periodical during the peak years of analysis, were also explicit in their reports on the Commission on Social Justice in 1926 and 1929.[28] Emphasizing the importance of positive eugenics, their 1926 report noted that "birth control is already practiced virtually everywhere by the well-to-do classes" and argued that it was "requisite to urge parents possessed of high-grade physical, mental and moral qualities and adequate economic resources to beget more children than those types of families at present have."[29] The next report expressed more concern about the "many serious evils caused by uncontrolled parenthood among those who lack the prerequisites of health and a reasonable measure of economic resources and intelligence to give to their children the heritage to which they are entitled."[30]

As another example of race suicide concerns, take the following sermon submitted to the AES competition for the best sermon on eugenics in 1926, during which a Congregationalist minister extolled his congregants that

> to have a better America and a better world . . . the people with the best qualities of character should be greater in number. Here you and I can, in a direct way, do very much good. It is our privilege to let our tactful influence bear upon the better class of people and encourage them to reproduce their own kind. It is very obvious that people of the higher class, the people with strong minds and hearts, need to be encouraged to have more children. In order to keep the human race alive each family must have an average of 3.7 children.[31]

Likewise, a 1930 article in the Quaker periodical the *Friend* stressed that there was a "need for birth control among the poorer classes of society" and emphasized the "danger to society of the decline of the birth rate among the more educated and privileged classes."[32]

It is important to stress here that for these religious leaders, class differences were assumed to be hereditary. Thus, even though they mentioned education, for example, their solution was that the highly educated should breed more, not that all people should become more highly educated. These beliefs are especially apparent in statements that explicitly reference race suicide. For example, the *Congregationalist and Herald of Gospel Liberty* insisted:

> Every [good] marriage must have a minimum of three children in order to fulfill its social obligation in maintaining the present level of population . . . those who are able must average four or more in order to prevent race suicide. Right here we face the alarming situation that so far as the educated people are concerned race suicide has already begun.[33]

In their warnings of race suicide, the early liberalizers were often intentionally vague about exactly what "race" was threatening to kill itself. However, an article in the Unitarian *Christian Register*, which quoted the well-known Anglican minister and prominent eugenicist Dean Inge, suggested that their primary concern was the white, and not the "human," race:

> In birth control we have in our hands an instrument which is capable of being turned to great good and still greater evil. It may be so used as to further the cause of social hygiene, which indeed can hardly be advanced without it. It may be so used [by eugenics] as to secure the optimum population in every country, and to put a stop to the dysgenic selection which at present threatens the whole future of the white races. Or it may be an instrument of moral dissolution and racial suicide.[34]

For eugenicists and the religious leaders allied with them, the biggest threat to the "white races" came from the "hordes" of immigrants who had inundated the country over the past few decades and who were having children at alarming rates. In fact, the early liberalizers were probably more concerned about immigrants' fecundity than they were simply about the poor. And it is in their statements about immigrants that the religious nature of their concerns also becomes apparent.

Views of Immigrants

That birth control reform was the easiest and most obvious way to deal with immigrants' "runaway fertility" was widely acknowledged by the late 1920s. For example, one sermon submitted to the 1926 AES competition argued: "There should be the recognition and regulation of helpful methods of birth control. Many scientists wisely advocate a saner restriction of immigration from other countries. But equally necessary is a wiser control of the "immigration from Heaven.""[35]

Like eugenicists in general, the early liberalizers were vehemently anti-immigrant and in favor of immigration restriction, often quoting well-known eugenicists like Edward Ross or Dean Inge and using metaphors that conjured up "floods" and "tides" to describe immigration.[36] For example, in 1924 the Christian Church stated that it was "taken for granted" that "some restrictions are necessary to prevent the flood of undesirables which otherwise would come to our shores."[37] The *Living Church* reported positively on a book that analyzed "the onrushing tide of mankind, its ebbs and flows, across continents and hemispheres, its surges into urban areas of high concentration."[38]

Less metaphorical articles were common as well. The Methodist *Christian Advocate* argued that restrictions were needed to "guard carefully our own national heritage" and "maintain our standards—economic, social, educational, moral, *religious*" and in another article asserted that "the unassimilated foreign born are responsible for a very large share of America's crime and lawlessness," especially in "the Jewish ghettos and Little Italies, where the children learn to speak the English language while parents remain ignorant of our ways and language."[39]

As the immigration restrictions of 1924 and 1928 went into effect, these religious groups indicated clear approval. The Protestant Episcopal Church's periodical, the *Living Church*, excitedly announced, "With the passage of the new quota law . . . the responsibility imposed upon those who handle cases from the 'predominantly non-Roman Christian countries' is already registering a marked increase."[40] Other articles in the *Living Church* applauded the "new policy of restriction" because "it will certainly prevent the further dilution of our stock, which has unquestionably been in serious danger" and because "we now draw our immigrants from a better class than formerly."[41]

A *Herald of Gospel Liberty* article welcomed the new laws as "a big step forward in immigration legislation" and explained how the new quotas would favor "the countries of northern and western Europe from which the original stock has come." It added, contentedly, "Of the 150,000 admissible, Great Britain alone will be entitled to about 90,000 of the total number."[42] Another *Herald* article indicated that the leaders of the Christian Church were not only happy about who would be let in but also about who was being kept out. Unlike some threads of the eugenics movement that lauded Jews as great eugenicists, this periodical made it clear that cutting down on Jewish and Catholic (especially Italian Catholics, according to this article) immigration was a positive development. The article noted with approval:

> The new quota laws are causing a marked decrease in the immigration from Europe. This is particularly true of would-be European Jewish immigrants.

They are turning to other lands than the United States for their new homes. Last year, 11,598 Jewish immigrants passed through our Ellis Island gates, while some twenty thousand other Jews left Europe to become settlers in Brazil, Argentina, and other South American countries, whose laws are less rigid than ours. The difficulties placed upon Italian emigrants by Premier Mussolini will restrain Italians from coming to this country.[43]

In sum, all of the early liberalizers had strongly anti-immigrant views, supported immigration restriction, saw the racial stock of current immigrants as inferior to the stock of the Anglo-Saxon immigrants who had founded the country, and were deeply concerned about the high birth rates of the foreign-born—especially Jews and Italian Catholics.

Even Reform Jews fit within this description. Although they opposed immigration restriction (because it would prevent Jews fleeing from "political oppression or religious persecution" from entering the country), they shared early liberalizers' concerns about immigrants' greater fecundity and its implications for quality.[44] Thus, in 1920 they urged "the nation to keep the gates of our beloved republic open" and in 1922 "deplore[d] the action of the United States Government in virtually abandoning its policy of keeping America a haven of refuge for the persecuted and down-trodden of the world."[45] A few years later, however, they noted with concern that

grave inroads are being made upon the well-being of our nation and other nations viewed as a whole, through the bringing in of a disproportionate number of children born within those classes of society where destitution, unhygienic conditions or irresponsibility prevail; these circumstances resulting in a comparatively poor progeny, to the detriment of the families concerned as well as of the nation.[46]

They closed by noting the "growing and justified widespread opinion that the citizenship material ought to be more carefully and eugenically selected" with approval.[47] Reform Jews' eventual acceptance of immigration restriction is consistent with Rachel Ellis's findings that Reform Jews found newer Jewish immigrants to be so distasteful that they did not even consider attempting to attract them to their denomination, preferring instead to wait for the "Americanization of the immigrant."[48]

Of course, Jews were the exception among the early liberalizers. Because they shared, at the very least, a religious identity with the newer

Jewish immigrants, they were less harsh about immigration in general. The remaining early liberalizers did not share a common religion with many, if any, of these immigrants, and their awareness of these religious differences was plainly obvious in their statements.

Anti-Catholicism and Anti-Semitism

Although it was mentioned less often than their "foreign" status, research on the eugenics movement has established that religion was a key part of immigrants' undesirable status, as "Nordics were Protestant, Alpines and Mediterraneans were Catholic."[49] There were many ways in which it was apparent that the religion of the majority of new immigrants was a serious concern to the early liberalizers.

In 1931 the *Congregationalist and Herald of Gospel Liberty* painted a rather dire picture of the religious changes (and chaos) in Chicago:

> Chicago represents the chaos, not only of Europe and America, but of the world. . . . The contrast between the Catholic and Protestant methods of church planting is most significant. . . . Dire are the needs where the Protestant churches have died or departed. These regions reveal the most numerous cases of juvenile delinquency and family disorganization, the highest rates of infantile mortality and death by tuberculosis, the lowest percentage of people who own their homes and the smallest average incomes. . . . There are in Chicago, not including the suburbs, 256 Catholic churches, each with a distinctive parish and a logical location. Their distribution has evidently been carefully planned. The Protestant organizations number about 1,100. If the Catholic churches appear to be marching, the Protestant ones seem to be indulging in guerilla warfare. No one has guided the distribution of these groups. . . . One of the issues facing Protestantism in Chicago is whether or not it can make a concentrated attack upon the disintegrating influences of city life.[50]

That same year, a Unitarian article reported on a similar angle, but with a more national focus:

> The Catholic birth rate in this country is seventy percent higher than the birth rate for the country as a whole. The excess of Catholic births over—500,000—is nearly three times that of the excess of births over deaths for the registration area. Allowing for mixed marriages and the effect of the Catholic birth rate on the general birth rate, it is more than four and a half

times the excess of births over deaths. Catholics therefore, by this excess of births over deaths, should be increasing nearly five times as rapidly as non-Catholics.[51]

Although religious differences were most often referenced simply in terms of Catholics versus Protestants, sometimes these religious leaders did get more specific. For example, the Unitarians reported on a study of various religious groups' ability to reproduce "eminent sons":

> Baptist clergymen fathered 1,105 eminent sons; Methodist clergymen, 495 sons; Presbyterian, 4,325; Episcopal, 5,565; Congregational, 6,000. Data for Unitarians are not given, because the numbers of our body are small for such a computation; but ... Unitarians rank even higher than Congregationalists. Mr. Huntington [of the AES] draws attention to the decisive superiority, in this field of comparison, of the factors of persecution and selection.... Freedom of thought, economic comfort, educational standards, and of *course religious training*, are tremendous factors in making exceptionally strong men. By contrast, the limitations of the Methodists in this respect are attributed to the fact that they have suffered no persecutions, and *the process of selection* is by no means like that prevailing among other denominations. The Roman Catholics have been under religious authority, and they are poor. There are no Catholic sons for comparison, of course, but the rank of Catholic people in respect of both leadership and intelligence has been relatively low.[52]

The article closed with strong eugenic statements that illustrate just how connected religious group and "stock" were for these early liberalizers:

> By several stages in the process of natural selection, they attained ... high moral, intellectual, and competent character.... But whatever we do, we must not weaken our stock by halting or turning back. We must guard against such alleged fellowship as vitiates our moral vigor, relaxes our spiritual ambition, and stultifies our reasonable doctrine.[53]

Similarly, in a sermon given to his Brooklyn Heights Presbyterian Church in San Diego, one pastor equated religion, immigrants, and "a taint in the blood":

> The class of immigrants, who come to our country and do not sympathize with our common heritage of faith, will pass that lack of spirit on to their children.... It has a great effect upon the religious conditions of our country.... Religious leaders have a deeper interest because the basic principles

of life are involved. Think also of the biological effects of immigrants, especially if they belong to the group having a taint in the blood, or some form of mental or physical defect![54]

Often, immigrants' Catholicism was implied by both their nationality and descriptions (usually disparaging) of their beliefs or religious practices. For example, an article in the *Congregationalist* reported the following horrendous situation about Slovakians who, the author felt, persisted in their unhealthy ways despite, or perhaps because of, their church's belief in the Sacrament of Penance and Reconciliation (commonly called confession): "The Pittsburgh District has a general missionary . . . who goes from house to house among the Slovaks. He finds booze, incipient crime, poverty, sickness, and religion; the latter the kind that seems to be impotent to deliver from sinful conduct although the soul is given absolution."[55] A *Presbyterian Magazine* article focused on the large families of Czechs, whose Catholicism was made apparent when the article compared them to "the neglected condition of these Protestant Czechs . . . brought to the attention of our Presbyterian Church."[56]

That religion, race, class, and fitness or desirability were seen as inseparable is also made clear from what is not said in the early liberalizers' periodicals. Despite the relatively common assertion that foreigners were un-Christian or "unchurched," calls to evangelize or convert immigrants to Protestantism were quite rare, occurring almost exclusively among the Southern denominations discussed in later chapters.

In fact, the Congregational Christian Church article that focused on Chicago closed with the following acknowledgment of defeat:

> Apparently great major groupings of religion in Chicago—Protestant, Catholic, and Jewish—are permanent. Few hope to solve the problems of religious competition by one group converting all the rest. The greatest need is a procedure of cooperation. For the Protestant denominations there must be a "planned economy" which will involve more than the elimination of wasteful competition. We must find a new strategy in which overhead organizations and local church leaders will co-operate.[57]

Likewise, readers of *Presbyterian Magazine* were asked to "think of whole segments of our population, particularly foreign races, for example, almost wholly outside the influence of the church," who suffered from "superstition and ignorance."[58] However, they were never asked to consider evangelizing to them. Even the one article that appeared in the *Herald of Gospel Liberty* calling for greater evangelization to foreigners makes it clear that this call was new and in response to a general dearth of such activity on the part of American Protestants. They noted that "the churches and Christian forces of our great cities were for years almost wholly indifferent to their need, and sometimes even unkindly disposed towards them. If this has been true of churches, it has been excessively true of individual Christians."[59]

In an article published in the *Friend Intelligencer*, Rufus Jones, a Quaker elder who was on the AES Committee for Cooperating with Clergymen, equated poor whites with "savages" who do not make "homes" or hold "family life at all sacred."[60] However, rather than making a call to convert these "poor whites," Jones mentions missionary work only in relation to foreign missions:

> The Christian home is the highest product of civilization; in fact, there is nothing that can be called civilization where the home is absent. The savage is on his way out of savagery as soon as he can create a home and make family life at all sacred. The real horror of the "slums" in our great cities is that there are no homes there, but human beings crowded indiscriminately into one room. It is the real trouble with the "poor whites" . . . that they have failed to preserve the home as a sacred centre of life. One of the first services of the foreign missionary is to help establish homes among the people whom he hopes to Christianize.[61]

Given that their religion was seen as immutable and they were thus not convertible, the fact that they were uneducated (not to mention poor) made Catholic immigrants' high birth rate even more problematic. It was not only a serious threat racially but also a crucial problem politically for the early liberalizers. Either immigrants were intent on trying to "dethrone the Puritan tradition," as the *Christian Advocate* warned or, more commonly, were "easily exploited" by urban political machines that sought to end these elite groups' dominance in the American political system.[62]

Political Power

General anti-Catholic sentiments were often framed in terms of "Rome's" political ambitions and general lack of deference to democracy and rights. For example, the *Christian Register* wrote:

So long as there is opposition to her control, Rome will strive to overcome it, in every department of life. She always has done so. It is true in all things that "whosoever usurps a share of her commission is not a shepherd but a ravening wolf," as *America* says.[63]

Anti-Catholic statements were particularly common during Al Smith's presidential campaign of 1928. For example, an article titled "Before We Vote" in the *Christian Register* wrote:

On one side stands a Church, absolute in its spiritual authority over all its obeisant children, which throughout its history has attempted to control, as spiritual, the political affairs of every state in which it has been able to gain power. It is consistent, patient, inexorable; and sometimes it seems, out of its marvelous and unbroken, if unhappy history, to be so sure that it will yet attain the great prize of terrestrial dominion in the name of its celestial infallibility, that those who stand opposed, though they are a vast majority, feel the atmospheric pressure of this Roman absolutism, and breathe heavily in the land of freedom. This is not rhetoric, but fact. . . . If we may not say we prefer a Protestant for President, without having our patriotism as well as our sanity doubted, we shall indeed have already passed under the control of that subtle power against which our souls should stand as adamant.[64]

The Methodist *Christian Advocate* seemed literally obsessed with the Roman Catholic Church's political ambitions, publishing sixty-eight articles in 1925 alone on Catholicism, many of which asserted, for example, that the Roman Catholic Church "has never promoted the spirit of democracy in any country where it has predominated."[65]

Many of these religious groups expressed outrage that the First Amendment was violated when the superintendent of a hall in Boston prevented Dr. James F. Cooper from giving an address titled "Sociological and Moral Aspects of Birth Control" to the American Unitarian Association, as an article in the *Congregationalist* complained:

It is not the first time that such a thing has occurred in Boston. When Curley, the Roman Catholic and Democrat, was mayor, he repeatedly used his power to prevent the Ku Klux Klan holding meetings in the city, and he also made it impossible for Margaret Sanger to speak on birth control or for the Socialist party to hold a peace demonstration.[66]

However, while there was plenty of material in the early liberalizers' periodicals about the Roman Catholic Church as an institution, what they were really worried about seemed to be Roman Catholics as *voters*.

Urban Political Machines

By the 1930s, Irish bosses "controlled such cities as New York, Brooklyn, and San Francisco."[67] Returning to table 2, note that the early liberalizers were among the oldest, most urban, and most northeastern of the denominations in our sample, with the smallest growth rates. Living in the areas with the greatest influx of Roman Catholic immigrants, early liberalizers no doubt witnessed these groups growing in proportion and political power. Thus, an article in the *Presbyterian Magazine* warned that "our great hoard of foreign-born or American-born of 'foreign descent,'" would cause Americans to "cease to be American in the Washington and Lincoln sense of the word, and become slaves of a foreign element which will eventually dominate our country, more in the future than in the past."[68]

Likewise, after asserting that "the political evolution of the United States is to be from Anglo-Saxon to a new cosmopolitan race called American," the *Living Church* asked, "Can the ideals . . . of Magna Charta [*sic*] . . . be safely confided to such trusteeship? God only knows. Whether we like it or not, the experiment is being worked out in the nation."[69] A large part of this political evolution was a result of urban political machines, which the early liberalizers believed merely sought to exploit these "ignorant" immigrants, as the following article from the *Presbyterian Magazine* explicitly noted:

> The coming together of immigrant populations has its challenge. While most immigrants were peasants in the old country, here they flock to the cities, living in their Ghettos, their little Italies, their San Juan Hills. Unaccustomed to our food, our manners, and our methods of living in general, they are often extremely unhappy for a time, *usually exploited (and by their own race)* needing friendship and kindness above everything else.[70]

In an article titled "Our Newspapers and Criminals," the *Presbyterian Magazine* indicated deep (and eugenic) concern about "a large proportion of adults who are too easily controlled by" politicians:

Other factors in the process of suggestion are in the person himself who is exposed to stimulation by acts of others, or spoken words or deeds. One of these is lack of experience, and it is children and adults of little experience or low degree of intelligence who are most suggestible because of this. It is that segment of society from which come the bulk of our prison population, the young and the socially inadequate. It is usual in discussions of causes of crime and causes of vice to confine one's self to the influence of environmental causes on children. The implication seems to be that they may be corrupted by their associations, but that the adult is somehow immune to such influence, and the causes of his depravity are to be sought elsewhere. Of course such a position is untenable; adults are suggestible in proportion to their lack of well inculcated attitudes and ideals, and there is a large proportion of adults who are too easily controlled by the process of suggestion, even when so crudely used as it is by politicians.[71]

Another article in the *Congregationalist and Herald of Gospel Liberty* questioned the utility of the "ward politician" in helping immigrants who were "bewildered by the strangeness" of their new environment:

Speaking a foreign language, many of them, bewildered by the strangeness of their environs, making no contacts with all that means America to us, save through *the ward politician* and the foreman in some factory, how are we going to build them into a worthful citizenship? . . . The problem seemed utterly hopeless while our immigration doors stood wide open. It is now clarified to this extent that we have largely stopped all fresh invasions. But we have millions of such people on our hands. How are we going to lift so vast a horde to the bare minimum of what constitutes real American manhood and womanhood? . . . Given ignorance and poverty almost anything can happen, and we have these forces at work in some form or other throughout almost half our population.[72]

Allusions to concerns about urban political machines are also often detectable in statements about voting and voters. Complaining, for example, that "recent immigration" had "made America the dumping ground of the least promising stock of the nations of southern Europe," Methodist Episcopal Church pastor Reverend Fetter told his congregants that "the largest percentage of future *American voters* were coming from the city's most unpromising environment and in many cases from its most deficient stock."[73] The *Presbyterian Magazine* referred to foreign *blocs*:

The country is vast. So is the population. The people are of all kinds and tongues. Many do not speak or understand English. They and the native-born live under conditions of kaleidoscopic variety. There are frontiers, rural regions and little villages that cannot provide for their own spiritual needs, much less help others. There are our cities—what a spectacle for God and man to contemplate! with their great foreign *blocs*, with the whole welter of "confusion, disorderly mixture, aimless conflict of creeds, policies, vices" of every great city.[74]

The issue was not just that immigrants were easily exploited and thus their votes easy to influence but that these votes influenced the politicians who were supposed to represent the people. For example, an article in the Protestant Episcopal Church's periodical the *Living Church* lamented that "foreign-born groups influence the action of representatives" in "our great cities."[75] A 1931 article in the *Christian Advocate* bemoaned "the power of politicians that pander to racial or ethnic groups."[76]

That political power was at the root of their concerns is clear not only from what they said but also from what these religious leaders reported doing. In addition to lobbying for birth control to be legalized, they also lobbied Congress for a constitutional amendment to change congressional representation. The *Living Church* argued that the amendment was nec-essary because "the immigration trend of the last two decades" has created an "alien influx to our great cities [which] gives these urban centers an unfair advantage over the rural sections and agricultural states."[77]

Controlling Catholic Fertility

At the root of all the actions and statements discussed so far, of course, was a deep concern that immigrants were having many more children than native-born WASPs. It was obvious to many that better-off WASPs had greater access to doctors and that a large part of the birth-rate differentials between the native and foreign-born was a result of this fact. As a Methodist congregation was told in a sermon submitted to the 1928 AES competition: "Those lower in the scale of intelligence and character are producing large families. Many who are not so seriously defective as to require segregation or sterilization, or for whom there are not at present adequate provisions for institutional care, should be taught the methods of birth control."[78]

As there was in the eugenics movement in general, there was considerable concern among the early liberalizers that reform efforts would be wasted because Catholics would not use contraceptives. Recall the article from the *Presbyterian Magazine*, quoted earlier, that argued that making contraceptive information available "would have no bearing or influence for good on our great hoard of foreign-born or American-born of 'foreign descent.'"[79] However, Sanger's efforts to chronicle Catholic and Jewish use of contraceptives at her clinics seem to have effectively eased these fears. In 1933 the Society of Friends' *Statement on Birth Control* reassured its members by citing the *Birth Control Review*'s finding that contraceptive information was being given out "mostly to the underprivileged mother."[80]

Thus, by the end of the 1920s, these denominations had become convinced that the race was in grave danger and that legalizing birth control was the best way to eliminate that danger, despite the Catholicism of those whose fertility most needed to be checked. However, their eugenic and anti-Catholic beliefs alone do not explain early liberalizers' willingness to officially change their doctrine on birth control, even when combined with the palpable anxiety they expressed about their losses of political power. As we will see in the next chapter, they shared their eugenic beliefs and anti-Catholicism with other denominations that did not officially liberalize.

What set the early liberalizers apart from these other denominations was the way in which their belief in eugenics and concerns about race suicide combined with their clear, undaunted belief in the rightness and importance of the social gospel—a belief that led them to become deeply concerned about poverty, war, and social injustice and, crucially, compelled them to take steps they thought would best help them to address these problems.[81]

BELIEF IN THE SOCIAL GOSPEL

Social gospelers deeply believed social activism was a necessary part of being a good Christian and that a focus on individual salvation was "not enough," as the *Congregationalist* insisted.[82] Thus, social gospelers continually juxtaposed the social, as opposed to individual, focus of other

Christians. For example, the following article from the *Presbyterian Magazine* insisted:

> The social interpretation and application of Christianity to the needs of the world is one of the primary functions of the Christian Church. The obligation of this function rests on the certainty that God in Christ has revealed to us not only a way of salvation for the individual, but an ideal which defines the proper relation of men, one to another, in every sphere of human interest and activity. . . . When followed to its highest expression, the social movement of our day with its demand for righteousness leads straight to Christ as its primary cause and deepest inspiration. The urgent social questions of today are those related to wealth and poverty, luxury and want, capital and labor, peace and war. These combine to voice a strong demand for a social interpretation of the gospel.[83]

In the strong biblical and messianic tones that prevailed throughout the movement, the *Presbyterian Magazine* also argued that

> organized Christianity . . . cannot rest satisfied with a mere improvement of the existing social order. . . . The Christian ideal [is] the Kingdom of God widened and extended until all men and all interests, everywhere, are brought beneath its sway—"Thy Kingdom come, Thy will be done in earth as it is in heaven."[84]

One of the key issues on Earth, as social gospelers saw it, was the vast inequality and horrendous living conditions experienced by immigrants living in urban slums.

A Critique of Urban Industrial Capitalism

The focus of social gospelers' activism was largely what they perceived as the unfairness of modern industrial capitalism. As such, they offered a steady and evidence-based critique of that system whenever they could. For example, in an article titled "The Challenge of the Modern City," the *Presbyterian Magazine* wrote in 1930 that "industrial unrest and extreme radicalism, not always of a wholesome character, is a feature of city life. Unemployment and hunger create riots. The chasm between classes grows wider."[85]

In its most radical form, social gospelers' critique of the industrial class structure sometimes resulted in outright calls for the institution of a new economic order—namely, socialism, as the following quote from an article in the American Unitarian Association's *Christian Register* exemplifies:

> The social gospel today, therefore, must go beyond supporting the demands for old-age pensions, or unemployment insurance, or collective bargaining, and must work for a new social order to replace capitalism. . . . Socialism, therefore, deserves the most careful *and sympathetic* study of everyone who takes the social gospel seriously.[86]

A key part of industrial capitalism was, of course, urbanization—something that did not escape the notice of social gospelers. For example, a *Presbyterian Magazine* article titled "National Missions and the World" focused on urban problems:

> The abnormal congestion of populations in cities within the last few decades is creating a series of problems in America with which we have yet found no effective way to cope. The census of 1920 awoke us to the fact that for the first time in the history of our nation the city population outnumbers the rural, which means a decided change in social attitude and outlook. It is changing the fibre of our civilization and threatens to revolutionize our national character.[87]

As shown by an article from the *Congregationalist and Herald of Gospel Liberty* that was briefly quoted in chapter 1 but is presented below in more detail, only those ignorant of urban poverty could possibly oppose the social gospel:

> Opposition to the social gospel must have found its genesis in editorial offices and preachers' studies, or in the hermitage of theologians. It never could have originated in the great throbbing marts of life. No man who opposes the social gospel ever has spent much time in the receiving ward of a great city hospital, where the bruised and maimed and dying are carried in from the shops and streets. . . . To imagine that God does not care about such things and that his Church must not concern itself about these and a thousand other vital matters of human relations is to malign God and pervert the very meaning of Christianity. And those who steel their hearts to this great field of applied Christianity known as the "Social Gospel" are not only misinterpreting the gospel of Christ but are also dwarfing and dehumanizing their own hearts.[88]

Thus, social gospelers were critical of capitalism, to the point of even openly promoting socialism, and deeply concerned about urbanization and what they saw as its inevitable effect of increasing and concentrating poverty. Of course, within all of these concerns, social gospelers were also aware of and openly discussed the fact that they were not, in general, the people who were suffering from any of these maladies.

The Religious Elite

There is no question that social gospelers, especially those in this chapter, were the elite. This is apparent when looking at the available quantitative data, like that presented in table 2, which demonstrate that the early liberalizers paid their ministers up to twice as much as other groups (more than 20 percent, on average). But it is also apparent from the news that these groups saw fit to print. For example, an article in the *Living Church* reported the following about the views of "88 Wellesley girls" (an elite all-women's college) who were asked "to write an essay on their views of the modern Utopia":

> Few believed in economic competition or the right of ownership of private property. Many were Socialists. . . . Eugenics was very much to the fore. Medical certificates were insisted upon. Indeed, the health and welfare of children were a first consideration. The students believed in birth control. Many of them advocated pre-marital experiment to ensure a happy and useful life together.[89]

Many articles promoting the social gospel often first acknowledged the privileged position of their readers vis-à-vis those they sought to help. For example, in a call that seems directed toward their more well-off members, the *Christian Advocate* insisted: "Vicarious sympathy for all classes of men is a prerequisite for preaching the social gospel. Given that sympathy, let all ministers of the gospel call men to follow Christ in all social relations and in the practice of the stewardship of all that they are and have."[90] Recall the *Congregationalist* article quoted in chapter 1, which acknowledged that "the people who bear the burdens of modern industry and suffer from its moral limitations are, on the whole, not in the churches."[91] Part and parcel of their critique of industrialism was an acknowledgment of and a focus on the unique problems associated with urban poverty and an acknowledgment that they were not the ones likely to suffer from that poverty. Thus, another author asked in an article titled "Facing the Down and Outs" in the same periodical:

> Who was I that I might enjoy a beautiful home in the suburbs, with dollars in the bank and a place in society, while these men were homeless, dollar-less and with no place to lay their heads except what charity provided? Why was my boy, studying his Latin for tomorrow's test, at my desk and surrounded by books, while this boy over in the corner, who cost his mother as much pain and who came into being at as much cost to creation, was bleary-eyed and facing a future of crime and remorse? Surely something was wrong. I saw it tragically portrayed in human life before me and my heart rebelled.[92]

Social gospelers were aware that immigrants were disproportionally likely to suffer from the effects of industrialization. For example, the *Herald of Gospel Liberty* gave its readers the following picture of urban child labor and poverty among Italian immigrants:

> Large numbers of children under ten years old, and some of them as young as three or four years, are employed in the manufacture of artificial flowers, in embroidery work, garment making, and other tenement occupations. . . . The artificial June roses which appear in the Fifth Avenue shops are made by the baby fingers of Italian children, who are paid twenty cents a gross.[93]

Such concerns about the plight of immigrants were in no way contradictory with eugenicists' concerns about differential fertility between desirables and undesirables. As one article in the Protestant Episcopal Church's *Living Church* noted, "Anyone who has had anything to do with social service work will heartily endorse the position of the conference on birth control."[94] Likewise, social gospelers saw birth control as essential to eliminating the reproduction of poverty, as another article in the *Living Church* made clear:

> Economic conditions [can] force upon unwanted children a premature life of labor, malnutrition, congested and unhealthy living conditions, and a pair of overburdened parents (broken by the economic struggle into which they are thrust and for which their strength is not sufficient). Chaining a man to a treadmill for the sake of unwanted children is a peculiar application of Christian principles![95]

When social gospelers' concerns about social justice and urban poverty came together with eugenicist concerns about race suicide, the seeds of birth control reform were sown.

The Eugenic Gospel

In their calls to eradicate poverty, social gospelers often invoked calls to "create heaven on earth." They often stressed that this new "kingdom" would come "not by divine magic" but from "sacrificial activity."[96] It is in these calls to create a "new Earth" where one can most often see explicit links to eugenic beliefs and, eventually, the importance of legalizing contraception. The following quote in the *Birth Control Review* from prominent eugenicist and Anglican priest William (Dean) Inge, quoted earlier in a Unitarian periodical, exemplifies the way in which social gospel beliefs could be easily combined with eugenics:

> Either rational selection must take the place of the natural selection which the modern State will not allow to act, or we must go on deteriorating. The Christian conception of the kingdom of God upon earth teaches us to turn our eyes to the future and to think of the welfare of posterity.[97]

The *Congregationalist* argued that "the Church from the highest motives imaginable, that of bringing in a present Kingdom of God," should encourage "more knowledge and practice of simple eugenic laws."[98]

Another article in the *Congregationalist* also equated birth control legalization with the evolution in thought needed to create "a Divine far-off event" (most likely Jesus's Second Coming):

> The vast process of evolution is still in progress [and] may [lead to] a Divine far-off event. . . . We have reached, wherever modern intelligence is in the ascendency, the assured conviction that a man is never more completely the child of God than when he is trying to shape the universe toward the very highest ideal which his understanding will permit him to conceive. If this means modifying or controlling the forces of nature, whether such control means the destroying of a malaria-bearing mosquito or the reformation of a long-standing economic order—in either case well and good, and "forward." Fundamentally, it is this idea which has inspired men's minds in relation to the subject of birth control. . . . Because children are born under certain conditions in the ordinary process of things, it does not inevitably follow

that those conditions must always bring children into the world. And it is not a perversion of the will of God if control to prevent the undesirable consummation is exercised. . . . We are dealing with a new step in man's attempt to regulate the ways of life in accordance with his highest intelligence.[99]

With a similar trust in science apparent, an article from the Universalist *Christian Leader* positively reviewed the book *The Genesis of the Social Gospel,* by Chester Charlton McCown, which argued:

> We have been able to discover the laws which make the radio and the aeroplane possible. We ought to be able to discover and apply the laws of social growth and control. We ought to be able to discover the how to bring the reign of God to earth. The process will be a long one, for the task is gigantic—a spiritual as well as a social task.[100]

In a quote that weds the early liberalizer concerns about race suicide with social gospel concerns about social equity, the *Congregationalist* asked, "For many years the wealthy and the educated classes have profited by modern knowledge of contraceptive methods and techniques. . . . *Why must this knowledge remain a class privilege?*"[101]

In the end, eugenic beliefs merged with the progressive Christianity of the social gospel movement into a single cohesive belief system. This is perhaps nowhere as elegantly exemplified as in a Methodist Episcopal Church sermon submitted to the 1926 AES competition:[102]

> The problems confronted by the Church and by the Eugenicists are the same, the motive is the same. United their program is complete. Cooperative effort will accomplish the task. And the result will be a new Humanity and a new earth, which is, in reality, the Kingdom of Heaven.[103]

The nine religious groups examined in this chapter became America's religious leaders on the issue of contraception. They did so because they had deeply racialized, classed, and geographically specific political concerns about immigrant fecundity—concerns that overlapped with many of the issues the social gospel movement sought to address.

Of course, not all of the religious groups in my sample that professed a concern about race suicide liberalized on birth control during the first wave. In fact, the next chapter will show a few groups that were, if even possible, more convinced of the importance of the white Anglo-Saxon race for America but chose not to make official statements on the issue. These groups did not see such pronouncements as within the purview of their religious duties because they rejected the main tenets of the social gospel movement. It is to these groups, the unofficial supporters, that we now turn. It is when contrasting the deeply religious meanings the early liberalizers attached to their support for birth control versus the more removed stances of the unofficial supporters that we can really see religion, and religious beliefs, vis-à-vis the social gospel movement, mattering.

4 The Supporters

Amid the flurry of pronouncements and debates that ensued between the early liberalizers and their critics (who are examined in the next chapter), four denominations tried to pick a middle ground by expressing often quite strong support for birth control but by refraining from making that support official: the Evangelical Synod of North America, the Northern Baptist Convention, the Norwegian Lutheran Church, and the United Presbyterian Church of North America.[1] Also concentrated in the Northeast, as map 3 illustrates, these groups nevertheless had large proportions of members in the Midwest.

Because there were no official liberalization statements to code, there was a bit more diversity of opinion among these "supporters." Thus, to be clear, only groups that showed general support in their official periodical or in their annual meeting minutes are included in this category. Groups in which a few pastors spoke out in favor of birth control but whose periodical said either nothing or only negative things were not included. Groups were kept in this category even if strong dissent was noted as long as approval was the overarching view of the periodical, as was the case with the Norwegian Lutheran Church.

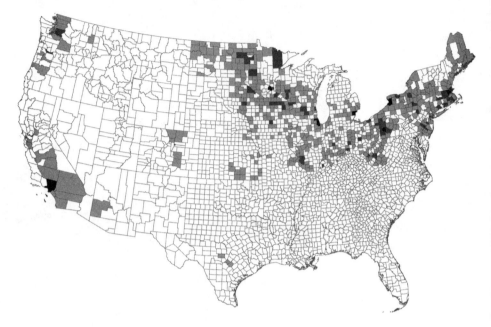

Map 3. Unofficial supporters.

Examining these four middle-of-the-road supporters brings a key analytical point into stark relief: if racialized beliefs in the eugenics movement and concerns about birth-rate differentials between native-born and
foreign-born Americans were the only factors that predicted liberalization
on birth control, the denominations examined in this chapter should not
only have been early liberalizers—they should have been the first. Fervent
promoters of eugenics, a few of these groups were even more extreme than
the groups chronicled in the previous chapter. Devout white supremacists,
they virtually trumpeted their belief in manifest destiny and the importance of the Anglo race to the nation to anyone who would listen. In terms
of the factors that pushed groups to liberalize, these supporters could not
have been more deeply concerned about race suicide.

But they differed from the early liberalizers in the central, religious,
and, some would argue, theological, causal factor examined in the previous chapter. Unlike the early liberalizers, they were ambivalent about,
or downright dismissive of, the social gospel. Rather than having a deep

and abiding belief in the importance of improving society to bring about the Messiah, these groups saw saving individual souls as their primary responsibility. Suspicious of groups that focused on social reform and not salvation, the four denominations examined in this chapter refrained from making official pronouncements. While they saw the wisdom in making contraceptive information accessible to those of "lesser stock," these denominations, all of whom were less urban than the early liberalizers, rejected the idea that such pronouncements were their religious duty.

UNOFFICIAL SUPPORT FOR BIRTH CONTROL

The Northern Baptist Convention published sixteen articles on birth control in the three years between 1929 and 1931. These articles either simply noted approval for a variety of reasons, most of them eugenicist, or reported in a positive tone on resolutions by other religious denominations or groups. For example, in 1929 the *Baptist* reported approvingly on the Universalist General Convention's resolution:

> A resolution favoring legalization of the giving of information on birth-control and the establishment of birth-control clinics under careful medical attention was passed by the Universalist General Convention in session recently at Washington, D. C. Gradually the churches become aware of their responsibilities in the line of social betterment.[2]

As it did in regard to other official pronouncements, the *Baptist* also wrote approvingly about the Lambeth statement:[3]

> We venture to say that it was in large part because this company of Christian leaders expressed themselves in a clear, succinct and positive fashion upon some of the questions with which the Christian conscience of our time is most deeply concerned. It had something very definite to say as to marriage and divorce, sex relations and birth control, race prejudice, peace and war, and Christian unity.[4]

In a more elaborate statement, the *United Presbyterian* also wrote approvingly about the Lambeth conference:

It is curious to note that the chief interest in the Lambeth Conference this year has centered around quite another matter. It is the deliverance of the conference on the subject of birth-control and the subject of divorce. The conference, after long and heated debate, with a strong minority holding out against the action, gave a guarded approval of birth-control. The whole matter is wisely stated. It is urged that any practices in this direction must be in harmony with Christian principles. Perhaps the resolution will be criticized because it does not attempt to point out with any clearness the Christian principles that must govern in such a matter. It does, however, condemn any disposition to limit or avoid parenthood from mere selfishness, luxury, or convenience. The deliverance is quite in line with those made by certain of our American Churches. But it has called out a great storm of discussion in the English papers.[5]

The *United Presbyterian* reported actively on other Presbyterian denominations. Thus, it reported with approval about the pending liberalization of its close relative the Presbyterian Church in the United States of America (with whom it would eventually merge):

> Approval of birth control by the next Presbyterian General Assembly is to be recommended. . . . This subject demands attention today as never before. Economic conditions and a worthy standard of living clearly make it wrong to bring children into the world without adequate provision for their nurture and proper consideration for the health of the mother.[6]

The article closed by making it clear that the eugenic reasons behind birth control reform were not lost on either group:

> The proponents of birth control claim that under the new regime there would be healthier children, healthier mothers and that the human stock would be greatly improved; more children would have the advantages of education, of comfortable homes, of good environment; quantity would lessen and quality would increase; the criminal, the mentally defective, the decadent, the abnormal type of life would be greatly lessened; the whole general standard of our common life would be lifted and coming generations would share liberties, opportunities and felicities which are largely unknown to the masses today. Those favoring birth control realize the very grave dangers inherent in the kind of education they propose to give the new generations, but they say they are willing to assume these risks and responsibilities in view of the ultimate blessings they believe will accrue to humanity as a whole.[7]

The Norwegian Lutheran Church published eight articles on birth control between 1930 and 1932 in its periodical the *Lutheran Church Herald*. The majority of the articles on birth control during the peak years of discussion were neutral, simply providing information about birth control laws, the results of the Lambeth Convention, or the Federal Council of Churches resolution. The following quote from the *Herald* made the strongest case for liberalization:[8]

> When once our pastors recognize the ethical challenge of the estimate that in America today 50 per cent of those who purchase contraceptive means are unmarried, that there is one criminal abortion for every 2 ½ births, and that 5 per cent of the illicit sex experiences outside of wedlock result in pregnancies, then they will come to feel the seriousness of the situation. While we may theorize about birth control, companionate marriage, and "consecutive polygamy," as Bishop Fisk calls it, the truth is that we face a condition and not a theory. Illegitimate parenthood is after all merely an accidental symptom of our modern sex obsession.[9]

Even the Evangelical Synod of North America, which said the least about birth control among these four denominations, came out very clearly in support of the FCC's statement in 1931:

> The birth control movement and the recent report of the Federal Council Committee on Marriage and the Home should be considered and studied. Those who would practice birth control for immoral purposes no longer need to be informed; most of them are far too well informed already through secret, vicious channels. That report, by the way, which created such a widespread interest, and which deserves thoughtful study, will be fully understood and appreciated only upon the background of a previous report of that Committee, "Christian Ideals of Love and Marriage." ... Is it not reasonable to assume that the word "knowledge" there used includes intelligent, pure, reverent sex information, of which birth control, in the best sense of the term, is but the climax?[10]

However, although these groups seemed to be in agreement that "the problem has wide implications and should be attacked also from a community point of view," they also made it clear they did not feel it was their duty to make a similar statement.[11] In a long article on birth control in 1931, part of which was quoted in the introduction to this book, the Norwegian Lutheran Church likened its refusal to make an official pronouncement to Jesus's decision to stay silent on difficult matters in the Bible:

> Jesus stooped down, and with His finger wrote on the ground, as though He heard them not." The Master was confronted with a delicate question, and instead of talking He wrote in the sand with the result that the accusers of the guilty woman "convinced by their own conscience, went out one by one." We draw the conclusion from this incident that it is the part of wisdom, at times to be silent rather than to write and talk about certain questions. We have no authority to make any *ex cathedra* pronouncement for the Lutheran Church [but] we can give some information.[12]

The article went on to discuss various resolutions of the Lambeth Conference and the Federal Council of Churches, as well as proposals in the Senate, books by Margaret Sanger, and the legal situation regarding contraception in various US states and even Holland.[13]

Simply put, these denominations saw the issue of birth control as disconnected from religious concerns. For example, the *Baptist* said:

> The nature of the subjects involved are such that it is peculiarly true of them that every individual must ultimately face and settle them for himself. Let all the light that may be shed upon them from every angle be welcomed. Only indirectly are religious issues involved. Primarily they are social and economic, and the religious element must be determined not upon authority, not on any one's say-so, but upon the nature of the results for human welfare and fullness of life that would follow from the practices adopted.[14]

This suggests that these denominations' reluctance to make a pronouncement was a result of their lack of belief in the social gospel. With such an individualist outlook, birth control was "only indirectly" related to religious issues or institutions despite its "social and economic" implications. To understand how groups similarly concerned about race suicide could reach such different decisions regarding their official stance on birth control, we must examine their views about the importance of the white Anglo-Saxon race in the history of the United States, investigate their skepticism about the social gospel movement, and, ultimately, come to understand how those views were related to their more rural and midwestern locations.

BELIEF IN EUGENICS

Without a doubt, the groups chronicled in this chapter stand out for their eugenic beliefs, even when compared to the early liberalizers. The Northern Baptist Convention had more members on the American Eugenics Society (AES) Committee on Cooperating with Clergymen (CCC) than any other denomination (see table 8). Its periodical the *Baptist* published at least one article per year between 1929 and 1931 promoting eugenics or the AES.[15]

The *Lutheran Church Herald* and the *United Presbyterian*, the Norwegian Lutheran Church's and the United Presbyterian Church in North America's periodicals, respectively, published even more, averaging two articles per year between 1930 and 1931 that promoted or were supportive of eugenics or a eugenic point of view.[16]

The *Evangelical Herald* discussed eugenics the least frequently, publishing only one clearly pro-eugenics article during the peak years of discussion (1929–31). But that article left no doubt about its views as it decried the use of birth control by the "cultured classes" and quoted the founder of eugenics—Francis Galton:

> Especially if practiced by our more or less cultured classes, and in such a way as to result in permanent birth-prevention, birth control seriously interferes with the progress of race culture and to that extent is a sin against church and state because through it too many families of good blood die out and the burden of progress in civilization is shifted to shoulders least able to bear it. . . . Francis Galton, in his book on "Hereditary Genius," says: "Whenever a man or woman was possessed of a gentle nature that fitted them to deeds of charity, to meditation, to literature or art, the social condition of the times was such that they had no refuge elsewhere than in the bosom of the church. And as the Church enforced celibacy, the best blood of society died without children, and thus the rudest portion of the community became the parents of future generations." The Protestant Reformation abolished this abuse also and as history proves many evangelical parsonages have become centers of culture and education and the headquarters for higher ideals for the whole congregation and neighborhood. Our cultured classes—for it is they which are in greatest danger—should be taught that the practice of birth control in such a way as to lead to permanent birth prevention is a *sin*—a sin against nature, against one's better instincts, against one's life-partner, and that it is also unpatriotic.[17]

The periodicals of the other supportive denominations were even more emphatic in their concerns about eugenics and race suicide. Reporting on the resolution by the FCC, the *Lutheran Church Herald* stressed that "very large families tend to produce poverty, to endanger the health and the stability of the family, and to limit the educational opportunities of the children."[18] That article did not, however, refer to its own flock. Neither did the following article, titled "What about Illegitimate Parents?," from which this quote was taken:

> We do know that in thirty-eight states [the illegitimate] birth rate is going up. That the average age of the unmarried mother is eighteen and that of the father about twenty-one; that the mentality, especially of the mother, is slightly sub-normal; that most unmarried mothers come from "broken" homes, and generally from big families.[19]

When discussing the fertility of its own flock, the *Herald* openly accused them of causing race suicide:

> Race suicide is [one] cause [of our limited growth]. We do not grow from within. We are going backwards. I baptize in my congregation five or six children a year. We have over 500 communicants. Formerly the confirmand classes numbered about 40. Last year I had 21, and this year I had no class. This condition is found all over.[20]

No doubt because of its stronger connections to the AES, the *Baptist* frequently reported on AES activities. In 1925, it matter of factly informed its readers that "through the committee on cooperation with clergymen," the AES would "bring to the attention of the churches the message of eugenics."[21] Five years later the same periodical reported approvingly on an AES committee recommendation to encourage clergy to have larger families via stipends:

> Having pointed out the steady decrease in the number of offspring from superior racial stock, he said, "We know from reliable factual data that the best quality of leaders arises, and rises in the greatest frequently, from the progeny of the clergy. Any proposal to encourage breeding and to increase the progeny of the clergy by supplementing their stipend for the proper rearing of such progeny is not only a human obligation which few would feel able to repudiate, but a eugenic measure which contains the greatest promise of sustaining and increasing our most valuable racial stock."[22]

As with the quote above, many of the group's statements on eugenics made its concerns about race suicide more than apparent, and as with the early liberalizers, articles in the *Baptist* demonstrated over and over again how closely concerns about race suicide were linked to concerns about class (and religion). For example, an article in 1924 criticized "successful individuals" who "place ambition, ease, luxury, and freedom of travel before marriage and rearing a family. They are practicing race suicide."[23] A 1929 article from the *Baptist* explicitly linked intelligence tests and birth rates:

> When the results of scientific mental testing are tabulated statistically, and graphically represented on the normal frequency curve, the range of intelligence becomes apparent: Grouped about the median will be seen the number of persons of normal average intelligence and below this group the subnormal and defective group, while above will be arranged the more intelligent and superior group. In the study of Doctor Goddard on "American Intelligence," he finds not more than 50 per cent of the American people in the average normal group, less than 25 per cent in the superior group and more than 25 per cent in the inferior group. By the study and practise of eugenics this condition in American population could be progressively changed for the better; but the facts are that the superior group is decreasing and the inferior group rapidly increasing, and it would seem that if this condition prevails for a period of years we are headed toward mediocrity and inferiority, and the very foundations of our democracy are threatened notwithstanding our repeated affirmations in politics that we are all born free and equal.[24]

Although it may be difficult to believe, the United Presbyterian Church in North America (UPCNA) periodical the *United Presbyterian* was even more emphatic about a belief in the importance of superior bloodlines. In 1929 it insisted:

> There is no doubt that the influences of heredity are tremendous. The language of the Second Commandment makes this plain. It speaks of visiting the sins of the fathers upon the children unto the third and fourth generations. That old biblical declaration is in harmony with the findings of modern science. It is a familiar and true saying that the blood will tell. Children inherit many of the characteristics and tendencies of their ancestors, not only of their own fathers and mothers, but of those farther back along the ancestral line.[25]

The UPCNA's greater emphasis on eugenics seems to have been connected to its stronger belief that superior genetic material was restricted to Anglo-Saxons. The *United Presbyterian* argued repeatedly in article after article that Anglo-Saxons' superiority was made evident by the crucial role they played in the founding and settling of the United States. For example, in 1930 a *United Presbyterian* article titled "Why the Anglo-Saxon?" argued:

> God loves all men. It is just as true, however, that the missionary value of all men is not the same. Men are born equal in their rights, but they are not equal in their fitness and ability to serve. They vary in their talents and powers. . . . Does it not look as if God were not only preparing in our Anglo-Saxon civilization, the die with which to stamp the peoples of the earth, but as if He were also massing behind that die the mighty power with which to press it? My conviction that this race is eventually to give its civilization to mankind is not based on mere numbers—China forbid! I look forward to what the world has never yet seen united in the same race; namely, the greatest numbers and the highest civilization. God needed the white Anglo-Saxon race. . . . In the discovery and colonization of America, God was opening the way for the Anglo-Saxon people, imbued with the spirit of the evangelical gospel, to become a great nation. . . . Deep-seated in the mind and plan of God, lay the Anglo-Saxon race and country, America, strategic in position, powerful and rich in numbers and wealth.[26]

A follow-up article in the next issue, titled "The Fitness of the Anglo-Saxon," elaborated further:

> The American, certainly, thinks quicker, if not more profoundly, and acts more promptly, moves more swiftly and is more inventive and adventurous. In no other country in the world can there be found among the masses so many men capable of handling large enterprises and dealing with large questions. In addition to this, it is said, "The advent of the United States of America, as the greatest world power, is the greatest political social and commercial phenomenon of our times. . . . In other words, two-thirds of the human race, yellow, brown and black alike, are governed by the other third of the human race, the white man, who is in control of ten-elevenths of the world's surface. Does this not answer the query as to why Paul was turned away from the yellow, brown and black races to the world-dominating, rich and powerful white race, culminating in the American Anglo-Saxon?"[27]

In sum, the religious groups examined in this chapter were absolutely devoted to the idea of manifest destiny and the role that Anglo-Saxons played in that destiny. Of course, the United States of America, the land of the free and the home of the brave, was also a land of immigrants—something these groups were well aware and proud of and indeed even claimed as a part of their relatively recent heritage. However, the immigrant heritage that these groups were proud of was quite distinct, ethnically and religiously, from the wave of immigration that so concerned eugenicists. The unofficial supporters of birth control were quick to emphasize the differences between the new and old immigrants, which they saw as inherent, inherited, and deeply problematic for the future of the country.

Views of Immigrants: Old versus New

The denominations examined in this chapter, those who only unofficially supported birth control liberalization, made constant comparisons between "old" and "new" immigrants. It might go without saying that the "old" immigrants always fared better. For example, the *Evangelical Herald* argued: "A tremendous change has come over the character of the immigrant. Formerly the finest class of Europeans came over, now some of the worst class come over. In the various institutions in the country, such as those for insane, etc., the foreign born predominate."[28]

The *United Presbyterian* claimed that new immigrants were responsible for a disproportionate amount of crime in the United States:

> We have been talking for years about the perils of immigration. We have pointed out that immigrants largely come, not as formerly, from western and northern Europe, but from eastern and southern Europe and from Asia. We point out that a large part of our lawlessness and our crime are perpetrated by these people.

Another *United Presbyterian* article argued that these newer immigrants, especially the Sicilians, had already destroyed American society, character, and institutions:

> The vast alien invasion of our shores destroyed our distinctive American character, perverted our institutions, displaced American labor from its

rightful position and gave America its present evil fame as the most lawless nation in the world. Sicilians and aliens of that type have built America's underworld and have made gangland a power before which even Federal authority, our chief executive being the spokesman, has confessed itself helpless and undone.[29]

These sentiments hold true even for the Norwegian Lutheran Church, which expressed great pride in its own immigrant heritage but lamented the fact that Scandinavians were being turned away by the same immigration restriction laws affecting Southeastern European immigrants in an article that quoted leading eugenicist Harry Laughlin:

> This country has never experienced any difficulty in assimilating Scandinavians. As settlers they rank among the true empire builders, bringing new lands under the plow, dotting the prairie with substantial homes, rearing large families and building solid communities. Their zeal for education supports great state universities well attended by their children. They take their political responsibilities seriously and dominate elections in several states. In addition to being strong, home loving, and assimilable, the Scandinavians in the United States are thrifty and law abiding. In Dr. Harry H. Laughlin's report on the origins of the inmates in more than 700 of our penal and public charitable institutions the Scandinavians make an excellent showing with respect to crime and dependency. They produce only one-third as many criminals, compared to their numbers, as the total population of the United States produces, and only three-quarters as many dependents. This raw material of good citizenship is now being shunted away from the United States by an unwise piece of legislation. What is Canada's gain is America's loss.[30]

Many of the frequent comparisons between new and old immigrants were explicit about the fact that they saw the old crop of immigrants as much more desirable than the new, as did an article from the *Lutheran Church Herald* aptly titled "They Were Desirable Because They Were Healthy and Strong . . ."[31] The article began by explaining that the previous cohorts of immigrants were "desirable because they were healthy and strong, accustomed to thrift and frugality in the country from which they came." After emphasizing that those qualities were "badly needed to conquer the wilderness, to till the soil and to build the cities of America amid the hardships of nature and the dangers from wild men and savage beasts," the article emphasized that the old immigrants had been more easily assimilated than the new:

> America desired and needed an immigration that should be easily assimilated. In the immigration from the Lutheran lands they received in the main those already accustomed to liberty and self-government and a fair degree of democracy. They were also people believing in education, largely free from illiteracy and unusually well adapted to a ready assimilation with other peoples of the country and trained into a fine, strong type of citizenship. They were not people who clustered into cities and crowded communities, but tillers of the soil, builders of homes and believers in government and obedience to constitutional law and authority.

As with the quote above, which emphasized the literate and well-educated nature of Lutheran immigrants, there was often an explicit emphasis on class, as there was in another article from the *Lutheran Church Herald* reporting on "The Johnson Immigration Bill":

> The Norwegians that one encounters at the American Consulate in Christiania seeking visas for America are very different from the people that one meets on the same errand in the consulates of Eastern and Southern Europe. They are not the middlemen, the sweatshop workers, the peddlers, the petty tradesmen, the under-sized, dazed-looking, excitable, illiterate folk from the agricultural and town slums of the south and east who pour into the slums of America each year under the 3 per cent law in sufficient numbers to populate a good-sized city.[32]

Newer immigrants were not only problematic because of their foreignness, lack of education, or general low class standing, however. As the above quote implied with its mention of "under-sized" folk, there were plenty of indications within these periodicals that immigrants were disliked because of what were seen to be racial characteristics. The *Lutheran Herald* made it clear that Norwegian Lutherans saw themselves as racially distinct from and superior to newer immigrants and directly countered critics of immigration reform who argued that the new immigration restrictions were founded on unscientific, racist principles:

> "The whole idea of relative race values," declare the antirestrictionists, "is objectionable, unreasonable and grossly offensive. It is not science, but pseudoscience." . . . The Bureau of the Census, which won't for a moment

admit that it is pseudo-scientific in its activities . . . shows that whereas the percentage of naturalization among the English in America was 63.1, among the Scotch 60.1, among the Welsh 72.9, among the Irish 65.7, among the Norwegians 67.3, among the Swedes 69, among the Danes 69, and so on, it was only 28 among the Poles, 28 among the Italians, 16.8 among the Greeks, 12.1 among the Bulgars, and so on. They have all had an equal chance, as has everyone in America; but they weren't born equal in intelligence or ability. Consequently the bulk of the Northwestern European immigrants have become a part of America while the bulk of the Southeastern European immigrants have remained Southeastern Europeans.[33]

Indeed, these denominations were more upfront about the undesirability of recent immigrants than most of the early liberalizers. For example, the *Baptist* published the following story of an Irish immigrant, soon to become a single mother, whose untimely death was part and parcel of her status as unfit to come to "our shores":

> Mary Brennon arrived on the "Celtic" and went to Ellis Island. Three days later she was ordered to be excluded. . . . She was not married and was about to become a mother. While detained six days on Ellis Island the girl caught a severe cold, which developed into pneumonia two days after she left New York on the "Baltic." The baby was born and died, and the mother died the next day. . . . Our missionaries at Ellis Island could tell us many stories equally tragic. It goes without saying that the doors of America cannot be thrown open to all who would come to our shores, but some method must be worked out to keep the unfit from leaving other shores.[34]

It will come as no surprise, then, that these groups heralded immigration restrictions. In 1925, just as immigration restrictions went into place, an article in the *Baptist* quoted eugenicist Edwin E. Grant's "interesting article in the *American Journal of Sociology*" that argued that stricter immigration requirements and easier deportation laws "eugenically cleanses America of a vicious element." The article went on to report that "a new system in handling the immigration problem is recommended, that is, a rigid test in American standards . . . before the prospective immigrant leaves his native land."[35] Four years later the *Baptist* reported with evident relief:

> To save ourselves from this mighty tide of immigration, congress threw up an emergency measure that temporarily stopped the flood. . . . Indeed, it was not until the "eighties" that we became firm as to the caliber of mental-

ity and morality that entered our land. . . . Fully eight million of these persons either will not or cannot take out papers that will establish them as citizens of this country. They have been called alien sojourners, and such they are. Further, much of the crime committed in this country can be directly traceable to this eight million. . . . In fact, much in this country that is undesirable is due to this large population which is among but not of us.[36]

Of course, as the quote regarding Mary Brennon's passage on the *Celtic* implied, religion was a key, inseparable element that distinguished the old from the new immigrants. The *Lutheran Herald* wrote:

> The churches follow exactly the coming of the people . . . when one race predominates, the churches of that race appear; when it recedes, the churches of other people appear. The newcomers bring with them their particular forms of faith. The Church is part of the imported social equipment and reflects the religious mind, memory, and traditions of the people.[37]

Indeed, new immigrants were fine if their religion was like that of the old immigrants. Thus, the *Evangelical Herald* argued in an article titled "New Americans" that more Protestants would be entering the country than had been recently, once the new immigration laws took effect: "In 1923, 220,000 people came in from Protestant countries of Europe. The new immigration law opens the door for even more Protestants."[38] Of course, most new immigrants were not Protestant but were Catholic, and therein lay the problem as far as these groups were concerned.

Anti-Catholicism

By the mid-1920s, the *Baptist* reported that Detroit was "more than half" Catholic and that conditions were "even more appalling" in New York and Chicago:[39]

> Our great American cities, practically all in the northern states, have been rapid in growth and are widely known as the melting pot of the nations. . . . Each of these racial and nationalistic groups presents its own problem and . . . one can only faintly appreciate the challenge they present to the Christian church. . . . In Detroit four out of every five people are unattached to any Protestant church. In New York and Chicago conditions are even more appalling. Such conditions militate strongly against a proper home life, an aggressive church life and the development of the higher nature of man.[40]

Similar articles in the *Baptist* chronicled the growth of the Roman Catholic Church in Saint Louis and another in the United States as a whole:[41]

> Authorities of the Roman Catholic church, led by the national director of the society for the propagation of the faith, have prepared and forwarded to Rome, there to form a part of the missionary exhibit of the Catholic church's Holy Year, a chart showing the growth of the church in America in the century from 1822 to 1922. At the beginning of the century there were nine Catholic dioceses in the United States. Today there are 103. There were seventy-eight Catholic priests then, now there are 21,164. Then the Catholic population was put at 600,000. Today it is put at 17,616,000.[42]

The *Evangelical Herald* published a two-part article titled "Is Catholicism Losing Ground in the United States?"[43] Although the author tried valiantly through creatively reported statistics to paint an optimistic picture, the answer was clearly no.

A telling quote in the "New Americans" article quoted above warned that "proselyting will not amount to very much."[44] Religion was, to them, almost as ascribed as the genetic characteristics they wrote about so disparagingly. Thus, although there were repeated calls in the *Baptist* for its readers to work harder at converting the "foreign-speaking elements," these articles make it apparent that such proselytization was not common. For example:

> The coming of the foreign-speaking elements or classes have greatly aggravated the city problems, but we have sneered at them and been satisfied to keep apart from them, uncontaminated. Little Polands, Italys, Hungarys, Russias, Roumanians, and other segregations have grown up in our larger cities where the English language is but little spoken, but where old country customs, methods, dress and religion persistently hold sway. . . . The Roman Catholic Church has flourished most by reason of this shifting of peoples. . . . The challenge to the Protestant communions is insistent. We have not gone to these peoples as we should have done in their home lands and native environments, and now God has sent them to us—to our very doors. . . . Baptists should be at the very front in this great task. As the foreign-speaking groups break away from Roman despotism, ignorance and fear, *The Baptist* faith appeals to them for its simplicity, its biblical standards and its liberty in Christ Jesus, the only head of the church.[45]

As the previous quote implies, like the early liberalizers these denominations "kept their distance" because they did not see Catholic immigrants as potential converts. As the *Baptist* acknowledged in 1929, "We were not Americanizing them, nor did we care to":[46]

> The Baptists began their organic life in Milwaukee in 1836. . . . The battle to win a place in the life of this great and growing city has not been without its difficulties. . . . Soon after 1880 there came great multitudes of people from central Europe, many of whom settled in Milwaukee. These people were members of the Roman Catholic church, or one of the Lutheran state churches.[47]

Another article, also in the *Baptist* and also reporting on the situation in Milwaukee, lamented that not a lot of effort was being made to convert Catholics: "Millions of the Polish people are unsettled in their religious convictions. They are drifting into skepticism, infidelity, atheism. Men of far-reaching influence with Polish people of this and other lands, not themselves Baptists, are repeatedly suggesting to us that *The Baptist* denomination make itself known to the Polish world."[48]

Political Power

Certainly, for these groups, as for the early liberalizers, concerns about race suicide were also concerns about political power. The following article from the *Baptist* begins by talking about differences in intelligence and ends by discussing how birth-rate differentials could threaten "the very foundations of our democracy":

> By the study and practise of eugenics this condition in American population could be progressively changed for the better; but the facts are that the superior group is decreasing and the inferior group rapidly increasing, and it would seem that if this condition prevails for a period of years we are headed toward mediocrity and inferiority, and the very foundations of our democracy are threatened notwithstanding our repeated affirmations in politics that we are all born free and equal.[49]

Similarly, the *United Presbyterian* lamented that recent immigrants "regard liberty as license to do what they wish. They do not value our institutions or our spirit. We ask, How can we incorporate such an heterogeneous mass into a political and spiritual unity?"[50]

However, for these more rural churches these concerns seem to have been more removed and more often centered on the political ambitions of "Rome," rather than particular issues in the United States. For example, these groups wrote fairly often of "the arrogant claims and the autocratic temper of the Church of Rome."[51] The *Baptist* promoted the Protestant League to "save the country from the Catholics" and "prevent the Romanizing of our institutions" but rarely mentioned urban political machines.[52]

In an interesting twist, and not one promoted by any other group in my sample, the *United Presbyterian* argued that the denomination's problems with the American Catholic Church would end if it would simply give up its allegiance to Rome:

> We give it as our candid opinion that if the day should come—as we hope against hope that it will come—when the Catholic Church of America will declare its independence of the Italian hierarchy and become an autonomous church, owned and controlled by American Catholics, that day will mark the beginning of the end of all misunderstanding between Catholics and Protestants in this country. And if in the course of events the American Church should repudiate the dogma of infallibility, declare herself as unequivocally opposed to the political establishment of any Church, and cease forth-with all opposition to state-controlled schools—popular suspicion of Catholic aims and purposes would entirely vanish. In such case Protestants would no more oppose a good Catholic who aspired to be President of the United States than they would oppose a good Presbyterian or a good Methodist or a good Episcopalian or a good Quaker. What Protestants fear is not the Catholic Church in America, but the Italian-controlled Catholic Church in America.[53]

The *Evangelical Herald* admitted its bias freely:

> Unfortunately there is very good reason to fear the election of a Roman Catholic president. But this fact is due not to the "prejudices" of the American people, or to the "intolerance" of Protestants, but to some stubborn and undeniable facts. One of these is the unalterable opposition of the Roman Catholic hierarchy to the American public school, which Americans consider one of the vital institutions of the republic.[54]

Unlike the early liberalizers' writings, there were no quotes about urban political machines and no quotes about corrupt political "bosses." Only one article out of the more than five hundred found in the related key word searches mentioned concrete political issues connected to new immigrants and their children. In that article, the *United Presbyterian* reported with approval on efforts to prevent "aliens" from being counted in congressional districts:

> Shall unnaturalized foreigners have a hand in shaping our government? A resolution calling for the submission of a Constitutional amendment to stop alien representation has been submitted to the present Congress. It proposes that the basis of representation in congressional districts shall be the number of American citizens in the district rather than the population. Congressional districts are now allocated on the basis of population. There are some 6.280.000 aliens in the country located chiefly in our large cities.[55]

This lack of concern about urban politics was certainly connected to these groups' more rural base. But, that was important for more than just their political orientation. It was also a key part of their deep ambivalence about the social gospel.

DOUBTING THE SOCIAL GOSPEL

The four denominations discussed in this chapter shared some crucial differences from the elite northeastern denominations discussed in the previous chapter—differences that explain their greater reluctance to embrace the social gospel.

Although the census data presented in table 2 is not precise enough to demonstrate this definitively (any county with more than two thousand people was counted as urban in the 1926 census), there are plenty of indications that the denominations examined in this chapter saw themselves as "rural churches," as the Norwegian Lutheran Church openly called itself, reckoning that it was, by its own account, "still 75 per cent rural and 25 per cent urban" in 1931.[56]

Distant from urban problems, these denominations sought to educate their readers via articles in their periodicals titled "The Problems of the Great Cities," "Can Our Large Cities Be Reached by Present Evangelistic Methods?," "The City Church," and "In the Slum of a City."[57] Rather than reporting on common goings-on, these articles focused on readers who were assumed to have a lack of familiarity with cities. They emphasized that things were "different" in cities.

Their more rural constituency meant that these groups were much more distant from the problems of urban industrialization than the early liberalizers, whose strong belief in the social gospel was discussed in the previous chapter. This distance is apparent in the tortured statements made by the Northern Baptists, who were deeply conflicted about the social gospel. During the six years for which I conducted analysis of the *Baptist* for the first wave of reform, I found six articles on the social gospel (about the average amount of most strong supporters gave the issue). However, the majority of these took a middle ground, asserting that all gospels needed to be both saving and social, as the following example demonstrates:

> Down in Kentucky they seem to be contrasting the "social gospel" with the "saving gospel," some advocating one, some the other and disputing about the two gospels. Bishop Warren A. Candler has a keen article in the Western Recorder in which he lashes certain "liberals" of that section who substitute a "social gospel" for a "saving gospel." In Chicago ... we can only express sympathy for our Kentucky brethren and pray that they may be able to deliver their brotherhood from any gospel that is not both and completely saving and social.[58]

One year later, another article in the *Baptist* argued for a gospel that was both "saving and social":

> On the one hand some emphasize personal evangelism. They seek to save individuals without giving any attention to their physical, social or economic needs. They often seek to accomplish this by mass movements called evangelistic meetings. The evangelists have one message for all people regardless of their needs; and if we may judge the effectiveness of these meetings by the number of adults who are permanently changed from non-Christians to Christians, and if we may further judge their effectiveness by the number of churches that became thereby stronger moral and spiritual agents in their communities, these meetings are of little value. ... The other position which is being taken by many who desire to make this world a better place in which to live and who have a passion to usher in the kingdom of God is an exclusive emphasis upon social service. ... There are a number of practical experiments which are now being tried, the purpose of which is to cure these ills of society.

No doubt much good is being done by these socially-minded people, even as some good is being accomplished by evangelistic mass meetings, in which the appeal is individualistic. . . . The spiritual and the social belong together.[59]

Social gospel historian Henry F. May also found that the Northern Baptists never embraced the social gospel fully, even though they possessed a "small but influential Social Gospel minority." He attributes this to the fact that the Northern Baptists had "a large rural membership" disconnected from the urban, industrial concerns of the social gospelers.[60]

The other groups were simply distant from the social gospel, as their limited statements on the issue suggest. Thus, the *United Presbyterian* and the *Lutheran Church Herald* mentioned the social gospel only once during the time period of our analysis. The *United Presbyterian* asserted that while "there is an important place for the 'social gospel' . . . individual conviction and conversion is the primary thing, and it needs to be kept in the *first place*" because of the following:[61]

The danger is that schemes of social improvement will be allowed to bulk so large in the thought of church leaders that the need for personal faith and conversion will be dropped into a secondary place. That is a significant sentence in the message: "Having lost the thrill of the gospel message, they have become content to put a program in its place." In our judgment that sentence goes to the heart of one of our difficulties. The average minister is beset with programs. Eager executives representing boards and committees and various schemes for human betterment are asking to program the work of each pastor, or at least are beseeching him to set apart various Sabbaths for exclusive consideration of particular religious interests. It takes some courage and resolution to resist all of these appeals and to keep the way clear for the old work of proclaiming the gospel message and appealing to men to be reconciled to God.[62]

Consistent with their rejection of the social gospel, the *United Presbyterian*'s authors did not attempt to disguise the fact that, unlike the social gospelers chronicled in the previous chapter who regularly criticized the excesses of capitalism, they were unabashedly procapitalist. In a 1924 article titled "Prosperity of the American People," they criticized the "red faced radical socialist" for failing to recognize the value of capitalist investment:

There are almost thirty million persons in the United States who are savings depositors. In addition there are more than 77,000,000 life insurance policies carried by the people of America representing a total of $48,000,000,000 in force, while the depositors of savings banks have over $18,000,000,000 to their credit. . . . These 30,000,000 thrifty savers receive over $700.000.000 a year interest. When the red faced radical socialist is bawling forth from his soap box on the street corner his lurid fancies concerning "the interests" and the "down-trodden masses" it will be of course to his interest to ignore any such little item as that given above.[63]

The one article found in the *Lutheran Church Herald* between 1924 and 1925 and 1930 and 1932 that mentioned the social gospel was clearly opposed:

The social gospel has confronted the modern church with a tremendous obligation in which there inheres a great peril. In a word, that peril can be stated thus: How can the Church function to make the social order Christian without ceasing to be a church? How can religion effectively apply its sanctions to the ideals of social morality without losing its character as religion? Such questions open up a vast problem. One thing, we may be assured, the Church must not do, on peril of losing its own soul—that is to make itself a political partisan agency on behalf of any cause, however ideal and desirable."[64]

A 1930 article titled "In the Slum of a City" makes the Norwegian Lutheran Church's lack of familiarity with urban problems apparent, as it also emphasizes that group's greater belief in the importance of focusing on individual salvation:

The first and foremost problem in the mission work, it seems to me, is therefore the city missionary himself. Can he, will he preach the saving Word of the Gospel at all times, in the midst of adverse conditions. . . . Or will he then condescend to a milder clime and attempt satisfying himself and other with a social betterment program lacking in what he earlier knew to be the only redeeming feature of all his missionary endeavors: the preaching of the Gospel. . . . Surely, this is of paramount importance to anyone engaged in missionary activities, especially so in our larger cities where, amidst all the social service activities of every cast and description, it is so tempting to let down our standard to a more congenial level. We can escape the brunt of suffering by condescending to a lower level, but can we thus escape the condemnation of having betrayed our Master, and of offering to starving, dying men a devitalized Gospel?[65]

With the exception of the somewhat tormented Northern Baptists, the other denominations examined in this chapter mentioned the social gospel less frequently. The *Evangelical Herald*'s views of the social gospel had to be discerned from related statements, as it did not mention the social gospel by name at all. However, these statements, particularly regarding religious activism, make it clear that it was dubious about both the value of and potential for religious activism:

> Those . . . who forget or ignore the fundamental fact that national morality and welfare depends not upon the laws which are upon our statute-books, but upon the spiritual influences which regenerate heart and soul and mold the personalities of our citizens, are grievously in error. We repeat what we have said before, the millennium is not in sight because national prohibition has been secured, and even if the new laws are rigidly enforced everywhere poverty and disease, vice and crime, corrupt politics, insanity and feeble-mindedness will still remain. The kingdom of God, that is, the reign of God in the affairs and relationships of men, is brought about not by legislation, even tho it be as wise and just as human effort can make it, nor even by education, religious or otherwise, no matter how thoro or universal it may be.[66]

The denominations featured in this chapter were devoted eugenicists who did not question the importance of heredity, the idea that some races were more likely to be endowed with superior genetic traits than others, and the belief that the most superior of these races, the Anglo-Saxon race, was ensuring its own demise via race suicide. However, unlike the early liberalizers, these groups were at best ambivalent about the social gospel. As a result, while they wanted birth control to be made legal, they did not see making a pronouncement to this effect as part of their religious duty. Thus, they tended to report positively on other religious denominations and organizations making pronouncements on birth control, as well as on evidence that birth control was being "effectively" or "properly" used, but did not themselves liberalize.

Such reluctance to make official pronouncements contrasts not only with the early liberalizers but also with the groups that did not hesitate to criticize the flurry of birth control liberalizations at the time. For a variety of reasons, which make for strange bedfellows, these "critics" rejected concerns about race suicide as well as belief in the social gospel and saw it as their religious duty to publicly criticize the spate of liberalizations. It is to these groups, some of whom were also eugenicists, but in very different geographic areas, with very different racialized concerns, that we now turn.

5 The Critics

In contrast to the religious groups chronicled in this book so far, six of the largest American religious denominations openly criticized liberalization. As table 4 indicated, these six denominations rejected both the social gospel and race suicide concerns. However, while they had these two crucial qualities in common, the reasons behind these beliefs, particularly their rejection of race suicide, could not have been more varied.

The first group of critics rejected race suicide because they rejected the assumptions inherent to the eugenics movement. These were predominantly immigrant denominations and were aware that they, and their fertility, were the targets of eugenicists: the Roman Catholic Church, the Lutheran Church–Missouri Synod, and Orthodox Jews.

The other critics chronicled in this chapter, the Presbyterian Church in the United States and Southern Baptist Convention who lived predominantly in the South, and the Church of Jesus Christ of Latter-day Saints who centered around Utah, were geographically much more distant from the population of Catholic and Jewish immigrants who roused concerns of race suicide in the Northeast.[1] The two Southern groups openly espoused eugenicist beliefs, but as whites who lived in the South, they did not share the same concerns about race suicide as their northeastern brethren.

THE CRITICS OF BIRTH CONTROL REFORM

The ways in which this group of denominations made their views about birth control clear were just as varied as the groups themselves. Some denominations, such as the Lutheran Church–Missouri Synod, did not officially condemn birth control but simply published many articles in their periodicals that were sharply critical, such as a 1934 *Lutheran Witness* article that warned that "the cloven hoof, forked tail, and horns stick out all over this birth-control agitation."[2]

However, most of the other denominations in this category officially indicated their disagreement. The Presbyterian Church in the United States (PCUS), the only critical denomination that had been a member of the Federal Council of Churches (FCC), finally acknowledged that its views were too different from the majority of other FCC members and withdrew its membership in protest after the FCC released its statement on birth control.[3]

The Roman Catholic Church, which already was and certainly became even more infamous for continually condemning birth control, reaffirmed its stance in the papal encyclical *Casti Connubii*, which Pius XI released on December 31, 1931, in explicit rejection of the Lambeth Conference, and has never changed that stance (although it almost did during Vatican II).[4]

The Southern Baptist Convention wrote the following scathing critique of birth control reformers in 1931 and went on the official record in their 1934 resolution:

> In the end economic pressure will speak and command a hearing where the churches and their bishops are dumb. . . . Birth control in the long run will be governed by bread and butter if intelligence becomes general. Divorce and remarriage will remain where they are today, resorted to by the selfish and shunned by those who regard the home and its benedictions. Just what effect these recent and obvious departures from the orthodox path pursued by our fathers will have upon the churches of the future remains to be seen. At the present time the new positions are repugnant to millions of church people and regarded as another step towards gilded paganism.[5]

The Roman Catholic Church Responds

The Roman Catholic Church was, without question, the most outspoken and visible critic of birth control.[6] Analysis of the Roman Catholic periodical *America* leaves no doubt that Catholics saw eugenicists' anti-immigrant stance as thinly (or not even) veiled anti-Catholicism. Articles emphasized that immigrants were their "brothers in the Faith" whose "efforts to remain Catholic" would be supported and accused birth control advocates and anti-immigration activists of shutting "out the immigrants from Italy [and] Poland" because they "were the Catholics who had large families and were the chief contributors to the growth of the Catholic population in the United States."[7]

The Roman Catholic Church directly took on eugenicists, accusing them of "preaching 'race suicide'" and critiquing other eugenicist arguments in articles such as "The Value of Later Children in Families" and "Birth Control and Prosperity," which directly took on the science of eugenics.[8] In "The Value of Later Children in Families," the author stated:

> Studies have supplied an explanation in biological terms of some of the failures of first born sons in the matter of intelligence, and especially their lack of self-control and their inability to take the place in life that their status among the nobility would seem to demand of them. The subject has a very special interest for us here in America and indeed for all the modern civilized nations because of the very common reduction in the number of children in families which has occurred during the present generation. This sociological development has left the civilized world to a great extent without whatever advantage might be derived from having a fairly good proportion at least of the increase in population recruited from among the later born of the families.[9]

The article concluded shrewdly:

> If the earlier children in families are not so intellectually well developed or endowed as the later children, the human race today is missing the contributions that might be made to it by the later children of families, since only rarely are families numerous enough to provide these valuable factors for humanity's progress.[10]

On a very similar note, another article questioned Malthus's theories and research and suggested that "one of the principal reasons why geniuses are rarer in our time than they used to be is that we are no longer getting the ends of families but only the beginnings of them and a great many of our geniuses have come very late in families."[11] The article titled "Birth Control and Prosperity" directly took on eugenicists' arguments that immigration restriction and lower birth rates would be good for the economic vitality of the nation. It noted:

> Now two things have happened which are already being felt in financial circles. First we cut off by one stroke all this new [economic] accretion to our foundations of prosperity; and secondly, we inaugurated a vigorous effort to reduce the population by artificial restriction of conception. We voluntarily deprived ourselves of what was probably the largest single cause of material prosperity, increase of adult population by immigration; and then we turned about and saw to it that the population would not grow naturally by births, which is a slower if more usual way of adding to the consumer power of the nation. . . . For years and years we have been accepting as gospel truth the idea that this country will in no distant day be overrun with people, all clamoring for food and no food to give them. It is the strongest social argument the birth-controllers have at their command. Now the economists destroy that fond illusion.[12]

Another letter to the editor regarding a recent article in *America* "drew attention to immigration (as well as other population increases) as our real source of prosperity," also questioning the economic wisdom of the new immigration quotas:

> I have just plotted immigration beside commodity prices for the last sixty-nine years. The restrictionists probably allege panics are due to immigration maxima. It does seem the maxima of the most rapid increases in immigration coincided with so-called panics, but the interesting and important indication is this: when immigration has decreased or remained depressed as the result of panics ('73, '84, '93), the country's recovery has been very slow, and when immigration quickly resumed a normal course after the panic year ('90, '03, '07, '20), the entire country's recovery was rapid. Unless this is a mere coincidence, we must lift the quotas, or look for bad business the next three years![13]

In addition to criticizing the soundness of their economic policies, *America* also criticized eugenicists for being classist, both in terms of whom they targeted for birth control efforts and in their understandings of the nature of the causes and consequences of poverty. For example, one author closed his article with the thought, "I am wondering whether, and to what extent, under the guise of welfare work, birth control is being spread among our working classes and among our poor all over the country."[14] The same author critically quoted the following statement by a social worker:

> It is generally the alcoholic, the mentally deficient and the criminally-inclined who are always in need, and who have the largest number of children; these as a rule inherit all the vices of their parents; generally such parents do not want so many children; they become an increasing charge upon the community; it seems imperative that this organization put at the disposal of such parents some scientific means to help them avoid the unwelcome burden; thus only can we at the same time decrease the number of unfit and of undesirables in the community, and make our own work more fruitful and permanent.[15]

Part and parcel of Catholics' critique of the classist nature of eugenicist views was Catholics' emphasis on the importance of environment, rather than breeding, particularly regarding the causes of crime. For example, in one article they criticized prominent eugenicists whose "permanent solution of the problem of crime is this: stop the breeding of criminals!" They then went on to directly quote what they saw as the most egregious statements by eugenicists: "The improvement of the mentality and character of the race ... can be done only through breeding. Environment, sociology, pedagogy cannot usurp the place of breeding—a cabbage will produce a cabbage and a rose a rose, in spite of all." Countering those arguments, the article continued:

> Potential criminality in all children of Adam and Eve we admit, and that impulse to wrong may be greater or less according to varied circumstances, such as time, place, and family. But that this impulse necessarily leads the person who is its victim into the path which it points out, we deny. The power of the impulse we admit, but do we not have a power greater than it to oppose against it and thwart it, the power of the grace of God?[16]

Another article in *America* titled "Sociology: The New Criminal Science" criticized eugenicist views of the biological nature of crime and complained, "The criminal has become a social menace just like a person afflicted with a contagious disease, that and no more. Criminality has been discovered, once and for all, not to be in man's free will. This does not exist. Crime is something purely biological in every case."[17]

In addition to critiquing eugenicists' focus on biology over environment, *America* directly took on eugenicist arguments for being anti-Catholic and attributed them to political concerns, both in terms of who would be elected and who was doing the electing: "Many Americans are still firmly convinced that Catholics, the laity as well as the hierarchy, are striving to control all political power with the ultimate purpose of transferring the Bishop of Rome from the Vatican to the White House."[18] *America* was clearly aware of the many critiques of American Catholics, especially debates over their political power and persuasion. One article in 1924 described "reports of discrimination against Catholics in practically every large city in the country." It went on to emphasize that those reports were from "even Boston and New York which, by popular but inaccurate tradition, are 'ruled by Catholics.'"[19] Another article the same year argued that Catholics should be given "rights at the polls," but their vote would not result in the subjection of the country to the pope, as many believed at the time: "When Catholics fight for their rights at the polls and insist that these rights be respected, they are not, let it be repeated, inaugurating a campaign for the subjection of the United States to the Pope, or for forcing their religion upon anyone."[20]

Finally, articles in *America* made it clear that the Roman Catholic Church intended to help Catholic immigrants remain Catholic and criticized "Nordic" pressures to speed up immigrant assimilation. For example, one author asserted that immigrants were "brothers in the Faith":

> We must, at all hazards, make every effort to let these people understand that we sympathize with their efforts to remain Catholic, that we appreciate their struggles and we do not look upon them with suspicion. We in short must welcome them as brothers in the Faith. In this our people have been remiss, but it is not too late to mend. The future of several millions of Catholic Americans depends upon it.[21]

Another article criticized the "extreme impatience" of "our 'Nordics'—wonderfully mouth-filling, though cryptic word—in respect to the assimilation of immigrant population": "Do it at once. Change it in one generation.

Become American, that, American as we see it!"[22] Whereas a slow process of assimilation is really to be preferred, since it evinces a disinclination to forsake old ideals without prior examination of the new ones to be adopted. Are "short-cuts" to citizenship preferable? Strictly speaking, why should not the immigrant change overnight?[23]

In sum, the Roman Catholic Church was far from blind and deaf to the anti-immigrant, anti-Catholic sentiments being trumpeted by eugenicists and the religious groups covered in the previous two chapters. On almost every point—questions of racial superiority, issues of political power and freedom, the speed and thoroughness of desired assimilation, the economic wisdom of immigration restriction—*America* published a response. This was no less the case with birth control. In fact, it was difficult to find quotes from *America* that criticized birth control but did not criticize eugenics.

Of course, the Roman Catholic Church was notorious for its opposition to birth control and Margaret Sanger in particular (especially after a very well-publicized incident when Sanger was prevented from speaking in Boston in 1929).[24] And many have attributed that resistance to the Roman Catholic Church's more centralized bureaucracy or fondness for more antiquated forms of religion, such as priestly celibacy and a refusal to ordain women. However, other groups shared Catholic skepticism of race suicide and eugenics. These other groups, the Lutheran Church–Missouri Synod, Orthodox Jews, and the Mormons, all shared one thing with the Roman Catholic Church—they were all outsiders in America.

Joining the Catholic Opposition: Other Outsider Critics

Like Catholics, Orthodox Jews condemned birth control and eugenics in the same breath in their periodical the *Jewish Forum*:

> Much could be said of the wisdom of the Bible on the subject of eugenics, and of its attitude on birth control. We scientists may justly condemn the extravagant opinions of some so-called preachers of the gospel, who actually rush in and air their views on a medical and scientific subject where—not the angels but—physicians and men of science fear to tread.[25]

In a 1924 review of the crucial book *Race Prejudice* by Jean Pinot, the *Jewish Forum* wrote approvingly of how the book criticized the "Nordic

myth" and "Anglo-Saxon and other supremacy claims." The review emphasized data and arguments that directly disputed eugenicist beliefs in the
importance of heredity by arguing that "practically all human differences,
in point of fact, can be laid to the milieu, or environment," asserting that
"the only thing certain about the study of races, the writer proves, is that
all people and peoples are the product of crossbreeding, which far from
being a degenerating process, has given the world its greatest men and the
whole American nation."[26] The author went on to note wryly, "If the Ku
Klux and Nordic supremacy experts" ever read this book, "there would be
the shock of learning that this is a work in which Jews had no part, and
throughout which the Jew is mentioned but rarely and meagerly."[27]

A few years later, as the eugenics movement was peaking in the United
States, the *Forum* published an article sardonically titled "Klintolerance."
The article chronicled example after example of racial intolerance between
groups, with a particular focus on "Jew and gentile, gentile and Jew."[28] The
most telling part of the article demonstrates that Orthodox Jews were
aware and disturbed that Reform Jews were involved in the eugenics
movement (as their early liberalization on birth control would suggest) and
especially sensitive to their elitism regarding newer Jewish immigrants:

> In the Jewish community of a certain charming city in Oklahoma, the
> "German" Jews were with rigid klintolerance segregated from that lesser spe-
> cies of Jew which emigrated, a generation or two or three later, from Poland
> and Russia. Amongst these communities, no less than among the dominant
> Protestant majority, there were certain klintolerances both manifest and
> muted. The group in power looked at its own theological habits, its own
> table-manners, and saw that they were good. Those habits and manners that
> were dissimilar were not merely *ipso facto* bad, but by inference a criticism
> and an impertinence. For they failed to realize, (and this is the basic foolish-
> ness of all Klintolerance) that this world is only the lovely place it is, despite
> all the Hitlers and the Heflins, precisely because of its differences—its "sacred
> and ineradicable differences," as D. H. Lawrence has called them.[29]

It probably comes as no surprise that Roman Catholics and Orthodox
Jews, the two most common whipping boys for eugenicists, were open
about their skepticism and concern about eugenics. But they were not
alone. The Lutheran Church–Missouri Synod, whose statements about its
"Americanness" presented below demonstrate just how much of an out-

sider this denomination still was at this time, was critical of eugenics early and often. In 1923, the *Lutheran Witness* directly took on eugenicists by using their own terms:

> Even in homes where children are still desired the opinion prevails and is gaining ground that their number should be regulated in accordance with the means of support. *"Fewer and better babies"* is the slogan. Birth control, frequently nothing but infanticide, once vigorously opposed and bitterly fought by the state, is in spite of adverse legislation still extant in some places, being advocated with ever increasing boldness.[30]

A year later, the same periodical again referred to the same slogan in another harsh critique:

> It is not our present purpose to discuss the various aspects of birth control, that odious movement which now seeks to obtain freedom through Federal and State legislation for the dissemination of its literature. Briefly, this movement advocates the use of drugs and contrivances by which married people and others may "cheat nature." And the devil's slogan which these destroyers of morality, and of civilization based on morality, have written on their banner is, *"Fewer children, but better ones."*[31]

In 1931 the FCC's pronouncement in favor of birth control inflamed tensions throughout the American religious field, especially among the critics. That year, an article in the *Witness* again argued, "If ever there was a slogan built up 100 percent of 'hot air,' it is 'Fewer children, but better ones.'" The article went on:

> Between the size of families and the goodness of the children there is no relation at all. Certainly we do not find that children of large families are more frequently than others poor, degenerate, vicious, or miserable, nor has it been our experience that the only child is more immune against sickness and death. . . . In our own observation there are more weaklings, both morally and physically, among the only sons than are in the same proportion found in large families. Nor does the voice of history confirm the proposition that smaller families will mean the production of more useful members of society, of talented men and women, of geniuses.[32]

The *Witness* did not only have problems with eugenicists' slogans, however. It also questioned the science behind those slogans. Like other critics of eugenicists, the *Witness* reminded readers that "Michelangelo, Beethoven, Wagner, Martin Luther, Moses, Aristotle, and Abraham Lincoln were the children of very plain people.[33] On the other hand, mediocre and even inferior children have had gifted parents."[34] In a similar vein, another article pointed out that "in any number of cases the most able men, who were an honor and joy to their parents, came from large families and very often were born after ten or more brothers and sisters had entered the home."[35] The following quote provides an example of how they often synonymously questioned both the science behind eugenics as well as eugenicists' personal morality:

> Just as the present time, when we hear so much about the sterilization of the unfit and when the falling off of births is so very evident, our people ought to be warned against the advice of quacks and unscrupulous propagandists of birth control. Another celebrated professor of medicine, Dr. Fishbein, has lately raised his voice in warning against interference with God's order. In the *Journal of the American Medical Association* he published an article in which he made this statement concerning the children of the poor or even of deficient parents: "Actually, we do not know enough to recommend any sort of mass action."[36]

In addition to referring to them as "quacks," the *Lutheran Witness*, quoting an editorial in the *Globe-Democrat* of Saint Louis, also referred to eugenicists as "the little band of professors and men and women busybodies" who were futilely "trying to apply to the human race . . . artificial stock-breeding rules" and closed with a call to "let our faddists quit their foolishness and help in properly educating children."[37]

The Lutheran Church–Missouri Synod seemed well aware of who should be considered allies in the fight against contraception. The same article quoted above noted that "there is no Church, other than the Roman Catholic, with the courage to stand out against the latest sin of the age."[38] Another article in the *Witness* published ten years later quoted *America* before concluding that birth control advocates were "making it safe to sin."[39]

Lutheran views of eugenics were certainly related to the importance and centrality of their recent immigration histories, which were ironically most apparent in articles that asserted their "Americanness" or critiqued other groups for their anti-immigrant views. For example, in an article titled "Is the Lutheran Church a Foreign Church?," the *Lutheran Witness* asserted: "The Lutheran Church in this country is composed of Americans, is officered by American citizens, and in that sense is an American church."[40] In what seems to have been a response to critiques of the Roman Catholic Church, which was infamous for not supporting a separation of church and state, the same article reminded readers that "we scarcely need to call attention to the fact that the Lutheran Church teaches the separation of Church and State, which is a fundamental principle of the American constitution."[41]

However, being an immigrant was not the only way a religious group could be aware of its outsider status vis-à-vis the Protestant establishment. Such is the takeaway point about the geographically and culturally more isolated Church of Jesus Christ of Latter-day Saints, or Mormons. While decrying declining birth rates in general, the Mormons directly countered eugenicists' central arguments about the importance of racial purity clearly in their periodicals.[42] Instead of simply dismissing eugenics arguments, they argued that they were fundamentally wrong. According to Mormons, the greatness of both the nation, and of Mormons as a group, was due to their "interbreeding":

> "Mormons" are the most composite people in the world today, since they have drawn, and continue to draw from the best nations of Northern Europe and from the most substantial citizenry of composite America. It is by no means an accident that the greatest nations of the past and of the present are of a mixed blood. . . . There is no doubt that the rapid ascendancy of the United States among the powers of the world is due in part to this admixture of blood in its people. Its fertile inventive genius, which has produced three-fourths of the world's inventions, and its development of the principles of democracy give the American nation a place by itself in the history of the world.[43]

Lest anyone question the centrality of geography for the racial views of all of the denominations examined in this book, the article concluded confidently that "the 'Mormon' people, occupying in the main the greater part of Utah and southeastern Idaho, with sprinklings in Wyoming, Colorado, California, and Arizona, are the most composite people in the most composite nation in the world."[44] All five of the articles found in the Mormon periodical the *Improvement Era* criticized birth control. Most did so on biblical grounds, arguing, for example, that

> the first great commandment of the Lord is, "Be fruitful and multiply and replenish the earth." (Gen 1:28) A married couple who refuse to have children disobey God's first commandment, and will have intense regrets both in this life and in the life to come. In advancing years, to see others have the joy of children in their homes that they might have had will be punishment in this world. In the next life, how can they face their Maker and explain their refusal to aid him in populating the earth? Then in sorrow and regret they will know the full meaning of the words: "Of all sad words of tongue or pen, The saddest are these, it might have been."[45]

The four outsider groups examined here, especially those with recent immigrant histories and identities as such, were open about their criticism of both eugenics and birth control. However, they were not the only denominations that rejected race suicide concerns. Indeed, they were joined by denominations that might seem like extremely unlikely allies, including those that were vehemently anti-Catholic, like the Southern Baptist Convention. To understand how these unlikely bedfellows came together, we must understand how racial concerns differed geographically and thus in conjunction with religious concerns. Whereas whites in the North were deeply concerned that Catholic immigrants were ruining America's racial stock, whites in the South viewed them as possible eugenic helpmates.

Southern Critics: The Geography of Race Suicide

Map 4 (which excludes Roman Catholics) demonstrates that for the most part, the critics lived outside of the Northeast, and a large portion lived in the South. With high birth rates and living where "the only socially inferior race was clearly separated by the accident of color" as eugenicist Prescott F. Hall wrote in 1919, Southern white denominations tended to be quite devoted to beliefs in white superiority and thus supportive of eugenic principals in general.[46] However, as Hall also noted in 1919, "until very recently there was no immigration at all" in the South.[47] Furthermore, Southern whites had a much higher birth rate than their Northern counterparts. In combination, these factors created religious denominations that were devoted to eugenics in relationship to blacks but relatively unconcerned about immigration or immigrant birth rates and tended to see white immigrants as potentially adding to the white genetic "lifestream," rather than destroying their racial stock. All of these factors lead to statements such as the following, which came from the Southern Baptist periodical the *Biblical Recorder*:

> These men argue at length for birth control. They give great emphasis to their argument that there are already too many laboring people in the world and that the proper way to remedy this is to limit the number of their children. They do not stop to think that their grandchildren will likely be working for the grandchildren of laborers today. They say: "There is surely no social wisdom in bringing 150 potential workers into the world when there are only 100 jobs to fill." It never seems to occur to them that a fairer distribution of the national income would create more jobs and keep the 150 employed. Race-suicide to prevent unemployment is a new doctrine.[48]

That they were eugenicists was blatantly obvious in both the Southern Baptist Convention's newspaper the *Christian Index* and the PCUS's periodical the *Presbyterian Survey*. The *Index* published seven articles supportive of eugenics between 1924 and 1925 alone. As an example, one of these articles included the following excerpt from Conklin's *The Direction of Human Evolution*: "We must seek through eugenics and euthenics to improve the bodies of men, through education, the minds of men; through religion, the morals of men."[49] The author concluded by asserting, "The key words of human destiny are eugenics, euthenics, heredity, sanitation, social improvement."[50] Still another *Christian Index* article argued:

> Heredity is a well-established fact in science. Through the whole realm of living things runs the great law. Like begets like. No grapes from thorns, nor figs from thistles. "That which is born of the flesh is flesh." "The great man," Grant Allen tells us, "springs from an ancestry competent to produce him."[51]

In fact, the *Christian Index* displayed such comfort with eugenic language that it used it almost flippantly in another article published in 1924:

> Do you like to look at good stock? Of course you do! Any normal man who does not delight upon a really fine specimen of nature is just not normal. And when that specimen of nature happens to be a horse, cow, hog, dog— that will do, the average man, especially down here in Georgia, will be very much pleased."[52]

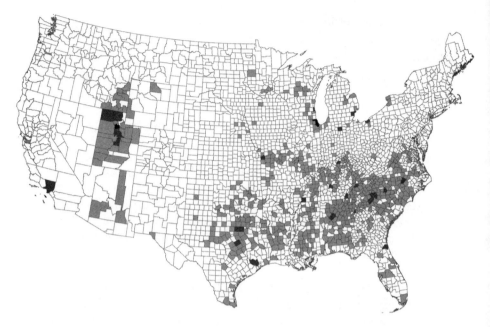

Map 4. Critics (excluding Roman Catholics).

The *Presbyterian Survey* did not question the importance of being wellborn. For example, an article in the *Survey* extolled its readers:

> The character of a child is chiefly the product of two forces, heredity and environment, and to both of these forces parents are more vitally related than other human beings. . . . There is in every human life a mysterious element of necessity. Everyone is born into a particular family which has a history and a character of its own, formed before he arrives. He has no choices in the matter; yet this affects all his subsequent life. He may be born where it is an honor to be born, or, on the contrary, where it is a disgrace. He may be heir to inspiring memories and refined habits, or may have to take up a hereditary burden of physical or moral disease. A man has no choice of his mother or father, his brothers or sisters, his uncles or his cousins, yet, on these ties which he has no power to unlock, may depend three-fourths of his happiness.[53]

Although steadfast in their beliefs about the importance of heredity and the science of eugenics, the *Survey* was much more likely to emphasize the importance of nurture over nature than the *Index*. For example, the following article, which began with an almost chilling portrait of genetic deficiencies, warned its readers of the importance of properly preparing their children for the "contests" of life in 1931:

> O what hopeless struggles some of us are preparing for our children! What tragedies are in store for them! Inherited appetites! Family traits and tendencies inherited from their forefathers coming with them into the world and largely determining their destiny! What would you think of a poor fellow trying to run a race with a hundred pounds of flesh, with a heavy suit of clothing on, and great iron balls bound round his ankles? Try to visualize such a contest: Running for a prize with half a dozen athletes properly trained for the race. The signal shot is fired, and here they go, some like the wind, and this poor fellows at a snail's pace, struggling hopelessly with the handicap that he has no power to overcome. Is that your child in life?[54]

Although it emphasized the burden created by one's parents, the article continued on, urging parents to be godly, to refrain from drink, and to otherwise train "themselves, so that inherited tendencies shall not be clogs to drag them down to defeat, but wings to bear them up and hurry them on to certain victory."[55]

Another article titled "The Illusion of the Horizon," published in the same periodical in 1934, argued similarly:

> The social and religious horizons of our lives are just as definite as any the eye discovers from a mountain top. Birth and breeding, class and creed set us within definite bounds where we live and move and have our being. Often they seem to us to be as fixed and irremovable as the stars. And yet we know that horizons do not exist . . . we may never arrive at the point beyond which our mental development cannot go. Whatever limitations circumstance may throw about us, we always possess a power to cope with them successfully.[56]

There are a number of important analytical points to make regarding these quotes. First, the *Presbyterian Survey* was focused on its own constituents and their ability to live up to their full potential in this article. The extent to which it would emphasize the importance of nurture over nature for other groups, especially in the case of this denomination, blacks in the South, is questionable. Second, and relatedly, while it emphasized the importance of nature, especially for child-rearing and especially for its own members, all eugenicist groups, at one point or another, emphasized the importance of religious instruction in that rearing—seeing it as a key part of what could ultimately be inherited.[57] Recall, for example, eugenicists' efforts to encourage ministers to have more children.

Third, and most importantly, these groups considered one population crucial to nurture. Both of the Southern groups that criticized birth control reform shared a quality that very much differentiated them from their Northern counterparts. In comparison to Northern white Protestants' scathing views of immigrants, Southern white Protestants actually welcomed them. In contrast to the Northern branch of their denominations' periodical that insisted, for example, that the "foreign born predominate among the insane," the *Presbyterian Survey* asserted, "It is not true that we receive the 'Scum of the earth,' for the so-called 'scum' seldom has the ambition to emigrate."[58]

Recall the intelligence statistics quoted by the Northern Baptists in the previous chapter. The title, "The Religious Implications of Modern Psychology," implies a focus on Catholics, who were known to be "rapidly increasing," although the article itself makes no such explicit connection. The article reported in part:

> When the results of scientific mental testing are tabulated statistically, and graphically represented . . . not more than 50 per cent of the American people [are] in the average normal group, less than 25 per cent in the superior group and more than 25 per cent in the inferior group.

The article went on to emphasize that "the facts are that the superior group is decreasing and the inferior group rapidly increasing."[59]

In contrast to the Northern Baptists' unquestioning acceptance of those statistics, look at how critically the same statistics were interpreted for the Southern whites reading yet another positive article on immigrants in the *Survey*. The article begins by reporting that "according to a recent experiment, the foreign-born is below the average intelligence. They do not contribute very much to the American intelligence." The article then went on to quote leading Northern eugenicists:

> Dr. Harry Laughling . . . is director of the Eugenic Bureau of the Carnegie Institution. He gives us the following conclusion: Out of the 13,920,692 men of foreign birth only 11.3 per cent make any definite contribution to our American intelligence. Twenty-six per cent are all of the average intelli-

gence; 800,000, or sixty-two per cent are below the average capacity of intelligence and general development.[60]

However, whereas the Northern Baptists seemed to simply take these statistics on face value as justification for immigration restriction, Southern Presbyterians questioned the reason behind these facts and even went so far as to argue that they were completely reducible to a lack of opportunity on the part of immigrants:

> What reason can be given for this fact? Of course the cause is obvious. It is due to the undeveloped element of the foreign-born stock that has migrated to this country. In their native countries they have no opportunity to develop themselves, and when they come to this country, thus they fall into the path of struggle for life, thus they remain undeveloped. Many among them are so illiterate that they cannot even sign their names. Most of them are slightly educated. What do we expect from such a stock? Apparently loss and not gain.[61]

Not according to this author. The article goes on to question this perspective, first arguing that immigrants might be *beneficial to the white* race on the basis of (what they saw as) sound eugenic science:

> There are certain definite contributions the foreign-born is making to . . . America. The first one we suggest is biological. The student of eugenics and social science knows that our "primitive" American stock is rapidly passing away . . . the Anglo-Saxon and Nordic stock. America is the most heterogeneous country in the world. Its population is becoming more and more complex. . . . We think it will save the country from stock deterioration. The history of the great nations of antiquity indicates that their downfall was largely due to the decay of the stock—new blood was lacking in the veins of the old weakened race. An homogenous people cannot last very long.[62]

The article continued on, quoting "a genius in the social and eugenic science" who claimed "(with convincing facts), that 'to keep a nation from deterioration, a mixture of race is the only necessity. A nation's culture lasts as long as the stock is sound, which is between 1,300–1,500 years.'" The article pointed out that "if this is true, the foreign-born population of America will be its savior, and is really making it stronger rather than weakening it, as it appears on the surface."[63] Continuing on, the article asserted that immigrants were already demonstrating the quality of their genetic material after only one generation on American soil:

> This [potential] is illustrated by the present condition of foreign-born fami-lies. Feeble-mindedness, for instance, is very rare among these people, while it is becoming a serious problem among the natives. A recent statistic shows 600,000 known cases of feeble-mindedness in this country. The foreign-born stock holds very well at present. Their children are intelligent, while they themselves are not. The old generation of foreign-born is passing away and a new one is emerging out of it. They leave us sound but undeveloped stock. They are the future fathers and mothers of America. They must be educated, but above all, must be Christianized. This is a work for Christian America.[64]

For Southern whites, immigrants could "save the country from stock deterioration," but only if their religion was "fixed." Deeply anti-Catholic, as the *Index* openly admitted, "We Protestants are crowded in with Catholics, and they get on our nerves."[65] Southern whites discussed con-verting immigrants to "Christ" much more than did Northerners.

That they had no affection for the Roman Catholic Church is undoubt-able. For example, the same periodical published a book review that was sympathetic to the anti-Catholicism of the Ku Klux Klan, if not the organ-ization itself:

> The Klan's opposition to the Catholic Church is due to that church's form of government which can be so easily manipulated for political ends. . . . The Catholic hierarchy has dominated politics in certain European countries and . . . has made its power felt in this country in opposition to our public school system.[66]

Another article in the *Index* elaborated on the historic reasons behind the Southern Baptist Convention's views of the Roman Catholic Church:

> History proves that for more than a thousand years the Roman Catholic Church has had political, as well as religious, ends in view. For more than a thousand years they have believed in the temporal power of the Church, and wherever Roman Catholicism has predominated religious liberty has perished from the land. . . . The Roman Catholic Church claims to be an infallible Church with an infallible pope and she never retracts and never changes. . . . We [Protestants] have purchased [absolute religious] free-

dom at a great price, and we are not going to sell it for a mess of political pottage.[67]

Despite the problems Roman Catholics might have posed for the nation's political system, they were not seen as a racial problem in the South. This is evident by the lack of concern these eugenicist denominations expressed about race suicide. The *Presbyterian Survey* did not mention race suicide or differential birth rates once during the eight years for which their periodical was examined (1919–20, 1925, 1930–35). The *Christian Index* published three articles in the four years for which we were able to obtain it that vaguely suggested the existence of differential birth rates and demonstrated an awareness of the issue, particularly for those in the North. This is most apparent in an article that listed the names and hospitals of some recent (presumably white) parents, after proclaiming happily: "We note with pleasurable satisfaction that Atlanta does not believe in race suicide. Recently we had nineteen babies in the hospital at one time."[68] This is perhaps why the *Presbyterian Survey* article, quoted at length elsewhere in this chapter, questioned the calls for political alarm coming from other (most likely Northern) quarters: "We cannot consistently assume that the foreign-born population of this country is extremely dangerous politically speaking."[69]

While the early liberalizers worked on curtailing immigration and immigrant fecundity, Southern groups discussed immigrants primarily as a missionary responsibility. The *Survey* showed a particular concern about Italian immigrants, often mentioning stereotypical qualities such as the following: "Did you ever walk down the streets of a foreign settlement in one of our cities? If you have done so, I wonder if you noticed the shrill jargon of the language, the garlic, the general air of dilapidation all around."[70]

The *Survey* also frequently gave updates on immigrant population estimates in Southern cities.[71] For example, a *Presbyterian Survey* article that continually elided ethnicity and religion with a focus on Italians started:

Does our religion mean anything to us? If so, we must propagate it. Visit with me some of our Southern cities and let us study the situation from a numerical standpoint: In New Orleans we find 75,000 Italians. In West Tampa, a suburb of Tampa, there are 12,000 Italians; in Ybor City, another of Tampa's suburbs, 18,000 Spanish-speaking people, besides many Italians. Thus it is in scores of Southern cities, and the Italians are here to stay, not to get rich and return to their native land. America is their home. They are building comfortable, attractive dwellings, their children are already American citizens, are rapidly becoming Americanized.[72]

Like other articles, this one goes on to ask, "But what of their religious status? Are they an asset to our country spiritually?"[73] The answer is clearly a resounding no:

> Come to Tampa and see. Porches lined with those not sufficiently interested in their soul's salvation to walk across the street to hear the Gospel message: various types of gambling dens in full blast continually; crowds of gaily-dressed young people on their way to the dance or ball game Sunday afternoon; many buying and selling on the Lord's day.[74]

The article urged readers to "gird up our loins and go into the battle with renewed strength [and] ... press on with undaunted courage and unflinching sacrifice to the goal of making America Christian by winning the immigrant to Christ."[75] Similarly, *Christian Index* articles gave various statistics regarding immigrants:

> Of foreigners in our Southland there are four million. They have come seeking liberty from oppression, and relief from poverty. They swarm our streets, work in our mines, commercialize our fruits, mend our shoes, open laundries and go far in breaking down our Sabbath. If we do not evangelize and train them, they will do us a great injury.[76]

To understand just how different their attitudes toward immigrants were from Northern Protestants, recall the early liberalizers' statements on proselytization. While Northern bodies sounded resigned to the demographic changes taking place religiously in the Northeast, Southern Protestants seemed genuinely interested in proselytizing to them. For example, the Congregational Christian Church wrote in defeated tones that "apparently great major groupings of religion in Chicago—Protestant, Catholic, and Jewish—are permanent. Few hope to solve the problems of religious competition by one group converting all the rest.[77] In contrast, a *Christian Index* article called readers to "evangelize these lost peoples in our very midst":[78]

Within a few city blocks of where the Southern Baptist Convention held its recent meeting in Kansas City, there are more than 20,000 Italians, 10,000 Mexicans, 5,000 Greeks, with Russians and other foreigners by the thousands, among whom so little is being done that we would blush to record it. Should I guide the minds of my readers to other sections of the territory of the Southern Baptist Convention, I could present facts so appalling and figures so surprising as to bring an ache to all but dead hearts. . . . There are more than 500,000 foreign farmers in the South, helping thus to make new frontiers in old territories. . . . But where will [we] be when Baptist farmers are supplanted by aliens in Tongue, Traditions, Blood and Beliefs? The sanest, most effective, and the most economical missionary work for the lost in other lands is to evangelize those of these lost peoples who come into our very midst, and have them return to tell the gracious story of the Cross. Why allow these who are our neighbors to remain right by us unevangelized while we spend thousands of dollars in sending hundreds of our own workers across seas to aliens just because they do not live next door. These converted foreigners are the rightful agencies for the evangelization of their own people in the regions beyond. . . . . Much more of this sort of assistance should be rendered.[79]

Of course, Northern groups occasionally mentioned evangelizing to immigrants. But the PCUS and the Southern Baptists did not just make idle calls for their readers to convert Roman Catholics to Christ. They offered concrete suggestions, such as the following two quotes (the first ended the article that quoted the intelligence statistics at length). After noting that immigrants "have their native religion but it cannot reach and hold the new generation," it advised:

We may suggest some concrete ways the Christians may help their foreign-born neighbors: The first and most important thing is to protect the foreign-born from exploitation. Many have come to my attention where they have fallen prey to some doctor or lawyer or business man, so called. This will help you to establish a point of friendly contact with them. Do not try to make them members of your particular branch of the Church, but keep them Christians. Tell them about Christ before you ask them to join your church. The children will open a way for you to reach the parents.[80]

Another article headline in the *Survey* reported with excitement that the gospel was now available "in Italian for One Cent."[81]

Of course, Roman Catholics were not of interest to these groups simply because of their (apparently impressive) potential to improve Southern white racial stock. They were also of interest because the PCUS and the Southern Baptists were aware that they suddenly and uncharacteristically found themselves allied with the Roman Catholic Church in relation to birth control. They actively discussed this development. Take, for example, the following lengthy discussion that appeared in the *Biblical Recorder* in 1935:

> On Sunday, December 1, Cardinal Hayes, "aroused by the recent movement to have birth control information supplied to mothers of families on relief," spoke in St. Patrick's Cathedral in the City of New York to voice his, "measured, deliberate and emphatic condemnation of the effrontery" of those who sponsored the movement. In the course of his remarks he said he spoke as an American citizen. In this we think he was correct. He did give expression to the sincere conviction our people generally hold that birth control as proposed by modern agitators is wrong, a conviction which finds expression in our federal laws making unlawful the broadcasting of such information on the subject as those who favor birth control would have given out. We know there are certain Protestant and Jewish clergymen, whom Cardinal Hayes classed as "prophets of decadence," who lend their support to the proposition. Cardinal Hayes reproached them and others who desire to "control the lives of the poor as if they were cattle," and declares that already the population of the country is not reproducing itself. We agree with him when he says: "The true lover of the poor today, and the true social scientist, knows that the right approach to the whole problem is not to keep people from having children, but is so to reorder our economic and social structure as to make it possible for people to have children and to rear them in keeping with their needs. Therein lies true social leadership: In birth prevention lies social degradation."

This is not to say that their eugenic views never extended to immigrants. They certainly did. For example, when discussing the implications of recent immigration restriction laws, they wrote agreeably, "Everybody is now agreed that we must have quality in the immigration of the future. That phase of the matter has been settled."[82] However, they went on to question the wisdom of the restrictions themselves:

> There is still considerable disagreement on the question of the quantity to be admitted and the methods to be employed in obtaining quality. Under favorable conditions as to taxes, the free capital resources of this country would be sufficient to employ a million or two more workers than they now do. A million or two more workers would enable us to utilize all of the so-

called surplus plant equipment developed during the war. Immigration restrictions that are based on quantity without regard to quality are already driving capital out of the country.[83]

In contrast to Northern whites who believed that all immigrants from Eastern or Southern Europe were of inferior stock than the "first" Anglo immigrants who had founded the United States, Southern whites seemed to have little concern about where exactly their immigrants were coming from—as long as they were white, their religion could be fixed. In their words, "It would be much better to make a hundred per cent Christians rather than a hundred per cent Americans out of the strangers now crowding our doors."[84]

This chapter includes the widest variety of religious denominations: Southern eugenicists, immigrant denominations critical of eugenics, combined with groups like the Mormons to openly criticize early birth control reform within the American religious field. Despite this diversity, however, they all shared one quality—a lack of concern about race suicide. And while the reasons behind their lack of concern about race suicide could not have been more different, their shared rejection of it led them to the same solution: they openly opposed birth control. This was the case so long as they also rejected, or at the very least were completely removed from, the social gospel movement.

DISTANT FROM THE SOCIAL GOSPEL

Newer denominations, whether because they were immigrant churches or just more recently founded than the groups that made up America's Protestant establishment, seemed almost completely out of the loop regarding the social gospel movement. Neither the Roman Catholic Church, Orthodox Jews, or the Mormons mentioned the social gospel once in the more than seven years of periodical analysis conducted for each of them. The *Lutheran Witness* mentioned it only once, in an article reporting on an FCC statement in 1934 and in an extremely critical tone:

> Now, while this message speaks of the good news of the Gospel, nowhere does it tell us definitely and explicitly it means by this Gospel. But after dismissing

this subject with a few vague and general phrases, it launches out upon the discussion of the present economic plight, cruel war, conflict with the liquor traffic, and corporate greed. And yet, in spite of all this, it never wearies of repeating the demand that we be "Christlike". Why, then, is this their very message so entirely unchristlike? God never forbade the government to use the sword. Far from it. He gave the sword to the government and expects the government to use it right. Christ never preached to reform social and economic inequalities. He never uttered one word forbidding the manufacture or the proper use of wine. Indeed, He used it in the Lord's Supper and taught His disciples to use it. But Christ taught doctrine, doctrine chiefly about Himself, and faith in Himself as the Only-begotten of the Father and about the Word of God and the Sacraments. Of all this these blind leaders say nothing. We must therefore choose between the Good Shepherd and these blind leaders. How could we hesitate when such is the choice? These men teach their own vain drama, but Jesus has "the words of eternal life," John 6, 68.[85]

In contrast to immigrant denominations that simply seemed disconnected from the social gospel movement, the Southern Baptist Convention and the PCUS knew all too well what sort of social activism was required by the movement and expressed very strong views against the social gospel. The Southern Baptist Convention asserted:

> The times are prolific of the ways in which men may be saved. There is salvation by eugenics and salvation by social service. There is salvation by talking spirits and salvation by pleasant thoughts. There is salvation by legislation and salvation by sanitation. But there is, in fact only one salvation. There is no other way but Jesus.[86]

With such strong feelings against the social gospel movement on the part of many of these groups (or a lack of engagement with it on the part of the rest) and lacking concerns about race suicide, this disparate group of denominations ended up finding consensus around one important belief: birth control reform did not make sense racially or religiously.

The importance of the geographic, and therefore the political and economic, context for racialization processes becomes apparent in comparisons between how both white immigrants and blacks were seen in the North versus the South. Although the analysis presented so far has emphasized how differently immigrants were seen racially in the North versus the South, we have yet to hear from any historically black religious groups. This is because, like the other ethnically marginal, more recent immigrant groups that we examined in this chapter, they were deeply skeptical of eugenics and unconcerned about race suicide. However, unlike the Catholics, Lutherans, and Jews chronicled in this chapter, these other ethnically marginal groups were deep believers in the social gospel movement. In contrast to those groups who were not and who thus openly criticized birth control reform and eugenics in the same breath, these other groups demonstrate that at this time in history, even silence was a statement.

6 The Silent Groups

The remaining denominations in my sample were completely silent on birth control during the first wave. Widely dispersed throughout the Eastern Seaboard and the Midwest (see map 5), these groups tended to be more solidly middle class than the other cells in table 4.[1] As Liston Pope wrote in 1948, "The Methodist, Baptist, and Disciples of Christ denominations are more typically associated with the middle classes."[2]

More important facts about the silent denominations examined in this chapter also tended to be groups that were racially marginalized in America more generally—either historically black or more recent immigrants—than most of the other denominations in my sample (except for the few openly critical immigrant denominations examined in the previous chapter). As such, the denominations chronicled in this chapter openly questioned eugenic beliefs. However, unlike those examined in the previous chapter, who were outsiders in terms of the Protestant establishment, these groups seem to have been in more of a bind. As strong believers in the social gospel movement, they had identities as religious activists. Given the frequent and public affirmations of eugenics made by their fellow social gospelers chronicled in chapter 3, the nine denominations examined here were aware that their fellow religious leaders' support for birth control reform stemmed from

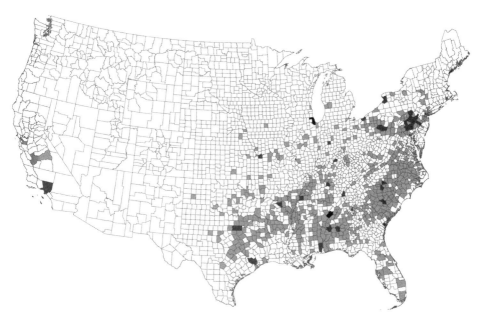

Map 5. Silent groups.

eugenicist concerns. When the statements these groups did make about other issues are examined, it becomes apparent that they did not remain silent on birth control out of apathy but rather because they found silence to be the only acceptable solution. Faced with the realization that their fellow religious activists were promoting birth control for reasons they could not support, silence seems to have become their safest course of action.

CRITICISM OF EUGENICS

The majority of the denominations that remained silent on birth control had racial or ethnic backgrounds that were more marginal than the early liberalizers' or unofficial supporters'.[3] Two of these denominations were traditionally black (the African Methodist Episcopal Zion Church [AMEZ] and the National Baptist Convention, USA). Both were openly critical of eugenics. In 1923, the AMEZ asserted:

To go back to the assertion that your fathers' character at the time of your birth will be yours also sounds very much like fatalism. The idea is antagonistic to progress. If the assertion were true, then there would be no advance in civilization.... Even Darwin in his plant life and animals proves that there is nothing in heredity.... Let the Christian get away from heredity. Heredity! what is heredity?[4]

In an article titled "Darwinian Law Given Unique Interpretation," the National Baptist Convention, USA, rejected Darwinian viewpoints in terms of race and argued:

It is "not those who fight that survive, but those who fit," was the unique interpretation of the Darwinian law of survival given to the students of Shorter College here in an address on race relations by Dr. R. B. Eleazer of Atlanta, Educational Director of the Interracial Commission. "Cooperation, not conflict is the law of progress," Mr. Eleazer asserted. "Those who learn to work together survive and grow strong; those who are always fighting inevitably destroy each other. Civilization goes forward as long as men work together; when they fall out and fight they head back toward barbarism." Applying this thought to the racial situation in America, the speaker held that the best interests of both races demand that they work together for the common good and that no hope is to be found in any other direction.[5]

In another article that discussed "white Baptists," the NBC warned emphatically, "God will not, God cannot, with reverence we say it, bless in full measure a people whose selfishness, prejudice substitute Christian affection."[6]

Criticism of eugenicists was not limited to the African American denominations, however, as almost every single other denomination that was silent on birth control also criticized eugenicist views. Although statistics on the percentage of their members who were foreign-born is unfortunately not available for any denominations at this time, this was particularly true for those groups whose periodicals suggested that they still had a strong identity as recent immigrants (the Reformed Church in the US, the United Lutheran Church in America, and Conservative Jews).[7] In 1927 the United Lutheran Church in America's periodical the Lutheran harshly criticized eugenicist reasoning in an article titled "The Heredity Fiasco":

You can take the baby son of respectable parents and put him in an environment where he becomes a thief, and you can take the son of thieves and make him a bank president. It is up to you and the environment with which you surround him. In other words . . . "Train up a child in the way in which he should go, and when he is old, he will not depart from it." . . . What will do wonders to make much talk about heredity look like "bunk" is Christian training, Christian discipline. That is the bedrock upon which character is built.[8]

The Disciples of Christ periodical *World Call* was disparaging of eugenicist attitudes in article after article. For example, in 1926 it published two articles criticizing the "superiority complex." The first, titled "Popular Fallacies about Race Relations," argued against "the most fundamental fallacy of all—the universal "superiority complex":

Each thinks itself better than the others, if it can. Jews thought themselves better than the Gentiles, Greeks felt superior to the Romans, and Romans to everybody. We white Americans are just as bad. We think ourselves the world, "God's last and best." Meantime Chinese and Korean and East Indians look down on us, in turn, as vulgar, excitable, noisy newcomers, superficial thinkers and crass materialists. Nor do Europeans think much better of us, if the truths were told. It is high time for the world to outgrow that fallacy. Nobody knows which is the superior race—or whether there be one. All we can say is that we differ in physical characteristics and in degree and kind of development. History shows that the backward race of one age often becomes the dominant race of the next, and vice versa. It behooves us all to be humble; to remember that we are all human beings, owing to each other respect and good will. And the more advantaged any of us happen to be, the greater is our obligation to serve the others.[9]

The second article harshly criticized prominent white supremacists such as Lothrop Stoddard, author of *The Rising Tide of Color*:

We have had the doctrines of racial superiority and domination consistently preached into our ears. The latest advocate of the Nordic myth is Lothrop Stoddard. The Nordic race must wake up in time, must shake off the mad dream of internationalism and reassert the pride of race and the merit to rule, in his doctrine. C.C. Josey is even now looking about for an inferior race upon whose broad backs we can lay the physical burden of our superior western world. In the middle ages men fought over religion; in the nineteenth century, over nationality; now the world is turning to race encounters. We must, in time, come forward with a Christian philosophy.[10]

These groups rejected or criticized eugenicists' focus on heredity and especially their focus on nature over nurture. Of all of these denominations, the Reformed Church in the US was by far the strongest critic, publishing eight articles that were critical of eugenics in 1924 alone.[11] In quote after quote, the *Reformed Church Messenger* emphasized the importance of environment over heredity:

> Chief Magistrate McAdoo, of New York, states that the Lombroso theories of criminal marks, that can be detected in men predestined to violent acts, have been largely abandoned and the young criminal today cannot in fact be distinguished from other men of his physical type. It is the observation of judges and other competent observers that the average young criminal is "a product of parental neglect and lack of discipline in the critical years when boyhood is turning to manhood, without the restraint of guidance."[12]

In another article that same year:

> Parents have little control over heredity. They have immense control over environment. Theirs is the responsibility of providing the best possible home atmosphere and environment for the children to grow up in.... Oliver Wendell Holmes said that if we want to have better babies we must begin with their grandfathers. If we want a better America and a better world two generations hence we have no time to lose; we must begin now to make our homes what they ought to be.[13]

And another:

> While we continually have cause to deplore the factors that enter into our problem through the door of heredity and can no longer be changed, the problem of the atmosphere is largely of our own making.[14]

However, while it was one of the most outspoken about its views about eugenics among the silent denominations, the Reformed Church in the US was not alone. Other churches with strong immigrant identities expressed similar sentiments, often in statements about current immigrants.

VIEWS OF IMMIGRANTS

In an article that seemed to be countering negative stereotypes about immigrants, the United Lutheran Church in America insisted in 1930 in the *Lutheran* that

> the vast majority of the present-day immigrants are good, clean, industrious Christian men and women, who are an asset to the land of their adoption and who come into a new environment perhaps with beating hearts, but with hope and expectation of a future before them, and with a determination to make good.[15]

Likewise, although their periodical the *S.A.J. Review* was not popularly oriented, the leader of the Conservative Jewish movement, well known for recruiting recent Jewish immigrants, Mordecai Kaplan, wrote in it in 1929 that Jews had "a strong antipathy against any attempt, be it scientific or religious, to make out a case for inherent distinctions between races and peoples."[16]

But even those that did not have strong identities as recent immigrants strongly criticized eugenicists' anti-immigrant views. For example, before concluding insistently that "God is the judge of racial equality, not America!," the Disciples of Christ urged readers of *World Call* to offer "sincere, wholesome friendship" to immigrants.[17] In another article the same periodical criticized eugenicist statements and general attitudes toward immigrants: "All foreigners are inferiors and we brand them so by the nicknames we give them. They are not in our class or on our level. We may accept services from them for which we pay, but friendship, never."[18] Another *World Call* article specifically called out racist statements about immigrants:

> When we say, "It has been my experience that the Russian-Jews are a dirty lot!" Or, when we see an uneducated Italian fruit vendor crying his wares along our streets, we say, "Ugh! Is that all Italy has to offer?" We forget that Italian children, in their homeland, sing operatic airs with the same familiarity with which our own, alas, sing the modern jazz. We forget, momentarily, the glorious history of Italy's art and sculpture. We forget that, was yet, America has not had as high a type of Italian immigration as we have had from other countries. Let us remember, that we can only justify a race by the

best of her history and education and most of all by the highest of type of her manhood and womanhood. Then and only then is that judgement desirable and fair.[19]

In a 1926 article, *World Call* condemned immigration restriction's racist reasoning. The article began by asserting that Christians must not discriminate:

> We affirm our unwavering faith in the great truths . . . universally recognized as essential principles of Christianity. . . . We believe that these principles are opposed to all discrimination based upon racial, national, or color prejudice.[20]

The article then quickly turned to the denomination's opposition to immigration restrictions:

> We deplore the recent action of the Congress of the United States in passing the exclusion clause in the so-called Immigration Act of 1924—for the following reasons: It violates the principles set forth above by regulating immigration according to racial discrimination rather than upon the personal basis of fitness according to equal standards for all. It constitutes a needless effort to a friendly nation since, without conference, it abrogates the Gentlemen's Agreement and secures by law that which could have been secured, just as easily, in mutual conference and so without hurt to a nation's pride and honor.[21]

The article concluded, "It brings hurt to the United States."[22]

Like the Disciples of Christ, the AMEZ was open about the fact that it saw anti-immigrant sentiment as thinly, if at all, veiled racism:

> If . . . you have been accustomed to look upon the Chinaman or the Italian who comes to our shores as an interloper, an alien, an inferior type of human animal [the Christian religion demands that you] put yourself to school to learn to think of him as a brother.[23]

Similarly, the Reformed Church in the US made strong statements about immigration reform in general, particularly in an article titled "Race Prejudice and the Immigrant," in which it argued that "instead of an impartial, fair and just consideration of the needs of the country, the determining factors [of immigration reform] were politics and racial prejudice." The article then went on to criticize the "gospel of the intrinsic superiority of the native-born American (and all Americans—with the exception of the Indians—were at one time foreigners) [and] its racial discrimination against the non-Nordic nationalities."[24]

The Reformed Church in America also came across as more welcoming to immigrants. For example, in an article titled "What Is Your Attitude toward the Foreigner?," the *Christian Intelligencer* urged readers: "Don't make the immigrant hate America. Make him love America. In other words, be an American . . . and be a Christian."[25] In an even more explicit criticism of eugenics, the Reformed Church in America argued forcefully against racialized views of immigrant inferiority in a *Christian Intelligencer* article as immigration restrictions were being debated:

> The Interpreter has no sympathy with the narrow views which find expression in the slogan "100 per cent American," for both America and Americans change with the passing of the years. We shall each of us make our contribution to the ultimate nation if, regardless of the racial stock from which we individually have sprung, we do our part in making the inevitable change a development of a better America.[26]

Thus, the denominations that remained silent on birth control were sharply critical of eugenicists and racist thinking in general.[27] Many of the groups that would remain silent on birth control openly identified as recent immigrants or racially marginalized. Those that did not had generally positive views of immigrants. All of these denominations (with the exception of Conservative Jews, who could not be) were members of the Federal Council of Churches (FCC) and, more importantly, expressed a deep belief in the social gospel movement and strong identities as religious activists. They were aware that their skepticism of eugenics put them at odds with their fellow social gospelers, religious leaders whom many saw as their colleagues, and it was this reality that pushed them to remain silent on birth control. Although they were circumspect regarding their fellow social gospelers' racist views, their concern was sometimes palpable. This was most often the case when they discussed their beliefs about the social gospel and questioned their fellow social gospelers' views of race.

BELIEF IN THE SOCIAL GOSPEL

All of the groups chronicled in this chapter were deep believers in the social gospel. In many of their statements, they sounded remarkably similar to the social gospelers who would become early liberalizers. For example, in 1929, in a statement that indicated they were clear on the divisions that existed regarding the movement, *World Call* wrote, "There is no guarantee that those converted to a gospel of personal salvation will welcome a gospel of social salvation; indeed they may become its most radical opponents."[28] A 1931 article used the same biblical imagery as the early liberalizers:

> A generation ago . . . the social gospel was in its swaddling clothes. Now we have become a compact world, in our thinking as well as geographically. We know that things we do affect us politically and things we do politically affect us economically. And religion—the search after the fundamental "why" of it all—influences every sphere of life. The fact that Christian laymen today are recognizing the direct bearing the solution of these problems has on the making of a Christian world affords a glimmer of hope that someday the Kingdom of God shall become more than a pretty phrase and Jesus shall actually reign among people who bear his name.[29]

Like the early liberalizers, the Disciples of Christ's social gospel beliefs were intertwined with concerns about social justice, labor, and immigrants and criticism of the capitalist exploitation of others via "great industrial organizations." In 1929 *World Call* asserted plain calls for "peace . . . brotherhood . . . and justice":

> [We seek] to inspire activity in the social gospel, to promote every form of church activity that touches social welfare, to educate in the use of ways and means to promote social justice and to cooperate with all who labor to bring in peace where there is strife, brotherhood where there is conflict, justice where there are iniquities, and good will where there is misunderstanding.[30]

A decade earlier, the same periodical had made it clear that the "immigrants in America constitute a vast neglected portion of our population." Referencing recent unrest, the article went on to tell readers:

> The nation has suddenly awakened to a realization of their presence. In the strikes and demonstrations and riots in our cities during recent months the

majority of those opposing constituted authority were of alien birth or parentage. In the Cleveland riot those who bore the red flags were nearly all immigrants. In the steel strike the charge is brought by the operators and owners that the majority of those who went out and who are causing the present disturbances are foreigners.

Questioning the anti-immigrant sentiment that had arisen in the country, the article went on to remind readers that immigrants came because they were recruited by capitalists:

> It has even been suggested that they be sent back to the countries from which they came! We need to remember how it happens that they are here. The truth is we sent for them. The agents of our great industrial organizations were sent to Italy and Austria and Hungary and Poland and Russia and other European countries to find the brawn and muscle needed in our great steel factories. Villages over there were almost depopulated or transferred in toto to industrial centers in America. Glowing inducements accompanied our invitations. The Immigrants were promised good wages and freedom and opportunity and all the such blessings of this land of light and liberty.

Consistent with social gospelers' concerns about the rapid urbanization that this industrial capitalism had created, the article then asked:

> And when they came, at the rate of almost a million a year, how were those promises fulfilled? We crowded them like cattle into the worst quarters of our great cities; we put them to work amid blazing furnaces twelve hours a day, with a twenty-four hour shift every two weeks. They were compelled to live in the most unsanitary quarters where normal childhood and the development of wholesome family life were impossible. Then we turned loose upon them the most wolfish elements of our civilization, until, maddened by mistreatment, plundered and betrayed, and knowing no other means of redress, when some wild Bolshevist comes among them and advises that they strike and join the revolution to overthrow their masters, they fall in behind the red flag. Then we shoot them down, for incipient rebellion must be quelled, and proceed to maintain civic order by force. But for how long? And what have we done for the immigrant? The church has done but little and the state less.[31]

The Disciples of Christ, the denomination *World Call* represented, was among the most adamant social gospelers in this group of religious denominations (and in fact, among all of the denominations in my sample). *World Call* reported that "some 300 addresses" about the social gospel had been delivered to its constituents in 1925.[32]

Most of the silent denominations were less vocal about the social gospel movement, but even so, they made clear statements in support of the movement. Take, for example, the Reformed Church in America's periodical, the *Christian Intelligencer and Mission Field*, which defended the social gospel against critics (many of whom appeared to be within the denomination itself) by insisting: "The so-called 'Social Gospel' is identified in the minds of some as an attempt to save the world *en masse* rather than by the slower processes of the redemption of individuals."[33] It asserted, "It is misunderstood, of course, when such an interpretation is put upon it."[34]

Similarly, the *Reformed Church Messenger* insisted that social reform was a key component of living a Christian life. In a 1924 article, it argued that efforts to change society, politics, and industrial relationships "into harmony with the standards set by the Lord Jesus Himself" glorifies God:

> The attempt to develop the spirit of worship, of piety and devotion, far from the madding crowd, isolated from the dust and grime of daily duty, is a will o' the wisp, the futility of which has been demonstrated in every era of history. . . . It does not spoil the true follower of Christ to busy himself in the effort to bring the social, political and industrial relationships of men into harmony with the standards set by the Lord Jesus Himself; on the contrary, it is such activity which glorifies the Christian life with most abundant fruitfulness. He who accomplishes most for mankind is the man who most truly "strikes the spiritual note" in his life.[35]

Another article published the following year in the same periodical and titled "The Social Obligation of the Church" asked readers:

> Should the Church . . . try to bring about any reforms other than spiritual changes in the individual? Surely . . . every Christian organization should . . . *use its influence in helping to abolish admitted evils and to change conditions which . . . militate against the formation of good character and the living of the Christian life.*[36]

Similarly, the Methodist Episcopal Church South (MECS) asserted:

Religion is designed to save men both in their personal lives and in all their relations. Its aim is a saved individual in a saved world. Therefore a study of personal salvation inevitably leads to a consideration of the questions in the field which has come to be known as "applied Christianity." . . . If the New Testament is lacking in specific directions for the tasks demanded by the social aspects of the gospel, the principles are all there. . . . While the social gospel is not directly proclaimed in the New Testament, it is implied upon every page. The Church can never make a Christian world merely by making individual Christians. . . . There is a gospel of corporate salvation as certainly as there is a gospel of personal salvation, and it is no less necessary to remind people of their duty as members of corporations than of their duty as individual Christians. Otherwise it is quite possible for a whole population to be Christian in private life and pagan in politics and industry.[37]

Importantly, even the groups that were arguably less integrated into the social gospel movement were, by 1930, discussing it and finding their previous level of engagement apparently lacking. For example, Conservative Jews (who only established their commission on social justice in 1931 as compared to Reform Jews, whose Commission on Social Justice was active by at least 1920) wrote:

It is therefore keenly to be regretted that our organization has not concerned itself sufficiently. . . . We have not as yet even a standing committee on social justice to study the relationship of Jewish life and tradition to such vital problems as unemployment, the ethical administration of business enterprises, collective bargaining, child labor, hours of labor, a more equitable distribution of wealth, questions of civil liberties, the relation of church and state, problems of international relations, disarmament, peace and the like.[38]

Likewise, the United Lutheran Church in America, which did not make many statements about the social gospel, seemed to be aware that it was a latecomer to the movement (and for that matter, to the FCC, since it only had a "consultative" membership in 1931). In 1925 it criticized itself in an article titled "Vision of Social Gospel" for being a "Church, composed of a comfortable middle class . . . far too much a soul with no body of social expression. It has been almost like a great gulf fixed between the Church and labor."[39]

All of these denominations likely became aware of what other religious denominations stood for via their memberships in the FCC, which, not surprisingly, was seen as the institutional location where the social gospel was being put into practice, as the *Methodist Quarterly Review* indicated:

> A generation ago a few men like Walter Rauschenbusch began to cry out for an application of the principles of Christianity in politics, commerce, and industry. At first they were misunderstood, neglected, despised, and opposed; but as their message gradually got home the attitude of leaders of thought changed, until at last the principles for which they stood have become commonplaces with the pulpit and press of the Church. The social implications of the gospel have found expression in the "Social Creed of the Federal Council of Churches," which is composed of thirty denominations . . . [which is] insistent in the demand that the welfare of the worker should be the first consideration in industry.[40]

COMBATING RACISM, AT ODDS WITH THEIR FELLOW RELIGIOUS ACTIVISTS

Unlike the early liberalizers, many of these groups took pains to mention that a key part of their social justice work was combating race and racism. The traditionally black AMEZ periodical was clear about this in a 1925 article titled "The State of the Church":

> Dr. W. E. B. DuBois has recently stated editorially in THE CRISIS that the National Association for the Advancement of Colored People would not have survived had it not been for the support rendered by the Negro Church and the Negro clergy. The Church today preaches more than ever before—the love of God and *social justice*—which preaching undoubtedly has wrought no small part in driving this blot upon American humanism into oblivion.[41]

A 1929 article from the Disciples of Christ periodical *World Call* made even more specific connections between the social gospel movement and efforts to combat racism in an article that reported excitedly about developments within the social gospel movement. It insisted that challenges to racial discrimination were one of the movement's most important new achievements:

> Thirty years ago the social gospel was practically unknown to the pulpit and when it did find an occasional pioneering voice it was limited to pleas for

philanthropy and uplift *without much challenge to a social and economic system that made* labor a commodity, *racial discrimination an alternative to social deterioration* and war the inevitable recourse of patriotic devotion.[42]

Another *World Call* article took on eugenic arguments:

> Dr. Stoddard assumes that race superiority is due to the germ plasm. Yet there seems to be no sound basis for discrimination biologically; indeed there is no pure race any more, as so many intermingling strains have flowed together. That determinism which operates in the field of heredity often seems to leave men bound and unequal rather than free and equal. . . . Today the Jew, the Nordic, the Japanese and the Chinese all assert their inherent superiority. Which one is really superior? The intelligence test reveal only part of the truth. Is the race horse or dray horse superior? Is the winner of the 100 yard dash or the three-mile race superior? Is the engineer or the poet superior? Stoddard laments the passing of the Nordic race, with the capacity of fighting, masterfulness and ability to collect the wealth of the world. . . . Who dares to say that the materialistic, industrialized, mechanized, militarized civilization of the West is the final or highest expression of the human spirit?[43]

Clearly, there was a racial divide among social gospelers. These social gospelers rejected eugenics and racism. The other better known social gospelers chronicled in chapter 3 did not. Given the frequent and public affirmations of eugenics their fellow social gospelers made, the groups examined in this chapter were no doubt aware that their fellow religious leaders' support for birth control reform stemmed from eugenicist concerns.

This awareness likely came from their mutual membership in the FCC and religious activism in general, as well as from deeper connections. For example, the *Reformed Church Messenger* reprinted a relatively mild article titled "Consequences of the Neglect of Childhood" from the *Herald of Gospel Liberty* in 1924.[44] The *Herald of Gospel Liberty* was the periodical for the Christian Church, an early liberalizer whose eugenic views were chronicled in chapter 2. The *Reformed Church Messenger* was the periodical for the Reformed Church in the US—one of the denominations examined in detail in this chapter that remained silent on birth control. The short three-week lag between the two publications indicates that there were strong connections and "affinities" between the two denominations.

Indeed, the two denominations ultimately merged in 1957. It also demonstrates, however, that leaders of the Reformed Church in the US had ample opportunity to be made aware that Christian Church leaders' views were much more eugenically inclined than theirs.

This is apparent in a rare article in the *Messenger* that sharply criticized their fellow Christians who focused on "physical and mental defects" in efforts to combat crime. Appearing in 1931, the article called such a focus "both pathetic and tragic":

> As Christians, we certainly rejoice that so much more attention is being paid today than in past centuries to methods of reclaiming and restoring the less fortunate children—who are underprivileged, defective and delinquent. It is both pathetic and tragic, however, that so much more attention is paid to physical or mental defects than to moral and spiritual shortcomings, and that so much has to be spent to pay the costs of crime because so little was spent in promoting the gospel of prevention and in sowing the good seed of truth in the hearts and minds of youth, both by precept and example.[45]

In another clear, but indirect, criticism of the group's fellow religious activists, the same periodical emphasized that "racial prejudice, unfair discrimination, hatred and economic oppression, will not bring about the kingdom of God" and stressed the need to show Christ's love for immigrants:[46]

> *Let us take Christ and His gospel of love seriously.* Racial prejudice, unfair discrimination, hatred and economic oppression, will not bring about the kingdom of God either in America or anywhere else: these always produced hell on earth. Why not try love? Do we really believe that Jesus was right when he preached conquest of the world by love? Let us be honest with ourselves. The immigrant problem involves not merely transformation of the immigrant, but also, and I would say chiefly, the transformation of the American.[47]

The social gospelers chronicled in this chapter rejected eugenics but deeply believed in the importance of progressive religious activism. They could, and occasionally did, criticize the eugenicist beliefs of other religious groups. However, when it came to the particular issue of birth control, there were simply very few ways they could question early liberalizers' views without directly calling their fellow religious activists who were making public pronouncements on the issue racists.

The FCC was likely an important place for these denominations to learn about their fellow religious leaders' views about birth control and the connection of their views to eugenics. It was clearly important to these denominations. For example, the *Reformed Church Messenger* lauded two denominations for maintaining their ties with the FCC despite their disagreements with the FCC's statement on birth control:[48]

> To those who realize the trend of things, it was a disappointment but not a surprise that the Assembly of the Presbyterian Church (South) should have taken an action withdrawing from membership in the Council and also from all further efforts at organic union with other Presbyterian and Reformed Churches. It is gratifying that the Presbyterian Church (North) and the Northern Baptist Convention realize more fully the importance of having some symbol of the essential unity of Protestantism, and continue to believe that the Federal Council is most suitable and necessary as such a symbol.[49]

If these denominations had not so deeply believed in the social gospel movement and been so connected to other progressive religious groups via the FCC, they would likely have openly criticized reform. But as deep believers in the social gospel movement and strong proponents of its institutional manifestation in the FCC, they stayed silent. Cognizant that birth control was a contentious issue in the country in general and within the FCC in particular and all too aware of the eugenic reasoning behind early liberalizers' stances, the denominations in this chapter decided that the best thing to do regarding birth control was to say nothing at all.

Most of the silent groups stuck to that decision for another thirty years—not liberalizing until after 1960 (unless a merger with an early liberalizer before that date spurred a statement, as was fairly common) and the invention of the pill. When they did so, however, their statements were qualitatively different from the groups that supported birth control during the first wave—all of which would become "America's promoters of contraception." It is to this story, and the second wave of birth control reform in the American religious field, that we now turn.

PART III From Legality to the Pill,
1935–1965

7 The Religious Promoters of Contraception

REMAINING FOCUSED ON OTHER PEOPLE'S FERTILITY

Between 1959 and 1961, the American Baptist Convention (the new name for the Northern Baptist Convention covered in chapter 4) released a series of statements about the importance of contraception as it related to preventing "world disaster." Its 1960 resolution provides a good example of its concerns at this time. It recommended that all the churches study seriously the "careful development of techniques of family limitation and birth control which will, as it now appears, be needed to protect the world against disaster."[1]

The American Baptists were certainly not alone in their anxiety. Many of the leaders of America's most prominent religious groups remained deeply concerned about the need to reduce family sizes, especially those of poorer countries. Talk of pending disaster was present in many other Mainline periodicals, such as the following from the United Church of Christ (UCC) periodical the *United Church Herald*:

> Two other acute problems of our mission must engage your attention. I speak of population and poverty. I am told that at the present rate of increase world population will double within the lifetimes of many of us. I do not doubt that scientific advances eventually will alleviate some of the suffering which the exploding population is visiting on mankind. But until that time

comes we can imagine all too plainly, the millions of ill-clad, ill-fed, ill-housed people who will live in misery if we do not move at once on two fronts to shape the future.[2]

Another article in the *United Church Herald* reported that "thoughtful persons in many countries are predicting that within a relatively few years the population explosion will "dwarf our present anxieties" even about nuclear warfare and Communist aggression."[3] The article went on to quote researchers who predicted that

> if present trends continue, famine will reach serious proportions in India, Pakistan and China in the early 1970's, followed by Iran, Indonesia, Turkey, Egypt within a few years and by most of the other countries of Asia, Africa and Latin America by 1980 . . . affect[ing] hundreds of millions—possibly even billions—of persons. It will be the most colossal catastrophe in history.[4]

The periodical *Christian Century*, the flagship publication for Mainline Protestantism, published eleven articles in 1965 alone on birth control.[5] Its calls for action were often quite urgent, no doubt because they also saw the issue of contraception and nuclear war as deeply intertwined:

> Prospects for the human race seem dreadful and forbidding. For if man continues to pursue one of the courses on which he is bent—unrestrained reproduction of his kind—there will soon be too many of us for this tiny planet to support. If he continues to follow another of the paths he treads—the race toward nuclear warfare—there will someday be none of us at all. These two crises confronting mankind are curiously related. The first will make the second inevitable and the second will eliminate the first.[6]

The article went on to explain just how and why the two threats of overpopulation and nuclear war were deeply intertwined, with overpopulation leading directly to everyone's worst nightmare:

> As the bid for inhabitable space and arable land increases, the probability of nuclear war increases, with the ultimate forms of destruction destroying the highest forms of life. . . . But neither of these crises is beyond man's control. He is not fated to commit global suicide nor does anything require a fatal multiplication of the species. He is not doomed to stay on the courses which lead toward death; he can choose life. But men will not choose life unless

they take the dreadful vision of death seriously; they must be told over and over again that the threat is real.[7]

In many of their statements, this new generation of religious leaders sounded shockingly similar to their predecessors, both in their level of alarm and in their solutions. For example, the *Register Leader* emphasized the importance of stopping the "unprecedented, malignant growth of world population which thwarts the industrial and educational development of the emerging nations . . . especially marked in Catholic Latin America."[8] In a review of the book *The Silent Explosion*, the Unitarian Universalist *Register-Leader* quoted the author: "We are breeding disaster—unless we can curb the silent upsurge of population that perils us all. Here is what America should do about it."[9] Months later the book was recommended again, this time with a grave message attached: "The most threatening problem facing mankind at the present time is what has appropriately been called the population explosion—an explosion, however, which in the title of his admirable book Professor Appleman makes quite clear is all the more difficult because it is so silent."[10]

Although most eugenic language had disappeared from their statements, its legacy was still starkly apparent. Take, for example, the following question asked by an author in the UCC's *Advance*:

> Why, it may be asked, are doctors and nurses striving to heal the sick and prevent disease in India when that country can't adequately support its present population? Under the circumstances is this a Christian or even a humanitarian service? These questions, not frequently propounded, present a problem of growing importance to the medical practitioner—especially to the Christian physician.[11]

Such blatant eugenicist views were now the minority, however. Discussions of "desirability" had been replaced by assertions of the need for "responsible parenthood" and its prerequisite, "family planning." Take, for example, the following quote from an article titled "A Christian Examines Planned Parenthood" in the *Presbyterian Survey* that quoted the retiring president of the World Bank in 1965:

> "I must be blunt. . . . Unless population growth can be restrained, we may have to abandon for this generation our hopes of economic progress in the

crowded lands of Asia and the Middle East." There is a single answer to this global problem—planned parenthood. The best way to solve the problem is to start with this positive answer in our own communities. Every city and village know the results of overpopulation—crime, juvenile delinquency, unstable family life, poverty, slums, and inadequate schools. We're always chipping away at solving these problems—more parks, police, jails, and schools."[12]

Their promotion of responsible parenthood and family planning made it clear that these religious leaders believed sincerely that many parents were irresponsible. The article continued by placing the blame squarely on the parents who could not seem to "learn to have the number of children they can care for": "We still avoid, except in a few isolated communities, dealing directly with the basic problem: the inability of couples to learn to have the number of children that they can care for and nurture into responsible citizens. This failure is the neglect of our society to share the meaning of responsible parenthood."[13]

As most of the quotes above suggest, there was a significant amount of consensus about the areas of concern: Asia, India, and Latin America were now the biggest worry, having largely replaced domestic concerns, as *Presbyterian Life* indicated in 1965:

> The American population explosion seems to be slackening off somewhat, and the American growth rate is not so menacing as that of parts of Asia and Latin America. India, for example, according to demographers, may well double its population within thirtyfive years. The growth rate in mainland China is said to be still faster.[14]

The ebbing concern about domestic population seems to have been due to the realization that "in the light of our present food surpluses and improved methods of agriculture, it does not appear that food will be a problem," as the *United Presbyterian* informed readers in 1955.[15] It might also have been due to the fact that the birth rates of the whitening Irish and Italian Catholic immigrants and their descendants had indeed plummeted.[16]

Others, such as Reform Jews, continued to insist that "the rapid growth of world population affects not only the underdeveloped areas throughout the globe, but the United States and the Western world as well."[17] As later sections of this chapter will show, however, the domestic populations whose birth rates were of concern had changed, with the focus on immigrants now turning to blacks in the inner cities. As Dorothy Roberts details in her chapter "The Dark Side of Birth Control," African American poor single mothers were of particular and growing concern.[18] An article in the *Christian Century* painted a bleak picture of these women's lives and marital prospects before recommending that any policies "should be based . . . on an understanding of the specific situation of urban Negroes whose chances for contracting stable marriages are severely limited by the unstable milieu within which they must exist."[19]

This chapter explores these trends—the deep concern about overpopulation in less developed areas of the world, the shift from explicit promotion of eugenics to a focus on responsible parenthood, and the changing domestic focus from immigrant to black fertility over the three decades following the first wave of liberalization. As the early liberalizers had hoped, contraceptives had indeed became more broadly available—a process that culminated with US Food and Drug Administration (FDA) approval of the pill and its soaring use in the early 1960s. As access increased, the same groups that fought for reforms in the 1930s continued their campaign to make contraceptives broadly available. Although their support for contraceptives never waned, two important changes did occur over the next decades. First, many of these groups went through significant organizational changes and would continue to do so up until the present. Second, as I will detail in this chapter, although their focus remained on other people's fertility and not their own, the populations whose fertility was seen as problematic had been fairly radically revised.

WHO WERE THE RELIGIOUS PROMOTERS OF CONTRACEPTION?

In an effort to help the reader keep track of the sometimes dizzying organizational changes many of the religious groups in my sample went through over the twentieth century, table 9 presents my sample of religious denominations as they are known today, in reference to their names as they were during the first wave of reform.

Table 9 American Religious Denominations Then and Now

Denominations	Periodicals[a] and Years Searched[b]	Date Liberalized
Religious Promoters of Contraception		
Reform Judaism	AJC Yearbook (1935–65)	1929
	Yearbook of the CCAR (1918–32)	
	Union Tidings (1919–30)	
Unitarian Universalist Association (1961)	Unitarian Universalist Register-Leader (1965)	
Universalist General Convention	Christian Leader (1926–50)	1929
(Universalist Church of America, 1942–61)	Universalist Leader (1955–61)	
American Unitarian Association	Christian Register (1919–55)	1930
United Church of Christ (1957)	United Church Herald (1958–65)	
Evangelical and Reformed Church (1934)	Messenger (1936–55)	
Reformed Church in the United States	Reformed Church Messenger (1919–32)	
Evangelical Synod of North America	Evangelical Herald (1916–36)	
Congregational Christian Churches (1931)	Congregationalist and Herald of Gospel	1931
	Liberty (1930–32)	
	Advance (1935–55)	
Christian Church, General Convention	Herald of Gospel Liberty (1918–29)	1931
Congregational Churches, General Council	Congregationalist (1918–29)	
United Methodist Church (1968)[c]	Christian Advocate (1919–65)	
Methodist Church (1939)		
Methodist Episcopal Church		1931
Methodist Episcopal Church, South	Methodist Quarterly Review (1919–30)	

Presbyterian Church (USA) (1983)		
United Presbyterian Church in the United States of America (1958)		
United Presbyterian Church of North America	*United Presbyterian* (1919–55)	1931
Presbyterian Church in the United States of America	*Presbyterian* (1935–45)	
	Presbyterian Life (1948–65)	
	Presbyterian Magazine (1924–32)	
	New Era Magazine (1919)	
Presbyterian Church in the United States	*Presbyterian Survey* (1919–65)	1960
Friends General Convention	*Friend's Journal* (1935–65)	1933
Society of Friends (Orthodox)	*Friend* (1945–55)	
	American Friend (1924–33)	
Society of Friends (Hicksite) (unified with Orthodox Friends in 1955)	*Friends Intelligencer* (1919–31)	
Protestant Episcopal Church	*Living Church* (1919–55)	1934
American Baptist Convention after 1972	*Christian Century* (1940–65)	1959
Northern Baptist Convention	*Baptist* (1920–32)	

Accept Contraception

Evangelical Lutheran Church in America (1988)		
American Lutheran Church (1960)[d]	*Lutheran Herald* (1934–55)	1966
	Lutheran Standard (1965)	
Norwegian Lutheran Church (known as Evangelical Lutheran Church after 1946) (1917)[e]	*Lutheran Church Herald* (1919–32)	
Lutheran Church in America (1962)[f]		
United Lutheran Church in America (1918)	*Lutheran* (1925–65)	1966

(continued)

Denominations	Periodicals[a] and Years Searched	Date Liberalized
Reformed Church in America	*Church Herald* (1945–62) *Intelligencer-Leader* (1935) *Christian Intelligencer* (1919–32)	1960
Conservative Judaism	*Conservative Judaism* (1945–2010) *S.A.J. Review* (1924–29)	1960
Christian Church (Disciples of Christ)	*World Call* (1919–55)	1972
Southern Baptist Convention	*Biblical Recorder* (1934–65)	1977
Lutheran Church–Missouri Synod	*Lutheran Witness* (1919–65)	1981
Church of Jesus Christ of Latter-day Saints	*Improvement Era* (1919–65)	1998
Seventh-day Adventist	*Liberty* (1935–65) *Signs of the Times* (1919–28) *Watchman Magazine* (1923–31)	1999
Assemblies of God	*Pentecostal Evangel* (1915–65) *Latter Rain Evangel* (1929–33)	2002
Churches of Christ	*Gospel Advocate* (1919–65)	Silent
African Methodist Episcopal Zion Church	*A.M.E.Z. Quarterly Review* (1924–65)	Silent
National Baptist Convention, USA, Inc.	*National Baptist Union Review* (1919–66)	Silent
Jehovah's Witnesses	*Watchtower* (1945–65) *Golden Age* (1919–35)	Silent

Table 9 (Continued)

Critics of Contraception

Roman Catholic Church	*Commonweal* (2014–16); *America* (1919–2017)	Never
Orthodox Judaism	*Jewish Social Work Forum* (1965); *Jewish Forum* (1919–55)	Never

a. Other periodicals researched: *Birth Control Review* (1912–40); *Christianity Today* (1956–present); *New York Times* (2014–16).

b. The years searched during the first wave of birth control liberalization were 1918–19, 1924–25, and 1929–31; for the second wave, 1935, 1945, 1955, and 1965; and for the modern era, 2014–17. In addition, regardless of year, any official statements on birth control, abortion, or homosexuality were gathered. If a periodical was not available for a particular year, the closest year available was searched. In addition to those searches, full key word searches were done during any year of mergers for all groups, as pending mergers tended to bring to light any remaining disagreements between groups.

c. The Methodist Church merged with the Evangelical United Brethren Church to form the United Methodist Church in 1968.

d. The Norwegian Lutheran Church merged with the American Lutheran Church and the United Evangelical Lutheran Church to form the American Lutheran Church in 1960.

e. The Norwegian Lutheran Church was formed as a result of a merger between the Hauge Synod, the Norwegian Synod, and the United Norwegian Lutheran Church of America in 1917.

f. The United Lutheran Church merged with the Augustana Evangelical Lutheran Church, the Finnish Evangelical Lutheran Church of America, and the Danish American Evangelical Lutheran Church to form the Lutheran Church in America in 1962.

By the second wave of reform I found little difference between those who had unofficially supported reform and the early liberalizers who had officially proclaimed it. This was mostly because, as table 9 indicates, all of the unofficial supporters except the Northern Baptist Convention (now the American Baptist Convention) had simply disappeared, swallowed up in mergers with early liberalizers.[20]

This chapter thus focuses on the eight denominations that became America's "religious promoters" of birth control in the postwar period. Among these are all of the denominations that were early liberalizers during the first wave, although only three of them remained intact: the Protestant Episcopal Church, Reform Jews, and the Society of Friends (now called the Friends General Conference).[21] All of the other early liberalizers are also included in this chapter, although their denominations went through various changes and appear under new names. The first new denomination included in this chapter is the Methodist Church, which formed in 1939 as a result of a merger between the early liberalizer of the Methodist Episcopal Church and the silent Methodist Episcopal Church, South. Another denomination name that is new to this chapter is the UCC, which formed when the Evangelical and Reformed Church (which initially formed as a result of a merger between the Evangelical Synod of North America and the Reformed Church in the United States) merged with the early liberalizer Congregational Christian Church in 1957.[22] Two other early liberalizers, the American Unitarian Association and the Universalist General Convention, merged in 1961 to form the sixth denomination examined in this chapter: the Unitarian Universalist Church. Finally, this chapter also includes the newly formed United Presbyterian Church in the United States of America, which was created in 1958 as the result of a merger between an early liberalizer, the Presbyterian Church in the United States of America, and an unofficial supporter, the United Presbyterian Church in North America.[23]

Before continuing with this analysis, an important caveat is needed. This book is not intended to be an evaluation of whether the concerns about the population explosion were legitimate. Certainly, many a learned man and woman deeply believed that the world was facing imminent doom at this time. Indeed, these population control advocates include many prominent members of my own discipline of sociology and its closely related subfield of demography. What the analysis that follows attempts to demonstrate, instead, is that whether the leaders of a religious group *believed* that the population explosion was real, and the extent to which they thought it threatened the world, seems to have depended on their initial openness to eugenic arguments. This is no accident—connections between the two movements are well established by scholars.

RACE SUICIDE TURNS TO POPULATION CONTROL

By the mid-1930s, the campaign to legalize contraceptives had been successful, culminating in a 1936 Supreme Court case that determined that distributing contraceptive information was not prohibited by Comstock obscenity laws.[24] By the time birth control was legalized, the American Eugenics Society (AES) had all but disappeared.[25] Researchers offer various reasons for the AES's demise—from rapid loss of popularity due to the taint of Nazism, to internal divisions and strife over the direction of the society, to the general decline of the field due to a significant drain in funding.[26] Most likely as a result of all of these factors, researchers agree that by the mid-1930s eugenics went from being a sign of progressive politics and enlightened scientific understanding to a dirty word associated with Hitler and by then, the AES was largely defunct.[27]

However, although the explicit mention of eugenics largely faded from public view, much eugenic thought and activism around birth control remained—but with two differences. First, although the focus was still on poor people of color, instead of nonwhite immigrants' fertility in the United States, activists became focused on fertility in the developing world and, to a lesser extent, African Americans in inner cities.[28] Second, instead of explicit talk about race suicide and open promotion of eugenics, most activists began to engage in a more "discreet and mild-mannered form of eugenics" in which they attempted to accomplish "eugenic control" through "population control."[29]

Efforts to convince the public that population control was desperately needed took advantage of the public's exhaustion and anxieties after the close of World War II. With the deployment of the atom bomb still a recent reality, eugenicists strategically promoted population control as crucial to preventing "the imminent destruction of human society" and the achievement of world peace.[30] In a quote that demonstrates this tactic, in 1945 Guy Irving Burch, who was the director of both the Population Reference Bureau and the AES, stated that "uncontrolled human reproduction . . . favors the least gifted of society . . . and in the long run will destroy human liberties and any chance for a world at peace."[31]

Many might bristle at the idea that simply taking stock of birth rates around the world was eugenicist, particularly when discussion of racial stock and "desirability" had been purged from all but the most openly eugenicist promoters. But connections between the two movements ran deep. For example, well-known eugenicist Frederick Osborn, who was a founding member of the AES, became president of the Population Association of America from 1949 to 1950. Unlike most other eugenicists, Osborn did not seem concerned about hiding his views as time marched on. He started the journal *Eugenic Quarterly* in 1954.[32] That same year, Osborn noted great progress in relation to the "growing concern with world population problems" and "the need to balance the concern over size of population with concern for the quality of that population."[33]

As another example, take AES president Henry Pratt Fairchild. Fairchild was the first president of the Population Association of America (as the AES began its decline from 1931 to 1934). Just a few years later, in 1936, he was elected president of the American Sociological Association.

Thus, the history of eugenics in the United States is well established, as is its relationship to concerns about world population and the organizations and academic disciplines (especially demography and sociology) that would study, and sometimes attempt to curtail, world population in the next few decades. However, although religious groups have always been central to debates over contraception, there has been very little systematic investigation of which groups supported birth control reform, and why. Likewise, until now there has been no investigation into how those religious groups who were advocates of eugenics adjusted their perspectives on contraception over time as eugenics became delegitimized.

This chapter explores the early liberalizers over the next three decades and demonstrates that by and large they remained staunch advocates of contraception. Like the former eugenics activists who became population control advocates, their focus shifted from the out-of-control fertility of immigrants and their children to the "population explosion" in the poorest countries of the world and the inner cities of the United States. Gone were open discussions of racial stock; these were replaced with vague references to "quality" but even more often simply substituted by a more concerted focus on "the poor" and their refusal to engage in "responsible parenthood."

"POORER COUNTRIES"

Early population control advocates focused on countries that have variously been called the *Third World*, *developing*, or *underdeveloped* in the decades since. At the time, none of these terms were popular. The most common descriptor used by the religious leaders studied here was "poorer countries." While this is certainly accurate, it fails to capture the racialized nature of their concerns. The areas of the world that were their primary focus—Asia, Latin America, and Africa, in that order—were all understood to be not just poorer but nonwhite. Thus, the key difference between the first and second waves of birth control activism was that instead of being worried about the fertility rates of immigrants in the United States, now the religious promoters of birth control were concerned about those in the poorer areas of the world who had never made it to America's shores. For example, one reader of the *Advance* stated in a letter to the editor in 1955:

> Our Protestant churches in this country, while giving support to family planning in their national organizations, have been very slow in really supporting the movement throughout the world. . . . India, Thailand, Japan and many more of the countries where resources do not balance with populations are making valiant efforts to start a program aimed at population stabilization. Even the World Health Organization is trying to help with this problem and has done a good deal. But it is hampered in the allout effort by the Catholic countries which are in the United Nations.[34]

The country seen to be in the most dire situation in 1965 was India. That year, an article in the Unitarian Universalists' *Register-Leader* read:

> It is horrifying to reflect that in India there are at this time eight million more people than there were last year at the same time; that a quarter of a

million people in a city like Calcutta have nowhere else to sleep but on the streets. India is but an example of what can happen to a country when its population remains uncontrolled. Every other country is similarly threatened with the disaster that has overtaken India.[35]

These religious leaders were not just writing about their concerns—they were actively involved in many governmental and nongovernmental agencies seeking to provide access to contraceptives around the globe. This is made abundantly clear in the following statement from the Methodist periodical the *Christian Advocate*, which mentions "Africa, Asia, and Latin America":

> Against the backdrop of the growing worldwide debate on the population explosion, the Board of Missions' World Division is joining other Protestant denominations and a unit of the National Council of Churches in an accelerated program of spreading birth control information and equipment to medical mission outposts and personnel overseas. Fifty hospitals, clinics, and dispensaries in Asia, Africa, and Latin America have been sent informational leaflets from the Planned Parenthood Federation of America discussing newly developed intra-uterine contraceptive devices recommended for use by village peoples. An accompanying letter from William Strong, New York, planned parenthood consultant of Church World Service (interdenominational relief and rehabilitation agency of the NCC), offered various services to overseas medical units, including: Information about new contraceptive devices and the names of doctors in the vicinity of various institutions who can offer help and advice; Educational materials in the field of birth control for varying languages and cultures; Supplies of contraceptive materials; and Funds to extend services or make new services available. Dr. Harold N. Brewster, medical missionary of the World Division, indicated strong support for the worldwide program of family-planning education and action which Church World Service has undertaken.[36]

Although there was consensus that the situation was perhaps the most dire in India, Latin America received almost as much attention in many of these religious periodicals. As the *United Church Herald* explained, population concerns, while "not limited to Latin America, of course," were "intensified on that continent where the population—which is heavily Catholic, at least in name—is expanding more rapidly than anywhere else." The article continued by reminding readers that "with a growth rate of nearly three percent annually the population [of Latin America] doubles every 23 years.[37] As another example, a bishop of the Protestant Episcopal Church who had visited Guatemala, Honduras, El Salvador, Costa Rica, and Nicaragua reported that "more children are being born in Central America than can ever be educated" and suggested that the only solution was "for all religious leaders in Central America to work out some approach to keep the birth rate down." If this did not occur, according to the bishop, "there is little if any hope for ever coping with the problems of illiteracy and the rising population."[38]

Latin America differed largely because, as Roman Catholics, the population was actually not supposed to use contraceptives. 1965 did not only mark the US Food and Drug Administration's approval of the pill, it also marked the end of the Second Vatican Council in the Roman Catholic Church.[39] As the council was coming to a close, the world was optimistic that the Roman Catholic Church would change its stance on birth control. For example, in 1965 the periodical for the newly merged Unitarian Universalist Church, the *Register-Leader*, published a review of the book *A Hope for Birth Control*. The review summarized the bleak and difficult life lead by a Catholic woman "in her desperate search for religious principles by which she can satisfy her husband, limit her family, retain her physical health, and remain a faithful Roman Catholic." After detailing her struggles with "producing seven children, without time for recovery from constant pregnancies . . . two miscarriages, and . . . a husband in the merchant marine [who] return[ed] in [an] expectant mood," the article closed with "The question now before the world is: Will the Pope's commission studying birth curbs rectify this shocking failure?"[40]

As I detail in my book *Vatican II*, although the religious leaders chronicled here certainly prioritized activism around birth control, they were far more concerned that the council liberalize Catholic understandings of church and state than they were about contraception. This might partly have been because they saw the issue of religious freedom as "stickier" than contraception—about which many signs pointed to Catholic liberalization. Of course, to the disappointment of the leaders chronicled in this chapter (and many devout Roman Catholics), the Roman Catholic Church did not ultimately liberalize on birth control, something that would create new divisions in the American religious field but is the topic of another book.[41]

AMERICA'S POOR

Eugenicists had always been concerned about making sure that the poor had access to contraceptives. Originally, the focus was mainly on poor whites in Appalachia and, later, particularly during the first wave of reform studied earlier in this book, on poor immigrants.[42] In 1965, American religious advocates of birth control remained concerned about the fertility of the poor in America. For example, in 1965 *Presbyterian Life* reported excitedly that "birth-control clinics are likely to be set up as part of the anti-poverty war in America, supported by Federal funds."[43]

Sometimes their references to the poor were somewhat oblique. For example, referring to two laws that were still on the books in 1965 that limited access to contraceptives to populations in the United States, *Presbyterian Life* referred somewhat vaguely "to the people who most need counsel and encouragement in managing the size of their families."[44] The Protestant Episcopal Church endorsed "placing of clinics services at the point of need, including public financed institutions with staffing and operations paid for from public funds."[45] Another article in *Presbyterian Life* emphasized that "rich and poor alike [have an increased understanding] of the need to limit families." However, as the article continued, it became apparent that the fertility of America's poor was the main focus. It informed readers that the poor in the United States have a "high rate of literacy" and would therefore likely limit their own fertility if given the means and knowledge to do so.[46]

Many of these articles emphasized the ignorance of the poor in relation to contraception and their corresponding relief upon receiving information about it. Take, for example, the following quote from an article titled "A Christian Examines Planned Parenthood" in the *Presbyterian Survey* in 1965:

> Listen to these voices that could have come from your community: "I had three babies in the hospital. The oldest is 4 ½ years old. No one ever told me a mother could plan her family. Why, this means that I can get my strength back and have the next one when I am stronger. Another woman, wiping away tears, said, "I've buried three babies and have more than I can feed at home . . . why didn't someone tell me this before?" Yet another quietly whispered, "I ain't never had a mother or no one talk to me about birth and

babies. . . . No one wants to tell you. Maybe if Joe and I can give this baby a good home, we can stay together. But we can't afford any more. Families with eight, nine, and ten children, in poverty, often deserted by fathers . . . are mute calls for concern.[47]

An advertisement in the same periodical made a powerful plea to its (obviously understood to be well-off) readers for help. It began, "You were singled out as the kind of person most apt to help make birth control work for all . . . for the poor as well as those more fortunate. Read how you can help!" The article then immediately painted a bleak picture, equating the situation in American inner cities with the slums of India:

> The need for birth control is obvious to all who have seen excessive population growth in our slums—some cities (inner cities) grow as rapidly as India—right here in America. These are centers of discontent—focal points of starvation and poverty. What we lack today in America's and the world's poverty stricken neighborhoods is adequate distribution of birth control information and products.[48]

After this call to action, the article then returns to its focus on the poor and why they, in particular, needed greater access to or encouragement to use, as the case may be, birth control:

> The poor get children. The crux of the matter is simple. The poor are ignorant about birth control. They do not understand it and could not afford it if they did. The higher echelons in our churches everywhere are in agreement that it is religion's obligation to establish clinical and field organizations that will teach the poor about birth control and provide them with birth control products.[49]

The article then made it clear that more work had been done regarding the poor in "foreign nations" than at "home."

> A beginning has been made, particularly overseas where medical missionaries are distributing birth control products such as EMKO FOAM in 31 foreign nations. Distributing information here at home is really a simple matter. We have found that mothers are happy to discuss the subject of birth control with men or with women without embarrassment. They need the information about reproduction . . . one of the most important subjects in the world . . . and are anxious to get it.[50]

The article closed by singing the merits of the Emko Company's experience distributing birth control information and products, both at home and abroad.

It was also clear, however, that the imagined recipients of contraceptive activism were not just poor—they were the poor in the "inner cities," which in 1965 typically meant that they were black. For example, an article in the Quaker periodical *Friends Journal* mentioned "urban unrest" as one of the key problems contraception could help curtail—along with, unique to the Quakers at the time—the destruction of the environment (most of the other early liberalizers mentioned the natural world in relation to food insecurity, if at all).

> We are deeply concerned as Friends that each (human) life created be enabled to flourish in family love, fully expressing divine potential, through responsible parenthood. . . . The grave approaching problems of urban unrest and world tensions, as well as conservation of the environment for future generations, require prompt attention.[51]

Sometimes, these periodicals were explicit about the populations they were most concerned about. The article from *Christian Century* that was quoted at the beginning of this chapter began by emphasizing both the extent of need among "Negro slum-dwellers" and the author's credentials as "an ordained minister" and case worker:

> A large proportion of today's welfare recipients are urban Negro slum-dwellers, and it is about them specifically that I speak, from my vantage point as an ordained minister who is presently a public aid caseworker in the Negro ghetto of Chicago. (The picture in other cities is, I understand, similar.)[52]

The article first sympathetically emphasized that the populations under concern were not actually simply lazy and listed the myriad of structural disadvantages they faced:

> Contrary to popular opinion, only a small percentage of the males and single females who receive public aid are able-bodied and capable of holding jobs. And the majority of these would support themselves were they not caught in a wave of chronic unemployment wherein unskilled laborers simply cannot find jobs. Many of them were laid off by large industries which moved from

the city or drastically reduced work forces because of automation. Not the least of their burdens is the knowledge that society as a whole—middle class Negro as well as white—thinks of them as "chiselers" who could support themselves if only they wanted to.[53]

However, the article then quickly turned to a discussion of the marriageability of "most of the men" available to inner-city African American women:

Most of the men with whom she comes in contact are poor marriage prospects, quite likely being unemployed and/or emotionally unstable, and they tend to be exploitative and irresponsible. They accept the sexual standards of their community, whereby sexual relations are an expected part of dating behavior, but usually are disinclined to use contraceptives even if they can afford them.[54]

It then quickly turned to a discussion of how and why these women lacked knowledge and access to contraceptives, arguing that "the A.D.C. mothers often lack knowledge of the whole subject of birth control, and most welfare departments do very little to enlighten them." According to the author, this lack of information, combined with the fact that "the typical A.D.C. mother is starved for attention," resulted in an unacceptably high number of pregnancies:

The truth is that the typical A.D.C. mother is starved for affection and tends to take it as she can find it, even though she realizes that life will be more difficult if another child is added to the family. Temporary though they may be, her love affairs serve to ease the feeling of lonely responsibility which plagues her existence as she tries to rear her children alone in a largely hostile environment. I have been impressed with the sense of stigma which most of these people feel simply because they receive aid. They are looked down upon and vilified by the entire community, Negro as well as white. They speak wistfully about wanting to "get off this thing" (they seldom refer to welfare by any term which implies dignity).[55]

In an indication of the taken-for-granted, much more privileged class backgrounds of the readers of the journal, the article also explicitly discussed how these women were seen by the middle class:

Middle class persons tend to find it difficult to understand why some A.D.C. mothers continue to bear child after child, and feel that they must be calculating and mercenary. . . . The middle-class Christian is not sure where he should stand on these matters, and he is infuriated by people who seemingly are untroubled about them and who simply enjoy themselves "doing what comes naturally." Consonant with these feelings, he is likely to be opposed to free birth control services for A.D.C. mothers on the grounds that this would allow sexual license without any "retribution" whatever.[56]

The article concluded with a clear call to "groups," such as those known to be the readers of *Christian Century*, to "consider steps to be taken to influence the community toward making them available."[57]

Throughout the article, two concepts were emphasized, although not as explicitly as they were by many other groups: voluntary family planning and responsible parenthood. Both implied a lack of planning and responsibility on the part of some populations in regard to fertility and a need for them to be taught those traits by others.

RESPONSIBLE PARENTHOOD—A EUGENIC LEGACY

As late as 1965, America's religious promoters of birth control were focused on other people's fertility in their contraceptive activism. Although this stance, in and of itself, could be seen as a legacy of eugenics, there is evidence that these religious leaders were aware of such concerns and actively trying to distance themselves. Much of this comes through in statements that indirectly reference eugenicists' promotion of involuntary sterilization, such as when the *Living Church* wrote in 1965 that the Protestant Episcopal Church would promote contraceptives, "respecting at all times [low-income persons'] complete freedom of choice."[58]

Certainly, part of this distancing was a result of the Roman Catholic Church's continued criticism of eugenic sterilization laws. As late as 1945, and in one of the very few articles on eugenics or sterilization found in any of the religious periodicals searched that year, the Roman Catholic Church kept up its criticism—and in doing so was one of the very few groups to publicly link the policies being promoted by eugenicists in the United States with those being used by Nazi Germany. An article titled "California's Disgrace" in the Roman Catholic periodical *America* stated: "The author reflects on the sterilization law enacted by the California State Legislature, which will permit the sterilization of certain patients. He compares the California law to a similar law enacted by the Nazis in Germany."[59]

Although the word *eugenics* was no longer used in the positive sense, as it had been in the early 1930s in polite society, eugenic language most certainly still was. For example, a 1965 article in the *Christian Century* reported that "William Shockley of Stanford University called for an intense effort to control population and expressed concern over the possible deterioration of humanity resulting from overbreeding by the world's unfittest."[60] The article then went on to report that R. Paul Ramsey, Paine Professor of Religion at Princeton University, had recently urged "churches take the lead in persuading couples who might produce defective children to remain childless."[61]

A eugenic legacy can also be seen in the terms America's religious promoters of birth control tended to emphasize. First and foremost among these was *responsible* parenthood, the very term implying that some parents—namely, those who were poor or who had more than two children—were *irresponsible*, as the following example from the *Register Leader* made quite clear:

> In the eyes of the state, a female has been a brood sow with the ultimate ideal of producing an annual litter . . . she is never a responsible parent, the mother of two carefully planned children. Most often she is a woman who has been so preoccupied and so successful with begetting that she has not had time to menstruate between pregnancies during her twenty years of marriage.[62]

Indeed, using their religious credentials, these groups stressed the morality of responsible family planning, as did the following article in the *Christian Century*:

> Churches and individual Christians . . . believe . . . that *responsible parenthood is a moral obligation.* Four years ago in a policy statement on responsible parenthood the National Council resolved that its duty "to help our fellow men overseas" included assisting "with various measures to alleviate population pressures and to extend family planning . . . as part of a wise and dedicated effort to advance in the underprivileged regions of the earth the essential material conditions conducive to human dignity, freedom, justice and peace." Resolution has now become action.[63]

America's religious advocates of birth control changed their focus on whose fertility concerned them between the first and second waves of liberalization on contraception. Initially concerned about race suicide in the 1920s, the groups examined here promoted the legalization of contraception during the first wave mainly so that poor Italian and Irish immigrants would use them. Thirty years later, the focus of whose fertility was the problem had radically shifted to the "poorer countries of the world" and America's "urban poor."

What remained the same, however, was that these groups promoted contraception out of a concern about *other people's* fertility. American religious advocates of birth control did not promote family planning out of a desire to reassure their flock that they were in good standing for using it—or even to reassure their members that they were fighting for their right to use it. In fact, rights entered the early liberalizers' periodicals and official statements only a few times and always in relation to others. For example, rights are implied in this relatively brief mention by the Quakers in a "Letter from in Pakistan" in 1965: "Of urgently needed changes, the position of women has priority. I must not omit to say that family planning is now getting a lot of support- and none too soon!"[64] However, even in this statement, explicit talk of "rights" does not appear.

When the issue of rights was discussed in these periodicals, the rights these religious leaders referred to are not those we have come to accept as part of the conversation today. Even in an article titled "Private Rights and Rising Birth Rates," which appeared in *Presbyterian Life* in 1965, the rights in focus do not appear to have been the right to *use* contraception (from the individual perspective) but rather the right *not to use* contraception or, rather, to reject sterilization:

> In other parts of the world however, even when contraceptives are available, people fail to use them. More than eight thousand birth-control clinics have been operating in India, according to a report by Ford Foundation population-expert Dr. Nicholson J. Eastman. But the attendance at the clinics has been "disappointingly small," and only a small fraction of the few women attending these clinics return for new supplies. Several answers to this problem have been proposed, among them the use of intrauterine coil or ring method of contraception, which in new tests has proved satisfactory. This method does not require continuous attention, and seems to be suitable to between 80 and 85 percent of women. Another possibility is the widespread increase of voluntary sterilization, a method useful when couples have had

as many children as they wish and "the only realistic answer," according to Dr. Buxton. Some see sterilization as too drastic to be widely acceptable, however.[65]

Only one article, in the Unitarian Universalists' *Register-Leader*, referenced rights in a way that could apply to both others and members of their group, in the following quote that bemoaned the slow state of progress in 1965:

> It should be easy to decide who owns the individual's fertility—the individual himself, the church, or the state. Yet such a decision is not simple. For centuries, fertility ownership has been contested by the three parties. However, I believe that the right of the individual to control his own fertility is slowly gaining ascendancy, but progress is slow, sometimes microscopic. Full emancipation is still distant, as the restrictive birth-control laws of Massachusetts and Connecticut (overturned by the United States Supreme Court in June), the punitive abortion statutes of all United States jurisdictions, and the reticence of physicians to perform sterilization operations all attest.[66]

However, as their focus on *responsible parenthood* implies, while there might have been some distancing from the language, and even the policies, of eugenics, it is also clear that many religious advocates of contraception were not distancing themselves from contraceptive activism more generally. To the contrary, it was clear that these religious leaders had identities as leaders in the movement to make birth control accessible to all. For example, the article quoted earlier from *Presbyterian Survey* reminded readers that "our Protestant churches have taken a stand favoring birth control" and then quickly continued by warning against resting on the laurels of their early support for contraception:

> There is a feeling that all we have to do is make a proclamation favoring birth control and all is well. This is like making a statement against sin and letting it rest there. More than words are needed. We need action in our home and foreign mission fields. In far too many communities, perhaps in yours, no action has been taken. This calls for immediate discussion within your church, in committee-room and from the pulpit to seek ways and means of getting action in this humanitarian activity.[67]

As another example, in 1965, with no sign of concern regarding their early motives, the *Christian Advocate* proudly reported on a seminar in which the "executive vice-president of Planned Parenthood World Population" reminded "nearly 50 church leaders" that Methodists were among the first to "say family planning was a moral necessity":

> Ministers are not doing the job they need to do in teaching their people about the disastrous implications of the rising tide of world population. . . . Because Methodists were the first denomination to say family planning was a moral necessity, the church has a particular moral responsibility to take the lead in seeing that their communities have family planning facilities.[68]

Of course, it is important to acknowledge that a focus on irresponsible parenthood was not limited to the early promoters. Eugenically inclined Southern groups that criticized birth control initially also used the term frequently. The Southern Presbyterian Church in the United States, initially a critic of birth control although always eugenicist in its orientation, came around fairly early (compared to most other critics and silent groups). Its 1960 "Message to the Nation" emphasized responsible parenthood not once, not twice, but five times:

> The God whose creative grace makes possible the blessing of children through marriage likewise vests man and wife with moral responsibility in the exercise of their procreative function. This responsibility is intensified by what is known as "the population explosion" and the threats to human welfare it involves. The bringing of children into the world is a privilege not to be lightly or selfishly evaded by married couples. On the other hand, the responsibility of prospective parents obligates them to consider how their children are to be provided with that which will make for their best physical, cultural, moral, and spiritual development. If man and wife are not to be denied mutual fulfillment in the sexual relation, and if society is not to be penalized by the unplanned and irresponsible production of children, it will follow that access to information regarding the best methods of birth control is the right of all married couples, and the provision of this information the duty of a responsible society.

An article in the same denomination's periodical *Presbyterian Survey* further emphasized the importance of responsible parenthood:

> There is a single answer to this global [population] problem—planned parenthood. The best way to solve the problem is to start with this positive answer in our own communities. Every city and village know the results of

overpopulation—crime, juvenile delinquency, unstable family life, poverty, slums, and inadequate schools. We're always chipping away at solving these problems—more parks, police, jails, and schools. But we still avoid, except in a few isolated communities, dealing directly with the basic problem: the inability of couples to learn to have the number of children that they can care for and nurture into responsible citizens. This failure is the neglect of our society to share the meaning of responsible parenthood.[69]

The Presbyterian Church in the United States merged with its Northern brothers in 1983, so it is covered in detail in this chapter. However, most of the other groups that were critical of early birth control reform ultimately liberalized on birth control as well but with a very different focus than the religious promoters of contraception. It is to these groups that we now turn.

8 The Forgotten Half

AMERICA'S RELUCTANT CONTRACEPTIVE CONVERTS

In contrast to the religious promoters of contraception who expressed a great deal of concern about world population and emphatically, even obsessively, covered every legal development regarding contraception, most of the remaining American religious denominations included in this study said relatively little about birth control. When they did so, they very infrequently discussed the population explosion, if they mentioned it in their periodicals at all. Instead, they seem to have entered the debate over contraception reluctantly and almost exclusively in reference to their own flocks and whether and when their use of contraceptives was religiously acceptable—for them, only within the bonds of Christian marriage.

In total, twelve (which would soon become eleven) of the groups in my sample of America's most prominent religious denominations fall into the category of *reluctant converts* to the norms surrounding contraception. Although diverse theologically, geographically, and historically, these groups have one crucial factor in common: all either openly rejected birth control or were completely disconnected from the movement during the first wave of liberalization but ultimately came around to reluctantly endorsing it by the second wave.[1]

Although many might attribute these groups' reluctance to publicly engage in debates about contraception to a reluctance to make pronouncements on social issues in general, there are two problems with this characterization. First, among these groups were some of the United States' most ardent believers in the social gospel movement. Here I refer to denominations like the Reformed Church in America, the Disciples of Christ, the Lutheran Church in America (formerly the United Lutheran Church in America), and the African Methodist Episcopal Zion Church (AMEZ), which expressed strong support for the social gospel movement during the first wave of liberalization but reservations about eugenics in its periodicals.[2] In addition, these same denominations actively commented on other social issues, especially civil rights. Their relative quietude was mostly restricted to contraception. While they seem to have begrudgingly accepted that contraception was part of humanity's modern existence (even if by never making an official statement about it), they remained distant from the concerns about other people's out-of-control fertility that so obsessed the religious promoters of contraception.

In addition to the four groups mentioned above, two formerly silent denominations (the only ones that also remained intact over the next three decades) ultimately became reluctant promoters of contraception: the National Baptist Convention, USA, Inc. and Conservative Jews. Thus, analytically, it is important to point out that all six of the original silent groups that remained intact through the next three decades took the same path and became the reluctant converts to contraception examined in this chapter (the other three merged with early liberalizers and became promoters of contraception).

In addition, while two of the groups who were initially strong critics of contraception never liberalized on contraception officially (the Roman Catholic Church and Orthodox Jews), the rest did eventually reluctantly endorse contraception and are included in this chapter.[3] These include the Southern Baptist Convention, which liberalized in 1967, as well as the Lutheran Church–Missouri Synod and the Church of Jesus Christ of Latter-day Saints (or LDS), both of whom eventually liberalized quite late—in 1981 for the Lutheran Church–Missouri Synod and 1988 for the LDS.

Finally, three new denominations are also included in this chapter. These denominations were too small and removed from the rest of the American religious field in the 1930s to warrant much attention in part II of this analysis but had become noticeably more important, and much larger, by the 1960s. These are the Jehovah's Witnesses, the Seventh-day Adventists, and the Assemblies of God. Despite important differences, all three denominations demonstrate how important the issue of immigration was for politicizing the issue of birth control. None predominated in the major cities of the East Coast, where immigrants were "flooding the shores," and with the exception of the Assemblies of God were quite neutral about birth control early on, refusing to take any political stance or condemn their members who decided to use it. Adding these relatively new religious groups to the analysis suggests that had birth control not become politicized because of the eugenics movement's desire to control immigrants' "runaway" fertility, other religious groups might have also liberalized in a way that focused more on their constituents' ability to use it and less on other people's irresponsible fertility.

BREAKING THEIR SILENCE

As contraception became accepted among most Americans and widely, safely, and conveniently available with the pill, the rest of the American religious field began to reluctantly make pronouncements in favor of it. Their statements were not just less frequent and later chronologically, however; they were also much more circumscribed. In comparison to the religious promoters, who quite simply wanted contraception to be available to everyone and anyone, especially the poor, these denominations examined in this chapter focused much more on when and how birth control was acceptable to their believers, barely mentioning the population explosion that virtually obsessed other groups.

This characterization applies to all of the groups that remained silent during the first wave, with the exception of two: neither the historically black denomination National Baptist Convention, USA, nor the Churches of Christ said anything about contraceptives in any of the years searched. The next most circumspect denomination in my sample, the historically Black AMEZ, published only one article in its *Quarterly Review* that mentioned birth control in the three years searched (1945, 1955, and 1965).[4] In contrast to the alarm and urgency expressed by the religious promoters, that article did not report on AMEZ views of contraception but instead, in one paragraph of a five-page article, it informed readers of the results of a recent meeting of the National Council of Churches' International Affairs Commission. The recommendation was that countries requesting contraceptive aid be given it.[5] The Lutheran Church in America was more vocal about birth control, publishing five articles on the topic in its periodical the *Lutheran* in 1965. But even so, with the exception of one article, which argued briefly that "information on responsible parenthood and family planning should be made available to all people" because these articles focused almost entirely on whether the Second Vatican Council would change the Roman Catholic Church's stance on "artificial means" of contraception.[6] This focus on whether the Roman Catholic Church would liberalize made sense, as the Lutherans, and the other denominations examined in this chapter, identified as fellow sexual conservatives by this time.

Along with being more circumspect, these reluctant converts were also much slower to change their stances on contraception. For example, by 1955, when America's religious promoters of birth control were expressing dire concerns about world population, the Reformed Church in America was telling its flock not to reduce their own fertility (lest they be overtaken by Roman Catholics—admittedly, not a new concern):

> There are several reasons why Christians should raise large families. Among them are these four. . . . *Not to do so jeopardizes the place of Evangelical Christianity in our land.* If present trends continue, the Roman Catholic Church will eventually become the majority group in our nation and when that happens, it will not be so much because of immigration evangelization as it will [be] because [of] a much higher birth rate. It seems rather strange to look upon parenthood as a missionary enterprise, and yet, in a sense, it is.[7]

Within the next five years, however, like the other silent groups the Reformed Church in America had decided there were good reasons to use contraceptive methods. A few years later, they acknowledged that the tide of public opinion had shifted.

The list of reasons the Reformed Church in America gave for its liberalization, first in 1960 and again in 1962, is illuminating. In its 1960 statement, it argued that "responsible parenthood is a God-given blessing to which Christian married persons should look forward (Gen. 1:28, Ps. 127:3). It is the readiest, most natural way of perpetuating and extending the Kingdom of God."[8] Note that although the Reformed Church was using the term *responsible parenthood*, it was doing so primarily in relation to its own flock. This becomes clear further on in the statement, when, still arguing against those who are skeptical that contraceptives are Christian, the article asserted:

> God apparently expects married couples to exercise responsible moral decisions in their sex lives and parenthood as well as in other realms of the Christian life. The argument against contraception to the effect that God knows when a child should be conceived and only allows contraception at proper times simply transforms the doctrine of sovereignty into an irresponsible parody that may be characterized as "magical determinism."[9]

Of the eleven reasons given in the document, only one referenced other countries and only in relation to giving aid if asked. There was nothing in the quote regarding the deep and disastrous concerns about the population explosion like those the early liberalizers had invoked. Instead, their pronouncement simply stated: "In the light of these conclusions, it would be right and proper for governmental, as well as private agencies to respond favorably to bona fide requests from underdeveloped countries for information and help in birth control problems."[10] In a final indication of just how differently the Reformed Church in America saw the issue from the religious promoters of birth control in the previous chapter, take its following statement from the same document. In a move made by other critics of the world population movement, it emphasized that economic growth, not access to contraception, seemed to be a more effective form of birth control: "Economic prosperity seems to have a larger impact on the birth rate than does the availability of information and materials for contraception."[11] Rather than arguing that those concerned about population growth should give contraceptives to poorer countries, the Reformed Church in America seemed to be suggesting that those concerned about population growth should focus more on encouraging economic prosperity.

The Reformed Church in America was not alone in its more reluctant endorsement of contraception and its suggestion that religious groups could do more than just promote it in poorer countries. Conservative Jews' statements also focused on whether their members could, in good conscience, use contraception and did not mention the population explosion or even the words *responsible parenthood*.[12] For example, in 1949, well after the religious promoters of birth control had begun sounding alarm bells about overpopulation in poorer countries of the world, *Conservative Judaism* published an article that focused strictly on the use of birth control for its readers:

> There should be general agreement between the two on plans for children. Not only is it true that a childless marriage is an incomplete marriage (since *piryah ve-rivyah* is one of the basic reasons for marriage), but disagreement between husband and wife on the desirability of children is a most serious matter. While the subject of methods of birth control is a matter on which they should have medical advice, any method utilized should be based on mutual agreement.[13]

Conservative Jews' focus on their members, rather than other peoples' fertility, was consistent over time. In 1960 they wrote in their official statement: "We are, therefore, justified in sanctioning birth control as a precaution against a danger to the life or health, physical or mental of the mother or her children, on the advice of a physician, or on the personal convictions expressing the private conscience of the individuals involved."[14]

The Disciples of Christ were much more actively concerned about contraception and world population than the other formerly silent groups, with four articles that positively mentioned birth control, two of which discussed the population explosion. Even so, the Disciples did not make an official statement until 1972. That official statement gives the best picture of their views. It begins much more focused on overpopulation and its environmental effects than would be expected from their initial silence:

> WHEREAS . . . "mankind's main problems today—increasing crime rate, overloaded freeways, airports, hospitals and colleges, poverty, air and water pollution and all other facets of environmental deterioration, the emergence of an impersonal society that encourages regimentation rather than individuality and creativity, failed school bond issues, increases in unemployment,

increases in taxes, hunger, and so on—either stem from, or are intensified by, overpopulation—sheer excess of people."[15]

However, after listing the multitude of problems that could result from overpopulation (most of which, it should be noted, were domestic in nature), the Disciples of Christ's statement turned to focus not only on domestic fertility (without any mention of "urban unrest" or the "inner cities") but on the fertility of its own members, never mentioning people in other countries:

> THEREFORE BE IT RESOLVED that the General Assembly of the Christian Church Disciples of Christ), meeting in Louisville, Kentucky on October 15–20, 1971 encourage congregations to support the Week of Compassion in its Family Planning Program, and that the Division of Homeland Ministries (Department of Christian Education and Department of Church in Society) be asked to draw up within twelve months a study document for local congregations of the Christian Church (Disciples of Christ), to the end that individual Christians and family units consider such matters as family planning, birth control, adoption and abortion as a part of a pressing need to curtail world population growth.[16]

It closed by emphasizing that "this action in no way diminishes the concern of this church for correcting unjust social systems."[17]

Thus, the groups who were initially silent about birth control did eventually liberalize. When they did, they generally demonstrated an awareness of changes in public opinion regarding contraception and concerns about world population, although those reports were more neutral in tone, as if they were informing their members about other folks' concerns, rather than expressing the deep anxiety that the religious promoters of contraception expressed. In comparison to the religious promoters of contraception chronicled in the previous chapter, all of whom had been active eugenicists that promoted birth control during the first wave, these groups had remained silent on birth control during the first wave—largely, it seems, to avoid directly criticizing their fellow religious activists for being racist. However, the reader will remember that there were other groups who rejected eugenics who had no such qualms about critiquing the early liberalizers during the first wave. Uninvolved in the social gospel movement, they had openly criticized both the eugenics movement and its promotion of birth control reform. Three of these groups also eventually liberalized on birth control.

Former Critics

The first of the former critics to liberalize was the openly eugenicist Southern Baptist Convention, which agreed in 1967 that birth control was a way to address world population concerns (something they were perhaps more open to as a result of their beliefs in eugenics than the other critics covered below), but only for married couples:

> WHEREAS, God has blessed us with the knowledge and skills of medical science for the benefit of mankind, and WHEREAS, Overpopulation and the threat of mass starvation is posing an increasing problem in many parts of the world, and WHEREAS, It is the responsibility of parents to determine the desirable size of families and the spacing of children so as to provide adequately for them as well as for the well-being of the parents, changes according to the times, and WHEREAS, The Biblical concept of marriage teaches sexual companionship of husband and wife, the procreation of children, the worth and dignity of a human life, Be it therefore RESOLVED, That the Southern Baptist Convention commends to those married couples who desire it and who may be benefited by it, the judicious use of medically approved methods of planned parenthood and the dissemination of planned parenthood information.[18]

Two other former critics, the Church of Jesus Christ of Latter-day Saints, otherwise known as the Mormons, and the Lutheran Church–Missouri Synod (LC–MS), liberalized much later than most other groups. The LC–MS provides another example of how, even when these groups reference fears about the population explosion that so concerned the religious promoters of birth control, their conclusions about what their responses to increasing population should be are illustrative. Instead of insisting on the promotion and dissemination of contraceptives, for example, a 1965 article in the *Lutheran Witness* emphasized to readers that they had a responsibility to provide "shelter, medical care, education, and the Gospel" in their missions.[19] The LC–MS did not liberalize until 1981. When it did so, it exclusively discussed birth control in the context of marriage:

> In view of the Biblical command and the blessing to "be fruitful and multiply," it is to be expected that marriage will not ordinarily be *voluntarily* childless. But, in the absence of Scriptural prohibition, there need be no objection to contraception within a marital union which is, as a whole, fruitful.[20]

Making it clear that they were primarily focused on their own members, the statement continued: "There may be special circumstances which would persuade a Christian husband and wife that it would be more responsible and helpful to all concerned, under God, not to have children. Whatever the particular circumstances, Christians dare not take lightly decisions in this area of their life together. They should examine their motives thoroughly and honestly and take care lest their decisions be informed by a desire merely to satisfy selfish interests.[21]

Even later than the Lutherans, the Mormons did not make an official statement on contraception until 1998—nearly seventy years after the first wave of liberalization and more than thirty after the second wave. When they did so, their entire statement was only two paragraphs long, so I quote it in full below:

> It is the privilege of married couples who are able to bear children to provide mortal bodies for the spirit children of God, whom they are then responsible to nurture and rear. The decision as to how many children to have and when to have them is extremely intimate and private and should be left between the couple and the Lord. Church members should not judge one another in this matter.
>
> Married couples also should understand that sexual relations within marriage are divinely approved not only for the purpose of procreation, but also as a means of expressing love and strengthening emotional and spiritual bonds between husband and wife.[22]

Such more circumscribed liberalization was not limited to the denominations that have, until now, filled the pages of this book. Three groups too small to play a significant role in the American religious field during the first wave had come into their own by the second wave. Their take on liberalization indicates that the more circumscribed liberalization on birth control might have been the most common path followed by all of America's religious denominations had birth control not become so politicized by the eugenics movement.

Emerging Denominations

The Jehovah's Witnesses, the Seventh-day Adventists, and the Assemblies of God provide interesting analytical leverage for this analysis. As denominations that were neither social gospelers nor eugenicists, they should have been critical of reform—and indeed, the Assemblies of God were.

However, perhaps because they were largely newcomers to the American religious field, both Jehovah's Witnesses and Seventh-day Adventists simply accepted birth control—fairly early on—but with the same focus on their own flocks as the reluctant converts.

ASSEMBLIES OF GOD

I will begin with the most conservative of the emerging denominations, the Assemblies of God. The denomination grew out of a Pentecostal revival in 1914. Quite critical of birth control reform during the first wave, the Assemblies of God saw only negative consequences for the growth of their denomination if they were to allow birth control, which they discussed in numerous articles. As an example, in 1934 a column in the *Latter Rain Evangel* reported that a church had to close its doors

> because the practice of birth control among its members had reduced the congregations to the vanishing point. The Gospel's function is to spiritually procreate. But in 10,000 churches every bit of worldliness tolerated. . . . Evangelism is discouraged, revivals are denounced and new-birth control is practiced as it was in the days of the Pharisees. Thus history repeats itself.[23]

The Assemblies of God were also very critical of eugenics, with two articles appearing in back-to-back issues in 1933. The second of these was one of the few publications to link eugenic thought with Nazi Germany in a section of a regular column titled "The Pulse of a Dying World," with the subtitle "Sterilization or Regeneration":

> Germany, through its stringent sterilization law taking effect January 1, 1934, expects to attain in time racial purity through the decrees of a Eugenic Court. Scores of states, including Russia, are discussing this means of arresting the propagation of undesirables. God's method is not race but grace, purification by regeneration, positive not negative—a new birth.[24]

The Assemblies of God had only one article on birth control in their periodical *Pentecostal Evangel* in 1945, 1955, and 1965. Unlike the other emerging denominations, that statement was not an indication of acceptance but instead noted concerns about with birth control pills, stating that their use would lead to immorality.[25] However, like the formerly crucial Mormons and Lutherans discussed in this chapter, today the Assemblies reluctantly allow contraception, stressing that "there are valid reasons for delaying, limiting, or not having children."[26]

In comparison to the Assemblies of God and in contrast to all of the other denominations explained in this book, both Seventh-day Adventists and Jehovah's Witnesses were, interestingly, quite neutral about birth control early on, refusing to endorse it like the early liberalizers, but also talking openly about it early on, unlike the strict groups. Together, adding these two relatively new religious groups to the analysis suggests that had birth control not become politicized due to the eugenics movement's desire to control immigrants' "runaway" fertility, other religious groups might have also liberalized in a way that focused simply on their constituents' ability to use it. And, in a sense, these emerging denominations heralded what was to come, especially those who had remained silent during the first wave.

SEVENTH-DAY ADVENTISTS

A relatively new denomination founded only in 1863 in Michigan, the Seventh-day Adventists were talking openly about contraception, and publishing relatively often on the subject, even during the first wave of liberalization. Thus, in 1931 an article in their periodical *Watchman Magazine* carefully refused to take a stand on the issue. Instead, in a response directed clearly to their own members, they discussed the various more and less biblically acceptable ways to limit children and concluded with a rejoinder to "obey civil laws" regarding contraception:

> *What is your stand on birth control?* Our stand is the Bible stand, as far as we are able to interpret it. If by birth control is meant any kind of method of limiting the world's population,—celibacy, contingency, contraception, abortion, onanism,—all of which, and more, are included in the broad meaning of the term, then we must qualify our answer. The bible sanctions celibacy in certain very rare cases (Matthew 19:10, 12), but it is left as a voluntary matter. Onanism met with God's displeasure (Genesis 38:8–10), though there is some question here whether God was displeased with Onan's refusing to comply with what afterward became a law in Israel (Deuteronomy 25:5,6), or because of his method of prevention of conception. Abortion is murder. It would seem to us that contraceptives are allowable in cases of disease coupled with weakness of body or will power, but they can be justified only comparatively, as the lesser of two evils, and their users should have a full knowledge of what all that resort to them involves, remembering to obey civil laws concerning them. Continence is no doubt the best way to limit the number of

children, where limitation is either desirable or necessary to the health and adequate economic provision for the family. Continence, however, is not the killing of sex desire, but the control of it. We hesitate to make hard and fast rules on the marriage relation. Situations and conditions differ so widely that each case should be dealt with according to its own peculiar needs.[27]

Their views thirty years later, during the second wave of birth control reform, were remarkably consistent with their views during the first wave, with a focus on how Adventists could, in good conscience, limit their families (and in fact seemed to be encouraging them to do so). Their periodical *Review and Herald* published the following advice for married couples:

> Before increasing their family, they [those professing to be Christians] should take into consideration whether God would be glorified or dishonored by their bringing children into the world. They should seek to glorify God by their union from the first, and during every year of their married life. They should calmly consider what provision can be made for their children. They have no right to bring children into the world to be a burden to others. Have they a business that they can rely upon to sustain a family, so that they need not become a burden to others? If they have not, they commit a crime in bringing children into the world to suffer for want of proper care, food and clothing.[28]

While the tone of these articles made it clear that Seventh-day Adventists were in favor of legal access to birth control, they lacked the sense of alarm about world population expressed by the religious advocates of contraception. Even in articles that argued in favor of family planning for economic reasons, the discussion seemed focused on their own constituents and not those in other places of the world or country.[29] By 1974, that feeling is clearly laid out:

> How does the Seventh-day Adventist Church stand on abortion and birth control? The Seventh-day Adventist Church has no official actions on either of these matters. It is safe to say that the great majority of married members practice some form of birth control. But this is guided by a family's capacity to impart emotional warmth and financial support to a reasonable number of offspring. It is not guided by a church dictum on the matter.[30]

This position on birth control is consistent with many of the other denominations that rejected eugenics during the first wave, a view that Seventh Day Adventists were open about sharing early on. For example, in

1927 they were quite critical of white supremacists in an article titled "Is the White Domination of the World about to End?"

> There are many voices today calling us in all sorts of ways, in all sorts of circumstances, to show a united white front against peoples of other color. Well, let us face the fact squarely. A solid white front certainly and inevitably means a solid yellow front, and a solid brown front, and a solid black front; and that, in the end of the day, can have only one meaning. It means war.[31]

That same year the Seventh-day Adventists' periodical explicitly criticized eugenicists in their own language in their magazine *Signs of the Times*:

> In the days of Spartan supremacy, the weaklings and the ill were heartlessly placed out on a rocky promontory, where the elements and the prowling beats might do away with them so that Sparta might contain only "superior" men and women. But Jesus Christ brought into the world a vastly different conception. He taught us that to care for the weak is not only a duty but a glorious privilege. Of Him the prophet had said, "A bruised reed will He not break, and a dimly burning wick will He not quench." Isaiah 42:3, A.R.V. Orphan homes, hospitals, rescue homes, Salvation Army homes, Red Cross Societies, *et cetera*, have all come into existence because of this phase of the teaching of Jesus Christ.
>
> But the Evolutionist, seeing plainly that his theory is not working out today before his very eyes, is ready to condemn the means we are putting forth to care for our sick and deficient, He is ready to sacrifice them on the altar of Evolution! But what will the outcome be? You may ask. If it is really true that the subnormal are multiplying so rapidly, and leaders and thinkers are decreasing at so alarming a pace, what does the future hold for the race?[32]

Consistent with their rejection of eugenics, the Seventh-day Adventists seem to have been largely concentrated in the Midwest thus noting that early Adventists concentrated on ministering "'Danes and Norwegians' . . . in the nearby state of Wisconsin," and proudly claiming today to be early integrationists who entrusted.[33] African Americans with leadership positions in the church in its early days.[34]

In sum, the Seventh Day Adventists suggest that groups that were critical of eugenics but not incumbents in the religious field like the Lutheran Church-Missouri Synod, or the AMEZ, had a different take on birth control. Able to remain largely neutral on the topic, they did not initially feel compelled to stay silent, but instead focused on finding the best religious solution for their members who wished to limit their family sizes during, and long after, the first wave of reform.

Jehovah's Witnesses were an even newer denomination than the Seventh-day Adventists—only taking their name in 1931, the same year that the first wave of birth control liberalizations peaked. With theological roots in the Seventh-day Adventist movement, Witnesses soon became well known for their rejection of blood transfusions, Christmas and birthday celebrations, and incredibly active proselytization activities both in the United States and abroad.[35] Although more political than Seventh-day Adventists, Jehovah's Witnesses channeled their political activity into critiques of World War I, patriotism, and organized religions—stances that did little to win them fans in governments in many parts of the world. Jehovah's Witnesses are included in my sample only because of their impressive growth in the United States after the first-wave analysis. However, their statements and stances on the issues examined here are still instructive, if only as a window into how a group very much removed from mainstream America saw the issues of the day. As early as 1923, the Witnesses made it clear that they had no particular problem with birth control:

> Perhaps those who object most strongly to birth-control are the people who argue that it is against religion. Many Bible students tell us that there is nothing in the Bible which condemns the use of preventives. The simplest way is for all who believe it wrong to refrain from using those means, but not to try to force their morals on people who are guided by different standards of morality. "Religion is a matter of faith, not reason."[36]

In 1932, just after the rest of the American religious field was riven by statements in favor of birth control by America's most elite groups, Jehovah's Witnesses published another article on birth control. That, too, intentionally refrained from comment, noting that "we do not see our way clear to open our columns to a general discussion of this subject, despite its importance." The article then went on to note that even so, "this article is expressed in language which cannot offend the most fastidious." It closed by recommending particular passages of the Bible for their readers who wished for more on "this great problem."[37]

Such acknowledgment that birth control was a "great problem" was likely connected to the fact that Witnesses were aware of the eugenic undertones of the early birth control movement and found them to be problematic. Thus, in 1934 their periodical the *Golden Age* wrote that sterilization of the "feeble-minded" seemed to be a relatively futile undertaking:

> Dr. C. Leonard Huskins, professor of genetics at McGill University, Montreal, points out that if all the feeble-minded were sterilized, the proportion of feeble-minded to the population would be decreased by only about 11 percent; it would take many generations of sterilization to make a decrease of 20 percent, and the percentage could never be decreased by more than 50 percent, no matter what steps were taken. To entirely wipe out feeble-mindedness, it would be necessary to wipe out all the relatives, including parents, brothers, sisters, uncles, aunts, and cousins.[38]

Although data about the racial and ethnic makeup of the early Witnesses (or of any religious groups, for that matter) are unfortunately not available, the Jehovah's Witnesses today are one of the most ethnically diverse religious groups in the country, with African American members numbering more than one-third and another 12 percent claiming to be racially "other" than white. If these proportions have held over time, that might explain why Witnesses had such a disparaging view of eugenics, even while they were critical of immigrants, especially Roman Catholics.[39]

Regardless of why they rejected eugenics, their stance on birth control became very much like that of the other groups who did so by 1969. That year the *Watchtower* published an article that answered "Questions from Readers" regarding contraception. None of the answers to these questions referenced the population explosion. More importantly, like the other reluctant converts to contraception examined in this chapter, the answers are intentionally circumscribed to focus on their own believers and what would be acceptable for them to use within the confines of Christian marriage. The article emphasized decisively that "the Bible does not directly discuss birth control, and so each couple [should] . . . reach their own conclusion" and explicitly stated that "those who seek to avoid having children now are not violating any command of God to Christians."[40] The article failed to "recommend or endorse" any particular methods of birth control, simply noting that "side effects" and "Christian principles" should be considered:

There are numerous birth-control methods. It is not our place as a Bible society to recommend or endorse any of these. If a married couple want to practice—and let us emphasize that this is entirely a personal decision—they have to conclude how to do that. There might be physical side effects from certain contraceptive methods. Hence, that should be considered. Another aspect to evaluate is whether a particular method might violate Christian principles in some way.[41]

Even the one article that did mention world population (quite late, in 1989) seemed to do so only to point out that things are different from the time of Adam and Eve and to emphasize the Jehovah's Witnesses' consistent stance that "nowhere in the Bible is birth control or family planning discussed.[42]

Although they are often left out of popular debate, a wide variety of American religious groups liberalized on contraception not out of the worries about other people's fertility rates, which motivated America's religious promoters of birth control, but due to concerns about whether their constituents could use birth control in good conscience. These denominations include groups as varied as the historically black AMEZ church and the relatively new denomination of the Jehovah's Witnesses. What all of these groups had in common was a rejection of early birth control liberalization and with the exception of the Southern Baptist Convention, of eugenics more broadly.

Conclusion

In 1926 the American Eugenics Society announced its first competition for the best sermon on eugenics: "Prizes of $500 for the best, $300 for the second, and $200 for the third best sermon are the rewards."[1] The call for submissions made the goals of the competition clear. The society's members wanted to bring the message of eugenics to a wider audience. Buoyed by eugenicists' belief that those churches were a "natural selective agency," a place where certain types of people of "the intelligent classes" could be found, they wrote: "Since the churches are in a measure a natural selective agency and since a large percentage of the intelligent classes are church members, it is hoped that the message of eugenics will be received by thousands of people in the United States who otherwise would not hear it."[2]

The call ended by emphasizing that if ministers were successful in their efforts to educate their parishioners about eugenics, there might be more "good people in America": "It has been said that good people make the churches and that the churches seldom make the people good. Even if this is so, the American Eugenics Society hopes that this award will be a help toward the increase of good people in America."[3]

Increasing the good people in America was only a small part of eugenicists' strategy, one referred to as "positive eugenics." By the time of this first competition for the best sermon on eugenics, the AES had decided to focus on its negative eugenics campaigns. Beyond working to increase involuntary sterilizations of the unfit, something at which they were incredibly successful but found inadequately addressed their larger race suicide concerns, they had decided to focus on making birth control more accessible to those they considered to be just generally undesirable. When the AES did so, it asked for, and ultimately received, the backing of the same religious groups whose pastors had submitted sermons to that competition—the whitest, wealthiest, most urban, and most highly educated members of America's religious establishment.

Thus began a series of vigorous debates within the American religious field about whether contraception was sinful and whether or not it was, whether religious groups had a duty to promote it. The first groups to liberalize on birth control did so with the sort of moral certitude that can only be gained by deep-seated religious beliefs—beliefs that many would reject today but that were deeply motivating and widely accepted at the time. These beliefs continued to inform their birth control activism for decades—as they remained America's religious promoters of birth control well into the 1960s.

It is certainly a stretch to argue that America's religious promoters of birth control continued to promote contraceptive access to poor people (who were mostly of color) in American inner cities and the rest of the world because they were still, secretively, eugenicists. However, while very few of the religious promoters of birth control would have embraced the eugenicist label by the mid-1960s, comparing their concerns and statements to those of the reluctant converts is illustrative. Doing so helps us to see that whether or not they considered themselves to be eugenicists, the overall focus of their contraceptive activism remained the same. They wanted to decrease not their own, but other people's fertility.

Such was not the case for the groups that more reluctantly converted to society's more accepting views of birth control. In comparison to the religious promoters of birth control, who saw themselves as, and arguably were, a part of America's elite, the reluctant converts were of more common and ethnically or racially marginal origins. As either historically black groups, more recent immigrants or, at the very least, situated in places where immigrants were not "flooding the shores," these groups did not see much value in the "science" of eugenics during the first wave of reform. As a result, whether or not they believed in the social gospel movement, they did not see it as their religious duty, or even their right, to comment on other people's fertility. Instead, when they did liberalize, the reluctant converts focused simply on the religious implications of contraception for their members.

This more truncated liberalization on the issue of contraception coincided with an entirely different take on sex and sexuality as the sexual revolution gripped America's religious groups. Rather than see themselves as "leaders in a movement," as the Methodists had, the reluctant converts were more likely to speak out, condemning "The New Morality" and the "moral decline and confusion" it was bringing, than they were to promote contraception.[4]

Of course, the story of those differences is a tale that goes well beyond the focus of this book, which is birth control. It is certainly a tale for the pages of at least one, if not many, future books.[5] However, it is also true that, as the saying goes, history repeats itself. Debates about religious views of contraception recently returned to center stage in our nation's politics. In many ways, these debates demonstrate that a great deal has changed since the mid-1960s. In particular, the debates today are much more about women's rights and much less about controlling undesirable fertility. But it is also true that much about them, especially what side of the debate a particular group is on, has remained the same.

HOBBY LOBBY AND THE LITTLE SISTERS OF THE POOR

In 2014 David Green, founder and chief executive officer of the Hobby Lobby chain of craft stores, and his family sued the federal government for mandating that his company provide health insurance that covered four contraceptives they viewed as abortifacients.[6] The Greens are evangelicals who attend a congregation that is a member of the Assemblies of God. They are prolife.[7]

The case was argued before the US Supreme Court on March 25, 2014. On June 30, 2014, the court decided that closely held companies like Hobby Lobby with religious objections were no longer to be compelled to cover contraception in their health-care plans. In 2015 the Obama administration created a procedure that allowed affected employees to receive contraceptives at a cost to the federal government. This compromise ultimately resulted in the Little Sisters of the Poor case, when the sisters, a group of Roman Catholic nuns, sued the Supreme Court, arguing that even filling out the required paperwork to help their employees obtain those (and any artificial) contraceptives was a violation of their religious beliefs. Ultimately, the Supreme Court ruled that the Little Sisters case should be settled in the lower courts but banned the government from fining institutions for not complying with regulations for religious reasons.

Both cases were seen as victories for religious groups, or for "religious freedom," as supporters emphasized, and as a loss for women and abortion rights groups. Both cases, especially Hobby Lobby, which was seen as the watershed, received a great deal of attention from both the popular and religious press. Within a few months, the issue had gained national prominence, with articles in the *New York Times* appearing almost daily at some points and with more than fifty appearing in 2015 alone.

THE SIDES REMAIN THE SAME

While the contours of the debates have changed, the sides remain astonishingly similar.[8] A website known as the Layman, dedicated to helping evangelicals "discern" whether to stay in the Presbyterian Church of the United States of America, summarized the sides of the debate especially clearly prior to the Supreme Court decisions. The religious groups at the front and center of the progressive view will be familiar to the readers of this book:[9]

> The United Methodist General Board of Church and Society, along with the Religious Coalition for Reproductive Choice, which includes the Episcopal Church, Presbyterian Church (USA) and United Church of Christ (UCC), have endorsed the HHS mandate that requires employers to provide insurance coverage for contraceptives and abortifacients. So too have the UCC's president, the Reformed Church in America's general secretary, the Episcopal Bishop of Washington, D.C.[10]

The article then went on to list the groups supporting the plaintiffs. Again, these are groups whose early opposition to birth control should be familiar to readers of this book—even if the reasons behind that opposition were varied: "In contrast, the United States Conference of Catholic Bishops, Union of Orthodox Jewish Congregations of America, National Association of Evangelicals, Southern Baptist Convention, Lutheran Church Missouri Synod . . . have identified the HHS Obamacare mandate as an assault on religious liberty."[11]

So what do we make of this, this century of division over contraception that began as a racial project among America's elite religious groups—this century of division during which the sides have not changed much? Perhaps the most obvious implication of this book is that the first issue connected to sex and gender that really divided the American religious field was not about gender at all, except, of course, to the extent that reproduction was and is always fundamentally about women's bodies. It was fundamentally about race and class—and which women they wanted reproducing and which they did not.[12]

Today, of course, gender is much more front and center, especially for progressive groups.[13] As the Right prayed that "the Supreme Court would rule in favor of the Green family . . . and the cause of religious liberty," the Left framed it as an issue of women's rights—and especially as an issue for poor women.[14] Take, for example, the United Church of Christ (UCC), which argued publicly against the Supreme Court decision on the grounds that it would have a disproportionate "impact on women of color." The UCC went on to assert, "For more than thirty five years the General Synod of the United Church of Christ has advocated for health care as a right and a priority for all people."[15] As this book demonstrates, the UCC, its precursors, and most other elite northeastern religious denominations have actually been advocating for contraceptives to be available and accessible, especially to poor women of color, for much longer than thirty-five years. Indeed, it has been nearly a century.

The reasons the religious promoters of contraception originally began promoting the legalization of contraception, however, are most likely understood in a very different light today than they were in 1930. Today, the eugenicist reasons for promoting birth control are at odds with the values espoused by progressive religious groups that pride themselves on fighting for social justice on all fronts, as does the UCC.[16] This fact brings me to an important point about the main takeaway of this book: race and conceptions of race are incredibly geographically and historically specific.

To give just one example: Many of the early liberalizers were progressive, even activist, in their stances on "the Negro" but utterly racist in their attitudes toward immigrants. Thus, in the late 1920's and early 1930's the Protestant Episcopal Church heralded the Immigration Restriction Act for preventing "the further dilution of our stock, which has unquestionably been in serious danger" but argued against the claim that "Negroes" were an inferior race.[17] Similarly, Congregationalists reported optimistically about eliminating the "very dangerous social malady" of race prejudice and questioned data claiming that "the Negro was of inferior mental and physical stock," all the while advocating eugenics.[18]

Such contradictions did not exist for Southern eugenicists who focused on blacks whose political or numerical threat was brutally repressed by a set of well-established institutions of racial domination. They saw Catholic immigrants as a racial boon or missionary opportunity, if they mentioned them at all. With high white birth rates, they had no fear of race suicide and its political implications. Southern groups like the Southern Baptist Convention remained critical of birth control reform well into the 1960s and remain steadfast sexual conservatives today. Yet we should not conclude this was because they were less racist than their progressive Northern counterparts. They were just racists of a different kind.

This brings me full circle to the other main takeaway of this book: religion intersects with other structures of inequality. It always has and it likely always will. From geography and its various systems of racial and class stratification to immigration and the people and places that see threat, versus opportunity, in new arrivals, religion is deeply, completely—even inextricably—linked with race, class, and ethnicity. It is these intersections that help us to understand both why religions change and why, even when they do, so much remains the same.

Notes

INTRODUCTION

1. "Protestantism Is Falling Behind through Unproductive Marriages," 40.

2. Carter, *Decline and Revival of the Social Gospel*; Phillips, *Kingdom on Earth*; Szasz, *Divided Mind of Protestant America*.

3. Collins, *Black Feminist Thought*; McCall, *Complex Inequality*; McCall, "Complexity of Intersectionality."

4. Many intersectional studies have focused on women of color. See Brewer, "Theorizing Race, Class and Gender"; Collins, *Black Feminist Thought*; Crenshaw, "Mapping the Margins"; Davis, *Women, Race and Class*; Espiritu, *Asian American Women and Men*; Glenn, *Unequal Freedom*; Hooks, *Ain't I a Woman*; Hooks, *Feminist Theory*; King, "Multiple Jeopardy, Multiple Consciousness"; Moraga and Anzaldua, *This Bridge Called My Back*; Robnett, *How Long?*

5. Recently, the study of class differences among religious groups has been revived, with a number of studies documenting that significant class differences remain between American religious denominations—for example, Keister, "Religion and Wealth"; Park and Reimer, "Revisiting the Social Sources of American Christianity"; Pyle and Davidson, *Origins of Religious Stratification in Colonial America*; Smith and Farris, "Socioeconomic Inequality in the American Religious System"; Wilde, Tevington, and Shen, "Religious Inequality."

6. For example, Baltzell, *Protestant Establishment*; Demerath, *Social Class in American Protestantism*; Niebuhr, *Social Sources of Denominationalism*;

Vidich and Bensman, *Small Town in Mass Society*; Weber, *Protestant Ethic and the Spirit of Capitalism*.

7. Wilde, "Complex Religion: Interrogating Assumptions"; Wilde and Glassman, "How Complex Religion Can Improve Our Understanding of American Politics"; Wilde and Tevington, "Complex Religion: Toward a Better Understanding of the Ways in which Religion Intersects with Inequality."

8. See, for example, *Moral Combat: How Sex Divided American Christians and Fractured American Politics*.

9. Omi and Winant, *Racial Formation in the United States*.

10. Omi and Winant, 55–56.

11. Waters, *Ethnic Options*, Emerson and Smith, *Divided by Faith*, and Alba, Raboteau, and DeWind, *Immigration and Religion in America: Comparative and Historical Perspectives*, are exceptions. Early sociologists of religion saw it as "a very important factor in the preservation of racial character" (Niebuhr, *Social Sources of Denominationalism*, 110), a key source of social identity (Herberg, *Protestant, Catholic, Jew*). Sociologists of religion have continued to emphasize the importance of religion for immigrants (Cadge, *Heartwood*; Cadge and Ecklund, "Immigration and Religion"; Chen, "Religious Varieties of Ethnic Presence"; Kurien, "Multiculturalism, Immigrant Religion"; *Faith Makes Us Live*; Warner and Wittner, *Gatherings in Diaspora*; Yang and Ebaugh, "Transformations in New Immigrant Religions") and African Americans (Emerson and Smith, *Divided by Faith*; Marti, "Affinity, Identity, and Transcendence"; McRoberts, *Streets of Glory*; Patillo-McCoy, "Church Culture as a Strategy of Action"; Patterson, *Rituals of Blood*; Wood, *Faith in Action*), but this work is often not in dialogue with the work on race or intersectionality.

12. Winant, "Racism Today," 756.

13. When discussing the "American religious field," I am explicitly drawing on theories of *organizational fields*, where organizations compete "not just for resources and customers, but for political power and institutional legitimacy." DiMaggio and Powell, "Iron Cage Revisited," 150; see also Martin, "What Is Field Theory?" During the early part of the 1900s, the American religious field included religious denominations; supradenominational organizations, such as the Federal Council of Churches; and religious movements, such as the social gospel movement. While all of these have had ample historical research conducted on them individually, they have rarely been examined for their separate influences on one issue, as they are here. See, for example, Carter, *Decline and Revival of the Social Gospel*; Hutchinson, *Modernist Impulse in American Protestantism*; Marsden, *Fundamentalism and American Culture*; Phillips, *Kingdom on Earth*; Szasz, *Divided Mind of Protestant America*; Tobin, *American Religious Debate over Birth Control*.

14. Omi and Winant, *Racial Formation in the United States*, 56.

15. The falsification of alternative explanations is perhaps one of the least emphasized but, I think, one of the most crucial components of the method—a

realization to which I am forever indebted to Kim Voss (c.f., Mahoney and Rue-schemeyer, *Comparative Historical Analysis in the Social Sciences*, 10). On the issue of big questions, see Skocpol in Mahoney and Rueschemeyer, *Comparative Historical Analysis in the Social Sciences*, 407. For an incredibly useful and simple differentiation of historical versus comparative-historical research, please see Edwin Amenta's table (Amenta, in Mahoney and Rueschemeyer, *Comparative Historical Analysis in the Social Sciences*, 94).

16. Of course, there are many studies of American religion. But few of these studies place race and class in a central analytical position the way that *Birth Control Battles* does. See, for example, *Moral Combat*. Likewise, James Davison Hunter's *Culture Wars* argues that progressive religious groups (and the nonreligious) are entrenched on the left and the "orthodox" on the right because of differences in "worldviews" and does not mention class or race at all. The most important study of American religion that has class as a key part of its explanation is Robert Wuthnow's *Restructuring of American Religion*, which highlights increasing and unequal access to higher education as the key factor behind divergent views within American religion. In *Restructuring*, Wuthnow examines factors, largely post–World War II that have to do with class and access to higher education, that explain increasing attitudinal variation *within* denominations. My study differs from Wuthnow's in that I focus on earlier differences *between* denominations to explain the first issue of sex and gender that really divided them (Wuthnow, *Restructuring of American Religion*, 154).

17. As Edwin Amenta notes in in Mahoney and Rueschemeyer, *Comparative Historical Analysis in the Social Sciences*, systematic samples are often difficult, if not impossible, for most comparative-historical research (p. 104). Not having them often makes falsifying alternative explanations difficult, if not impossible.

18. Only one denomination that met this initial threshold, the African Methodist Episcopal Church, has been left out. I was unable to locate any copies of its periodical, the *Christian Recorder.*

19. Hout, Greeley, and Wilde, "Demographic Imperative in Religious Change."

20. Of course, this means that hundreds, if not thousands, of religious groups are not included in my sample. While a study of them would certainly be fascinating in its own right, given the difficulties I had obtaining the periodicals for many of the larger groups in my sample, I suspect that most would have left few traces of their views from one hundred years ago. See Goldstein and Haveman, "Pulpit and Press: Denominational Dynamics and the Growth of Religious Magazines in Antebellum America" for a thorough analysis of the connection between geographic and economic resources and the growth of religious periodicals in antebellum America.

21. Pope also noted that some groups were harder to classify, especially Lutherans: "The Lutheran denominations are harder to classify, because of their closer association with farmers, with particular ethnic backgrounds, and with skilled workers" (88).

22. Cantril, "Educational and Economic Composition of Religious Groups."

23. These archives include collections from the American Birth Control League, Margaret Sanger Papers, Sophia Smith Collection, Smith College, Northhampton, MA; American Eugenics Society, American Philosophical Society, Philadelphia; Federal Council of Churches, Presbyterian Historical Society, Philadelphia; and numerous religious denominations, including the Disciples of Christ Historical Society, Nashville; Friends Historical Library, Swarthmore College, Philadelphia; Evangelical Synod of North America Collection, Eden Theological Seminary, Webster Groves, MO; General Methodist Collection and the New England Conference Commission on Archives and History, Boston University School of Theology, Boston; Halls Index of American Presbyterian Congregations, Presbyterian Historical Society, Philadelphia; Protestant Episcopal Church, Austin, TX; Quaker Collection, Haverford College, Philadelphia; and the Southern Baptist Convention Historical Archives, Nashville.

24. The 1926 sermons survived, as did the cover letters from the 1928 competition, which gave me a total of sixty-eight sermons (counting multiple submissions only once). I was able to place sixty-two, or 91 percent (forty-two out of forty-four from 1926 and twenty out of twenty-four from 1928), in a denomination after extensive research.

25. Thompson, "Rural Arguments for Birth Control," 1037.

26. "Birth Control," 451

27. Southern Baptist Convention, *Annual of the Southern Baptist Convention*, 112.

CHAPTER ONE. AMERICAN RELIGIOUS ACTIVISM IN THE TWENTIETH CENTURY

1. As a key example, Michael Young argues that religious activism on both abolition and temperance had grown to such popularity by the 1830s that they can be credited with forming the basis of all modern social movements, including the nonreligious.

2. Oshatz, *Slavery and Sin*, 130.

3. May, *Protestant Churches and Industrial America*, 29.

4. May, 29.

5. Denominations' abolitionist stances were found, unless otherwise noted on table 6, in Hinks and McKivigan (2007).

6. Hein and Gardiner, *Episcopalians*, 76–80.

7. Young, *Bearing Witness against Sin*.

8. Carter, *Decline and Revival of the Social Gospel*, 33.

9. Phillips, *Kingdom on Earth*, 202.

10. Szasz, *Divided Mind of Protestant America*, 64.

11. "National Prohibition a Reality," 3.

12. "National Prohibition," 1.

13. "Is National Temperance a Cure for All Human Ills?," 137.

14. "Editorial: Women at the Polls," 528.

15. Trager, "Jewish Women in Palestine," 1305.

16. "Woman's Best," 51.

17. "Suffrage Victory," 15; Should Women Be Included," 3.

18. "Editorial: White Baptists," 4.

19. Sanford, *Federal Council of the Churches of Christ in America*, 554–569.

20. Sommer, "Federal Council Under Fire," 185.

21. Chambers, *Tyranny of Change*, 105–107.

22. Chambers, 105.

23. Hutchinson, *Modernist Impulse in American Protestantism*, 2.

24. Baker, "Is the Protestant Game Worth the Candle?," 907.

25. Furthermore, although many have equated a belief in modernism with support for science, when one broadens the universe of religious groups beyond Protestants, it becomes obvious that support for science, or more specifically, evolution, was not a one-to-one correlation with modernism. The best example of this would be Orthodox Jews, who were by no means modernist in most of their views (or religious identity). In 1931 they wrote in their periodical the *Jewish Forum* that "no true Jew will ever dream of conflict between science and religion, even though he may not be able in every case to reconcile the teachings of the one with the other. 'To oppose them is to make a false antithesis; they are complementary and not competitive.'" Macht, "Torah and Science Twenty-Seven Years Ago and Now," 377. Likewise, the Roman Catholic Church, discussing evolution, argued that "despite its apparently scientific character, the whole row, on both sides, is chiefly emotional." Kane, "Row over Evolution," 125–126.

26. Carter, *Decline and Revival of the Social Gospel*; Hopkins, *Rise of the Social Gospel in American Protestantism*; Hutchinson, *Modernist Impulse in American Protestantism*; Marsden, *Fundamentalism and American Culture*; May, *Protestant Churches and Industrial America*; Phillips, *Kingdom on Earth*.

27. Carter, *Decline and Revival of the Social Gospel*; Hopkins, *Rise of the Social Gospel in American Protestantism*; Rosen, *Preaching Eugenics*.

28. May, *Protestant Churches and Industrial America*, 91–92, 100, 105–108.

29. May, 110–111.

30. May, 190–191.

31. May, 184–185.

32. May, *Protestant Churches and Industrial America*; Hopkins, *Rise of the Social Gospel in American Protestantism*.

33. Carter, *Decline and Revival of the Social Gospel*, 2, 4.

34. Carter, 4.

35. Carter.

36. For example, the Society of Friends mentioned "the present abnormal extent of unemployment and low income" in its statement on birth control. Special Committee of the Women's Problems Group of Philadelphia, *Statement on Birth Control*, 4.

37. "Council Findings and Resolutions," 1032.

38. White and Hopkins, *Social Gospel*, 36.

39. May, *Protestant Churches and Industrial America*, 190. I attempted to examine this factor in greater detail via the *Census of Religious Bodies* but found that the variable it provided that distinguished between rural and urban areas was far too generous in its definition of urban to be useful.

40. "Is Protestantism Middle Class?," 68.

41. "Concerning Infant Damnation," 1036. Ironically, this quote comes from the Christian Church, which was the most rural of the denominations that were strong social gospelers (a factor that might explain the implied lack of experience of most readers of the article). The Christian Church had only 15 percent of its members living in urban areas circa 1926 (see table 2). However, the Christian Church merged with the much more urban and devout social gospeler, the Congregationalist Church, in 1930, just six years after this article was published.

42. Elsewhere I explore whether that path might have been more indirect—that is, whether earlier movements, such as abolition and temperance, led to the social gospel rather than directly to support for birth control reform and thus ended up leaving a lingering progressive bent to the groups that supported them. This also does not appear to be the case. See Wilde and Hutchenlocher, "Who Were the Social Gospelers?"

CHAPTER TWO. MOBILIZING AMERICA'S RELIGIOUS ELITE IN THE SERVICE OF EUGENICS

1. "When Laws Prohibit," 13.

2. Margaret Sanger Papers, Sophia Smith Collection, Smith College, Northampton, MA.

3. The focus on sermons and clergy may obscure connections for the much less hierarchical Society of Friends, which seems to have also been more feminist in its orientation and also seemed to be friendlier to the ABCL than other groups. Although the Society of Friends had no clergy on the ABCL board, their statement on birth control mentioned "well established committees of the birth control organizations . . . working vigorously" and even quoted an article in the *Birth Control Review*. Special Committee of the Women's Problems Group of Philadelphia, 3, 5.

4. For a more thorough examination of the issue of feminism among the early liberalizers, including a review of the rich literature on women's roles within these religious denominations, please see Wilde and Al-Faham, "Believing in Women."

5. Quote taken from a popular eugenics "tree" flyer; Ludmerer, *Genetics and American Society*; Mehler, *History of the American Eugenics Society*; Whitney, "American Eugenics Society," 252, 255.

6. For example, Thompson, "Rural Arguments for Birth Control," 1036. Of course, other nonwhite groups were also the focus of eugenicist policies, particularly regarding immigration restriction (i.e., the Japanese and Chinese Exclusion Acts; Chang, *Citizens of a Christian Nation*), intermarriage between blacks and whites, and the involuntary sterilization of many African Americans (Zuberi, *Thicker than Blood*). However, because of their geographic distribution, these other nonwhite groups were not generally of concern to the early liberalizers. Alba, *Italian Americans*; Brodkin, *How Jews Became White Folks*; FitzGerald and Cook-Martin, *Culling the Masses*; Ignatiev, *How the Irish Became White*; Jacobson, *Whiteness of a Different Color*.

7. Baker, "Godliness of New York," 121.

8. Baker, 123.

9. "Protestantism Falling Behind through Unproductive Marriages," 40.

10. As an example of both the level of detail and alarm, take the following quote:

> The New England States, the original home of American Puritanism, are now important centers of Catholicism (Massachusetts shows 1,100,000 members of the Roman Catholic Church and 450,000 members of all Protestant Churches combined!). In Illinois there are about a million Roman Catholics, while the strongest Protestant body (the Methodists) cannot show more than 300,000 adherents. In New York state we find 2,300,000 Catholics and about 300,000 Methodists, while no other Protestant body numbers more than 200,000. "Protestantism Falling Behind through Unproductive Marriages," 40.

11. Beisel and Kay, "Abortion, Race, and Gender in Nineteenth-Century America"; Evans, *Playing God?*

12. Erie, *Rainbow's End*, 2.

13. Harper, "Some Neglected Aspects of the Immigration Problem," 28.

14. "Protestantism Falling Behind through Unproductive Marriages," 40.

15. Skiff, "Fecundity of Mothers in Dependent Families," 310.

16. Glass, "Geneticists Embattled," 140; Rosen, *Preaching Eugenics*, 150–152.

17. Inge, "Some Moral Aspects of Eugenics," 9–11.

18. Franks, *Margaret Sanger's Eugenic Legacy*; Gordon, *Woman's Body, Woman's Right*.

19. For example, Hunt, "Why Birth Control?"; "Minutes from February 14, 1929," American Eugenics Society (AES) Papers, box 7, fol. "AES Minutes 1927–1929," American Philosophical Society (APS), Philadelphia, PA.

20. Hunt, "Why Birth Control?," 129.

21. For example, "Catholic Woman's Opinion," 300; Lilien, "Birth Control among Polish-American Women," 1034; Marion, "What Catholics Say," 333;

Robinson, "Recent Statistics on Differential Birth Rates," 413–418; Yarros, "Objection Disproved by Clinical Findings," 15–16.

22. Wiggam, "Progress and Prospects in the United States," 5 (emphasis added).

23. Whitney, "American Eugenics Society," 257.

24. *Eugenics at Work*, AES Papers, box 11, fol. "AES Printing Orders, 1926–1942 #1," APS, 1931. See, by way of comparison, Rosen, *Preaching Eugenics*, 157.

25. Rosen's *Preaching Eugenics* (2004) is the main contributor to this field, although it has been criticized for portraying only progressive groups as eugenicists (an inaccuracy I correct with a more systematic sample), as well as Leon's (2004) work that focuses only on a few Catholic outliers. Leon, "Hopelessly Entangled in Nordic Pre-suppositions," 3–49. Neither of these sources provide much, if any, discussion of birth control reform; Black, *War against the Weak*; Bruinius, *Better for All the World*; Franks, *Margaret Sanger's Eugenic Legacy*; Gordon, *Woman's Body, Woman's Right*; Haller, *Eugenics*; Kennedy, *Birth Control in America*; Keyles, *In the Name of Eugenics*; King and Ruggles, "American Immigration, Fertility Differentials, and the Ideology of Race Suicide," 347–369; Kline, *Building a Better Race*; Larson, *Sex, Race, and Science*; Ludmerer, *Genetics and American Society*; Pickens, *Eugenics and the Progressives*; Rafter, *White Trash*; Rafter, "Claims-Making and Socio-Cultural Context in the First U.S. Eugenics Campaign," 17–34; Rafter, *Creating Born Criminals*; Ramsden, "Social Demography and Eugenics in the Interwar United States," 547–593; Reed, *From Private Vice to Public Virtue*; Reilly, *Surgical Solution*; Stern, *Eugenic Nation*.

26. For example, Carter, *Decline and Revival of the Social Gospel*; Marsden, *Fundamentalism and American Culture*; Phillips, *Kingdom on Earth*; Szasz, *Divided Mind of Protestant America*. The sole exception is Tobin's (2001) study. Her argument is consistent with mine, although her book neither examines a systematically drawn sample nor distinguishes between some denominations that I found had important differences. Tobin, *American Religious Debate over Birth Control*.

27. Mehler, *History of the American Eugenics Society*, 88; see also Leon, "Hopelessly Entangled in Nordic Pre-suppositions," 8.

28. AES Papers, box 11, fol. "AES Printing Orders, 1926–1942 #4," APS.

29. The CCC received $4,000 out of $18,375 spent on committees. "Minutes from January 3, 1927," AES Papers, box 7, fol. "AES Minutes 1927–1929," APS.

30. The 1926 sermons survived, as did the cover letters from the sermons submitted to the 1928 competition. Together, there were a total of sixty-eight sermons submitted by the pastors of sixty-eight churches (counting multiple submissions only once), of which I was able to place sixty-two, or 91 percent (forty-two out of forty-four from 1926 and twenty out of twenty-four from 1928), in a denomination after extensive research.

31. Sherbon, "Preacher's Part," 3.

32. "Prizes for Sermons on Eugenics," 48.

33. For details on the denominational coding of the sermons, please see the methodological appendix at https://www.ucpress.edu/book/9780520303218 /birth-control-battles.

34. For individual denomination maps other than those for Roman Catholics, please see the online methodological appendix.

35. "News and Notes," 34; consistent with these geographic realities, about one-third of AES charter members in 1926 were from the Northeast. With the exception of California and Illinois (other areas with high proportions of immigrants, a point to which I will return below), which each had about seventy members, most other states were represented by between one and ten members. Mehler, *History of the American Eugenics Society*, 82, 143, 149. Figures A1 and A2 in the online appendix demonstrate that the denominations most concerned about race suicide were concentrated in the same areas with the greatest numbers of Roman Catholics (many of these same areas had large populations of Jewish immigrants as well, but their relatively smaller numbers precludes showing them on national graphs).

36. Pope, "Religion and the Class Structure," 84.

37. "Protestantism Falling Behind through Unproductive Marriages," 40. Regarding the limited Catholic involvement in the AES, see Leon, Sharon. "'Hopelessly Entangled in Nordic Pre-suppositions': Catholic Participation in the American Eugenics Society in the 1920s."

38. This is not to minimize the important differences between earlier waves of Irish Catholic immigrants and later waves of Italian Catholics, who were also generally seen as embarrassing and in need of Americanization by the mostly Irish American Catholic hierarchy at this time (see Orsi, *Madonna of 115th St.*).

39. Ellis, "Marketing to Whom?"

40. See Rosen, Preaching Eugenics.

41. Mehler, History of the American Eugenics Society, 63–65, 312; Rosen, Preaching Eugenics.

42. See, by way of comparison, Rosen, *Preaching Eugenics*, 37.

43. AES Papers, box 16, APS.

44. AES Papers, box 13, APS.

45. AES Papers, box 15, fol. 2, APS.

46. Lutz, "Jew at Our Door," 596.

CHAPTER THREE. THE EARLY LIBERALIZERS

1. MacArthur, "Eugenics and the Church," 6.

2. For individual maps of each denomination, please see figures A3–A10 in the online appendix; of course, immigrants were also Jewish; however, Jews were much smaller in proportion than Catholics, making a map of their relative proportions difficult to read.

3. Rev. P. Olin Stockwell of the Methodist Episcopal Church in Lamont, OK, "Methodist Sermon on Eugenics (Third Prize)," AES Papers, box 20, fol. "Stockwell, F. Olin," APS.

4. "Professor Skinner on Censorship," 1314.

5. "Minutes of the Universalist General Convention at Washington, DC," 76.

6. The Protestant Episcopal Church's conversation extended slightly longer than most because 1934 marked the annual conference in which it formally approved of its statement on "Eugenics." McCracken, "General Convention," 551–552.

7. "Eugenics," 292.

8. Special Committee of the Women's Problems Group of Philadelphia, *Statement on Birth Control*, 4.

9. MacArthur, "Eugenics and the Church: The Church and Courtin'," 278.

10. Whitney, "American Eugenics Society," 258.

11. "Aids to a Better Race," 586; Cooper, "Birth Control and the New Morality," 567–568; "Instinct and Promiscuity," 66; "Law of Birth Control," 582; "No Longer Evolution's Pawns," 758; "Prejudices," 582; Wilbur, "Intelligent Control of Our Human Stock," 975–976.

12. Miller, "Religion and Eugenics," 516.

13. Miller, 516.

14. Evans, "Conflict of Science and Ethics"; Fletcher, "Social Issues," 663; Fletcher, "Suppression Which Results in Expression"; Raynale, "Michigan State Convention," 1459; Rose, "Notes on a Papal Encyclical"; Thompson, "Mrs. Sanger and Birth Control in Our Country"; "Unitarians Back Birth Control," 677; Warner, "Is a Moral Code Sufficient?," 1075.

15. Bevans, "Problems of Marriage," 631–632; Holmes, "Our Newspapers and Criminals," 220–222; Smith, "Parent-Child Relationships," 165–166, 174; Smith, "Parent-Child Relationships: Part II," 217–218, 223; "Whither Are We Drifting?" 257.

16. Smith, "Parent-Child Relationships," 165.

17. Smith, "Parent-Child Relationships: Part II," 217.

18. Finding the right periodical for the Methodist Episcopal Church's Northeastern Conference, which was the only regional conference to officially liberalize, was extremely difficult because many Methodist Episcopal Church regional conferences had periodicals with exactly the same name. I thus had to rely on data from only 1931 to assess the Northeastern Conference's views of eugenics. In that year only one article was published that related to eugenics, but it offered very strong support, with a Sunday school lesson text that asked, "By what law of the application of the spirit of Jesus are we increasing the percentage of defectives and imbeciles? . . . Jesus was always the foe of disease." Stockdale, "Lesson Exposition," 122–123.

19. Stockdale, 122.

20. Stockdale, 123.

21. "Prejudices," 582.

22. The Christian Church and the Congregationalist Church and their periodicals the *Herald of Gospel Liberty* and the *Congregationalist* were going through a series of mergers at this time, which finally culminated in 1930. I conducted an analysis of both periodicals prior to the merger and found three articles promoting eugenics in the *Herald of Gospel Liberty* between 1924 and 1925 (Deer, "Consequences of the Neglect of Childhood," 56–57; "Regulating Marriage," 436; "Trend of Events: Our Immigration Regulations," 101–102), one article promoting eugenics in the *Congregationalist* in 1929 (Bishop, "Eugenics and the Church," 342–344), as well as one countering eugenic arguments (Patten, "Eugenics Again," 511). After the merger the new periodical, the *Congregationalist and the Herald of Gospel Liberty*, ramped up its publication of articles promoting eugenics, publishing three a year between 1930 and 1932 ("Bookshelf: Eugenics and Marriage," 389; "Certain Areas Breed Crime," 239; Blanchard, "Birth Control," 474–475; Scotford, "Birth Control Seems to Be Working," 1069; Spoolman, "Other Side of the Birth Control Question," 1336–1337; Thompson, "Rural Arguments for Birth Control," 1036–1037).

23. Deer, "Consequences of the Neglect of Childhood," 56. With the exception of its statements about sterilization, this was a somewhat mild article—an argument that was popular with denominations that were much more critical of eugenics, such as the Reformed Church in the US, which reprinted the article three weeks later (Deer, 10).

24. Bishop, "Birth Control," 343–344; Bishop, "Eugenics and the Church," 344.

25. Cooper, "Birth Control and the New Morality," 567.

26. Fletcher, "Social Issues," 663.

27. "Aids to a Better Race," 586.

28. I used two periodicals to piece together Reform Jews' views: the *Yearbook of the Central Conference of American Rabbis* and *Union Tidings*. Neither was popularly oriented, and the latter was only available until 1930. Despite this, a total of three articles on birth control were published between 1926 and 1930, all supportive of birth control from a eugenics standpoint (Chronbach, "Social Studies at the Hebrew Union College," 3–4; Frisch, "Report of the Commission on Social Justice," 103; Israel, "Report of the Commission of Social Justice," 85–86).

29. Frisch, "Report of the Commission on Social Justice," 103–104.

30. Israel, "Report of the Commission of Social Justice," 86.

31. "Congregational Sermon on Eugenics," AES Papers, box 13, fol. "Carlson, Walter M. 1926," APS.

32. Furnas, "Report of Women's Problems Group," 571.

33. Spoolman, "Other Side of the Birth Control Question," 1336.

34. "Instinct and Promiscuity," 66.

35. Rev. P. Olin Stockwell of the Methodist Episcopal Church in Lamont, OK, "Methodist Sermon on Eugenics (Third Prize)," AES Papers, box 20, fol. "Stockwell, F. Olin," APS.

36. Woodruff, "Social Trend," 467–468; "Chicago Clergy Comment Favorably on Report of Lambeth Conference," 580.

37. "Trend of Events: Our Immigration Regulations," 101.

38. Woodruff, "What Is Prosperity?," 397.

39. Welch, "Some Considerations on the Immigration Question," 527 (emphasis added); Woolever, "Prohibition, Crime and Criminals," 1078.

40. Canaday, "New York City Mission and Cooperation in Immigrant Work," 50.

41. Woodruff, "New American Policy Regarding Immigration," 468; "Report on the Joint Commission on a World Conference," 14–15.

42. Johnson, "Immigration Problem in the United States," 1160.

43. "Trend of Events: The Census," 744.

44. Franklin, "Message of the President," 107.

45. Wolf, "Commission on Social Justice," 89; Wolf, 69.

46. Frisch, "Report of the Commission on Social Justice," 103.

47. Frisch, 103.

48. Ellis, "Marketing to Whom?"; Kohler, "Discussion of Dr. David Philipson's Address," 7722–7734.

49. Ludmerer, Genetics and American Society, 22.

50. Kincheloe, "Changing Chicago," 1479, 1507.

51. "Catholic Losses," 514.

52. "Factors in Eminence," 50 (emphasis added).

53. "Factors in Eminence," 51.

54. Rev. Alfred O. Elliot, AES Papers, APS, 5.

55. Leiper, "Finds Booze, Incipient Crime, and Primitive Religion," 336.

56. Miller, "Among the Czech Farmers in Texas," 551.

57. Kincheloe, "Changing Chicago?," 1507.

58. Morse, "Question Mark in National Missions," 123; Warnshuis, "Mexican Man-Power and Manhood," 222.

59. "Foreigner," 844.

60. Although only Orthodox Quakers liberalized early on birth control, there was a great deal of overlap between different Quaker denominations and periodicals at this time. This is indicated by the fact that Rufus Jones, by far the most important Quaker eugenicist, published extensively in many Quaker periodicals, including the *Friend Intelligencer*, which was a Hicksite Quaker periodical. I thus gathered articles from all major Quaker periodicals. Quaker historian P. J. Benjamin wrote that "Jones was a leading liberal Friend in Philadelphia Orthodoxy who did much to redirect Quaker thought and action in the Progressive Era. But like many leading . . . religious leaders of the Social Gospel movement,

Jones saw immigrants as a threat to democracy and the American economic order." Benjamin, *Philadelphia Quakers in the Industrial Age 1865–1920*, 283; American Philosophical Society, Philadelphia, PA, American Eugenics Society Collection, box 11, fol. "AES Printing Orders, 1926–1942 #4."

61. Jones, "Nursery of Spiritual Life," 344.

62. "Puritan's Detractor," 1156; Stelzle, "Challenge of the Modern City," 273–274.

63. "Make America Catholic," 267.

64. "Before We Vote," 840.

65. Woolever, "Parochial School Controversy Carried to Washington," 496.

66. "In Darkest Boston," 729.

67. Erie, "Two Faces of Ethnic Power," 263.

68. "Whither Are We Drifting?," 257.

69. "Our Foreign Religious Groups," 555.

70. Stelzle, "Challenge of the Modern City," 273–274 (emphasis added).

71. Holmes, "Our Newspapers and Criminals," 221.

72. Elmore, "America's Back Yard," 894–895 (emphasis added).

73. AES Papers, box 14, APS.

74. "Individual Responsibility," 545.

75. Woolever, "President Hoover Checks Immigration," 589.

76. "Growing into Our Full Selves," 754.

77. Woolever, "Is Congress Representative?," 1062.

78. "Methodist Sermon on Eugenics," AES Papers, box 14, fol. "Close, Kenneth R. 1928," APS.

79. "Whither Are We Drifting?," 257.

80. Special Committee of the Women's Problems Group of Philadelphia, *Statement on Birth Control*, 5.

81. Because of the nature of their periodical, which was one of the few not directed at a lay audience, I am unable to ascertain whether Reform Jews would have specifically referenced the social gospel in their periodical, as did the other early liberalizers. However, historians agree that Reform Jews shared social gospelers' concerns about inequality and were active in the movement, the influence of which can be seen in "certain doctrines of Reform Judaism" (Carter, *Decline and Revival of the Social Gospel*, 4). Interestingly, these were codified just as the social gospel movement was taking off and was at its peak. For example, Reform Jews spelled out the following principles of modern American Reform Judaism in the 1885 Pittsburgh Platform stated that: "In full accordance with the spirit of Mosaic legislation, which strives to regulate the relation between the rich and poor, we deem it our duty to participate in the great task of modern times, to solve, on the basis of justice and righteousness, the problems presented by the contrasts and evils of the present organization of society" (Heller, *Isaac M. Wise*, 465.). As another example, in 1920 the Central Conference for American Rabbis' Commission on

Social Justice made strong statements against the "inequalities of living and earning conditions" (Central Conference of American Rabbis, *Yearbook*, 88), which not coincidentally was the commission that made most of the eugenic and birth control statements (Frisch, "Commission on Social Justice," 144–146).

82. Chalmers, "It Is Not Enough," 959.

83. McDowell, "Applied Christianity," 335.

84. McDowell, 335.

85. Stelzle, "Challenge of the Modern City," 273–274.

86. Lewis, "More Adequate Social Gospel," 455.

87. Marquis, "National Missions and the World," 543–544.

88. "Concerning Infant Damnation," 1036.

89. "Conference Discusses Wellesley Girls' Views," 72.

90. "Message to the Churches of America," 14.

91. "Is Protestantism Middle Class?," 68.

92. Morgan, "Facing the Down and Outs," 477.

93. "Trend of Events: More Evidence That Low Wages Mean a High Death Rate," 221.

94. "Chicago Clergy Comment Favorably on Report," 580.

95. Ayres, "Lambeth and Moral Enlightenment," 307.

96. Hoyt, "Genesis of the Social Gospel," 370.

97. Wiggam, "Progress and Prospects in the United States," 5.

98. Bishop, "Eugenics and the Church," 343.

99. Blanchard, "Birth Control," 474–475.

100. Hoyt, "Genesis of the Social Gospel," 370.

101. Thompson, "Rural Arguments for Birth Control," 1037.

102. "Prize Winners in the Sermon Contest," 48.

103. Rev. Rufus C. Baker to First Methodist Episcopal Church in Albuquerque, NM, 1926, "Methodist Sermon on Eugenics," AES Papers, box 13, fol. "Baker, Rufus C. 1926," APS.

CHAPTER FOUR. THE SUPPORTERS

1. For individual maps of each denomination, see figures A11–A14 in the methodological appendix at https://www.ucpress.edu/book/9780520303218/birth-control-battles.

2. "Folks, Facts and Opinion: A Resolution Favoring Legalization," 1474.

3. "Bishop Stewart on Birth Control," 484; "Folks, Facts and Opinion: The Jewish Attitude toward Birth Control," 475; "Presbyterian Birth Control Report," 634.

4. "Guidance for the Common Man," 1467.

5. "Lambeth Conference," 6.

6. Marlin, "Presbyterian Commission Approves Birth Control," 2–3.

7. Marlin, 3.

8. For example, "Birth Control," 451.

9. Hering, "What about Illegitimate Parents," 105.

10. "Mother's Day—a New Angle," 363.

11. Hering, "What about Illegitimate Parents," 105.

12. "Birth Control," 451.

13. "Birth Control," 451.

14. "Report on Birth Control," 425.

15. "Folks, Facts and Opinion: A Resolution Favoring Legalization," 1474; Beyl, "Religious Implications of Modern Psychology," 1342–1344; "Folks, Facts and Opinion: Ministers' Homes Were Given," 183.

16. "Family a Divine and Holy Institution," 453; "Heredity and Individual Responsibility," 10; Hering, "What about Illegitimate Parents?," 104–105; Hutchison, "Fitness of the Anglo-Saxon," 4; Hutchison, "Why the Anglo-Saxon," 4; "Is Birth Control Hostile to Race Culture?," 683; Jensen, "Home Missions a Real Problem," 1161–1162; Marlin, "Health Tests before Marriage," 3; Marlin, "Presbyterian Commission Approves Birth Control," 2–3; "Psychic Expert Finds Child Is 'Born Criminal,'" 888.

17. "Is Birth Control Hostile to Race Culture?," 683.

18. "Resolutions by Federal Council of Churches," 452.

19. Hering, "What about Illegitimate Parents," 104.

20. Jensen, "Home Missions a Real Problem," 1161.

21. "Folks, Facts and Opinion: The Eugenics Society," 738.

22. "Folks, Facts and Opinion: Ministers' Homes Were Given," 183.

23. "Folks, Facts and Opinion: A Severe Criticism," 286.

24. Beyl, "Religious Implications of Modern Psychology," 1343.

25. "Heredity and Individual Responsibility," 10.

26. Hutchison, "Why the Anglo-Saxon," 4.

27. Hutchison, "Fitness of the Anglo-Saxon," 4.

28. Lehmann, "General Home Mission News: Will Immigrants Overthrow the Civilization of This Country?," 41.

29. Marlin, "Emigration Exceeding Immigration in the United States," 2.

30. "Canada's Gain Is America's Loss," 197.

31. "They Were Desirable Because They Were Healthy and Strong," 708.

32. "Johnson Immigration Bill," 453.

33. "Johnson Immigration Bill," 453.

34. "Folks, Facts and Opinion: The Following Story," 167.

35. McGuire, "World in Transit," 895.

36. McAllister, "Church Saw It First," 72–73.

37. Stub, "City Church," 39.

38. Lehmann, "General Home Mission News: New Americans," 463.

39. Lovett, "Detroit Baptist Doings," 1448; Gleiss, "Can Our Large Cities Be Reached," 57.

40. Gleiss, "Can Our Large Cities Be Reached," 57.

41. Watson, "Notes from St. Louis," 232.

42. "Folks, Facts and Opinion: Authorities of the Roman Catholic," 219.

43. Enders, "Is Catholicism Losing Ground, I," 6, 8; Enders, "Is Catholicism Losing Ground, II," 6, 8.

44. Lehmann, "General Home Mission News: New Americans," 463.

45. Finn, "Anent the Problems of the Great Cities," 1128.

46. McAllister, "Church Saw It First," 72.

47. Shaw, "Milwaukee Baptists," 353.

48. Hulburt, "Foreign Missions in Milwaukee," 413.

49. Beyl, "Religious Implications of Modern Psychology," 1343.

50. "Other Side of the Immigration Question," 4.

51. "Protestant Catholics," 6.

52. "Folks, Facts and Opinion: Another Protestant Organization," 611.

53. "Protestant Catholics," 6–7.

54. "Serious Danger," 497.

55. "Stop Alien Representation," 6.

56. See also the maps for these denominations: the Evangelical Synod of North America (map A12), the Norwegian Lutheran Church (map A11), and the United Presbyterian Church of North America (map A10); Stub, "City Church," 39; Stub, "City Church," 39.

57. Finn, "Anent the Problems of the Great Cities," 1128; Gleiss, "Can Our Large Cities Be Reached," 57; Stub, "City Church," 39; Anderson, "In the Slums of a City," 988.

58. "Folks, Facts and Opinion: Down in Kentucky," 214; see also Wells, "New Fashion in Evangelism," 451–452.

59. Wells, "New Fashion in Evangelism," 451–452.

60. May, *Protestant Churches and Industrial America*, 190. Their more rural nature is obscured by the urban data provided in table 2, which relies on data from the 1926 *Census of Religious Bodies*, which unfortunately coded any county with more than 2,000 residents as "urban"; May also argues that the Northern Baptists were also "affected by the growing influence of rich laymen, especially their great and pious benefactor, John D. Rockefeller" (who were not inclined to support anticapitalist or anti-industrial theology. May, *Protestant Churches and Industrial America*, 190). However, I see no reason why "rich laymen" would have held more sway among the Northern Baptists than they did among any of the other elite denominations, of which there were many, that expressed much stronger support for the social gospel.

61. "Federal Council Message on Evangelism," 6.

62. "Federal Council Message on Evangelism," 6.

63. "Prosperity of the American People," 8.
64. "Church Cannot Be a Political Agency," 357.
65. Anderson, "In the Slums of a City," 988.
66. "National Prohibition," 1.

CHAPTER FIVE. THE CRITICS

1. For individual maps of these groups, please see figures A23–A26 in the methodological appendix at https://www.ucpress.edu/book/9780520303218/birth-control-battles.
2. Graebner, "Birth-Control Bill before Congress," 60.
3. "Presbyterian Church in the US General Assembly," 112.
4. See Wilde, *Vatican II.*
5. "Divorce and Birth Control," 5.
6. Tentler, *Catholics and Contraception*; Underwood, *Protestant and Catholic.*
7. Keeler, "New Anglo-Eastern Entente," 200; Murphy, "Communications," 373.
8. K., "Reviews: Christianity and the Race Problem," 306.
9. Walsh, "Value of Later Children in Families," 5–6.
10. Walsh, 6.
11. K., "Reviews: Christianity and the Race Problem," 306.
12. "Birth Control and Prosperity," 151.
13. K. K., "Communications: Immigration and Prosperity," 268.
14. Howard, "Sociology: Welfare and Birth Control," 554.
15. Howard, 553.
16. Benedik, "What Causes Crime?," 173–174.
17. Burkett, "Sociology," 334.
18. "Editorials: The Screen of Prejudice," 135.
19. "Editorials: Victims of Persecution," 231.
20. "Editorials: Flag-Waving Patriots," 135.
21. Keeler, "New Anglo-Eastern Entente," 200.
22. De St. Denis, "Reformation or Short Cuts," 11.
23. De St. Denis, 11.
24. For example, "Professor Skinner on Censorship," 1314; Underwood, *Protestant and Catholic.*
25. Macht, "Torah and Science Twenty-Seven Years Ago and Now," 380.
26. Burstein, "Race Prejudice," 784–785.
27. Burstein, 784–786.
28. Golding, "Klintolerance," 106.
29. Golding, 110.
30. Spitz, "Motherhood," 161 (emphasis added).
31. Graebner, "Birth Control—and a Fair Jesuit," 199 (emphasis added).

32. Graebner, 120.

33. Because of their more recent immigration history and greater propensity for farming, Lutherans' class location was more difficult to nail down than other Protestant groups but was generally similar to Catholics, if much more rural. Pope argued that "the Lutheran denominations are harder to classify, because of their closer association with farmers, with particular ethnic backgrounds, and with skilled workers." Pope, "Religion and the Class Structure," 89.

34. Sommer, "Dr. Howard A. Kelly on Birth Control," 114.

35. Sommer, "Birth Control," 299.

36. Sommer, "Dr. Howard A. Kelly on Birth Control," 114.

37. Sommer, "Birth Control," 299.

38. Graebner, "Birth Control—and a Fair Jesuit," 199 (emphasis added).

39. Graebner, "Birth-Control Bill before Congress," 60.

40. Sommer, "Is the Lutheran Church a Foreign Church?," 197.

41. Sommer, 197.

42. For example, Boyer, "Sustaining the Glory of Motherhood," 575–578.

43. Evans, "Heritage and Promise," 131–132.

44. Evans, 132.

45. Perry, "Be Fruitful and Multiply," 679.

46. Hall, "Immigration Restriction and World Eugenics," 125.

47. Hall, 125.

48. Farmer, "Current Topics: Birth Control," 7, 11.

49. Mullins, "Christianity at the Cross Roads," 7.

50. Mullins, 7.

51. Porter, "Virgin Birth of Jesus," 8.

52. "Georgia Baptist Orphans Home Has Fine Dairy," 9.

53. Moore, "Religion in the Home," 70–73.

54. Cartledge, "Timeless Question," 554.

55. Cartledge, 554.

56. "Illusion of the Horizon," 329.

57. Eugenicist religious groups such as the Oneida Community, for example, which went so far as to actually breed children, choose parents on the basis of a number of attributes. Along with physical attributes, such as strength and attractiveness, spirituality was key. Wonderley, *Oneida Community*; Klaw, *Without Sin*.

58. Lehmann, "General Home Mission News: Will Immigrants Overthrow the Civilization of This Country?" 41; Harkness, "Stranger within Our Gates," 390.

59. Beyl, "Religious Implications of Modern Psychology," 1343.

60. Sparthey, "Contribution of the Foreign-Born to the United States," 715.

61. Sparthey, 715.

62. Sparthey, 715 (emphasis added).

63. Sparthey, 715 (emphasis added).

64. Sparthey, 715.

65. Herring, "This Little Room of Ours," 20.

66. Binns, "Book Reviews," 31.

67. Lingle, "Religious Liberty," 30.

68. "With the Hospital Family," 28.

69. Sparthey, 715.

70. Hoyt, "Christian Americans," 523.

71. See also Olgers, "What the Reformed Church Is Doing to Bring the Spirit of Christ in Race Relations," which chronicles the number of Poles, Germans, Russian, Italians, Swedes, Irish, and so forth in Chicago.

72. "Compelling Home Missions Task," 354.

73. "Compelling Home Missions Task," 354.

74. "Compelling Home Missions Task," 354.

75. "Compelling Home Missions Task," 354.

76. "Home Mission Board Departments," 17.

77. Kincheloe, "Changing Chicago," 1507.

78. Withoft, "W.M.S. and Y.W.A. Program for March," 16–17.

79. Withoft, 16–17.

80. Sparthey, "Contribution of the Foreign-Born to the United States," 715.

81. "Gospel in Italian for One Cent," 264.

82. Paxon, "Forecast of Business Conditions," 19.

83. Paxon, 19.

84. Sparthey, "Contribution of the Foreign-Born to the United States," 715.

85. Sommer, "Blind Leaders," 37.

86. Granade, "Light That Grows," 30.

CHAPTER SIX. THE SILENT GROUPS

1. For maps of each individual denomination chronicled in this chapter, please see figures A15–A22 in the online appendix.

2. Pope, "Religion and the Class Structure," 89.

3. That is, with the exception of the MECS. The collapse of the *Methodist Quarterly Review* in 1930, just as many groups were making their pronouncements on birth control, made conclusively coding the MECS's position on birth control next to impossible (it could have indicated unofficial support or open criticism of birth control reform at any point in the next year and a half after the journal collapsed, or it could have simply remained silent—there is basically no way to know for certain in the absence of a periodical). Its more positive views of immigrants and lack of concern about race suicide is generally consistent with the position of other white groups from the South. The only article that touched

on eugenics asserted that although physical descent matters, we determine the "growth or retardation" of our children (Hammond, "Human Races and the Race of Man," 624). Given the limited evidence, I do not focus on the MECS as evidence for any of my claims.

4. Evans, "Evolution and the Bible," 10–11.

5. "Darwinian Law Given Unique Interpretation," 2.

6. "Editorial: White Baptists," 4.

7. Unfortunately, there is no data on the percent of each denomination who were foreign-born. The 1926 *Census of Religious Bodies* did not gather individual-level data on each denomination.

8. "Heredity Fiasco," 13.

9. Eleazar, "Popular Fallacies about Race Relations," 30–31.

10. Ewers, "This Things of Prejudice," 27.

11. Barnett, "Responsibility of the Church toward the Problem of Crime," 9; Blemker, "Atmosphere," 9; Deer, "Consequences of Neglect of American Childhood," 10; Kern, "Proper Starting Point, 12–13; "Parents—Stop, Look and Listen!," 3–4; "Put the Accent on Evangelism," 5; "Religion in the Home," 4; Schaeffer, "Christian Endeavor Topic," 30–31. This was not a unique year for this periodical. In 1931 it published six articles that were critical of eugenics.

12. "Parents—Stop, Look and Listen!," 3.

13. "Religion in the Home," 4.

14. Blemker, "Atmosphere," 9.

15. Freas, "Port Work for Immigrants," 8.

16. Like the MECS's periodical, the *S.A.J. Review* folded in 1929, just as the wave of birth control liberalizations began. I have left them in the silent category despite this, however, because their official statements were available in *Proceedings of the Committee on Jewish Law and Standards of the Conservative Movement (1927–1970)* and *Proceedings of the Rabbinical Assembly of the Jewish Theological Seminary of America (1927–1932)*, and neither source mentioned birth control at this time. In comparison, Reform Jews' official statements made multiple positive comments about both birth control and eugenics, and they, too, did not have a popularly oriented periodical; Kaplan, "Why It Is Hard to Be a Jew," 10.

17. Butchart, "Reinterpretation of the Immigrant," 24.

18. Treudley, "Scaling the Tower of Babel," 8–11.

19. Butchart, "Reinterpretation of the Immigrant," 23–24.

20. "Christian View of Exclusion," 65.

21. "Christian View of Exclusion," 65.

22. "Christian View of Exclusion," 65.

23. Gordon, "Nature and Method of Religion," 8.

24. Spinka, "Race Prejudice and the Immigrant," 7.

25. "What Is Your Attitude toward the Foreigner?," 245.

26. Demarest, "Interpretations," 358.

27. The sole exceptions were the Churches of Christ, which simply said little about social issues in their periodical the *Gospel Advocate* and nothing at all about eugenics.

28. Taylor, "Why We Are Where We Are," 27–28.

29. "This Compact World," 4.

30. "Board of Temperance and Social Welfare," 45.

31. Burnham, "Unredeemed America," 14–15.

32. Taylor, "Work of the Board of Temperance and Social Welfare," 31–55.

33. It seems that many of the critics to whom this article was referring were within the denomination. Two earlier articles from the *Christian Intelligencer and Mission Field* ("Present Day Foes of Christianity," 532; "Social Gospel and the Community Church," 689, 696) on the topic were much more skeptical than the one quoted here.

34. Studens, "Point of View: Mass Production," 440.

35. Schaeffer, "Christian Endeavor Topic," 30.

36. "Social Obligation of the Church," 4.

37. "Corporate Application of Christianity," 719, 721–723.

38. Landesman, "Lessons We Can Learn from the Economic Crisis," 192.

39. "Vision of Social Gospel," 4.

40. "Corporate Application of Christianity," 724.

41. Spottswood, "State of the Church," 23.

42. Taylor, "Why We Are Where We Are," 27–28.

43. Ewers, "This Things of Prejudice," 27.

44. Although the fact that they reprinted this article could certainly be taken as an indication that the Reformed Church in the United States was in favor of eugenics, which I initially concluded, the overall tone of the journal makes this unlikely and suggests that it was reprinted not because of the article's argument that "subnormals" should be sterilized but because of this article's argument that "these are the children who may go either up or down according to environment and training. A recent estimate was made that eighty per cent of juvenile delinquents are in this class. Herein is our hope." Deer, "Consequences of the Neglect of Childhood," 56–57; Deer, "Consequences of Neglect of American Childhood," 10.

45. "We and Our Children," 4.

46. Ironically, the fact that the majority of silent denominations did not see themselves as racially distinct from immigrants meant that, like Southern whites, these denominations saw only the Catholicism of immigrants as a problem; one that could be easily remedied via proselytization efforts. Thus, for example, under the subheading, "The Italians," the United Lutheran Church of America mentioned that it planned to "gather the large unchurched, careless and indifferent of this nationality who have lost their faith in the Roman Catholic Church." Roehner, "United Lutheran Church and the Immigrant," 19.

47. Spinka, "Race Prejudice and the Immigrant," 7–8.

48. Both the Northern Baptist Convention and the United Presbyterian Church in North America were unofficial supporters of birth control, supportive of legalization in general but disturbed by the FCC's statement because they felt that it implied that they, too, as members of the FCC, were in favor of official liberalization.

49. "Criticizing the Federal Council," 3.

CHAPTER SEVEN. THE RELIGIOUS PROMOTERS OF CONTRACEPTION

1. American Baptist Convention, *Year Book of the American Baptist Convention, 1960, New York*, 69.

2. Herbster, "State of the Church," 9.

3. Bailey, "Crisis Demands Leadership," 24.

4. Bailey, 24.

5. Coffman, *Christian Century and the Rise of the Protestant Mainline*.

6. "More than a Bad Dream," 861.

7. "More than a Bad Dream," 861.

8. Montagu, "Too Many People," 3.

9. Beacon Press Book Ad, "Silent Explosion," 123.

10. Montagu, "Too Many People," 20.

11. Wilder, "Planned Parenthood in India," 11–12.

12. Cabell, "Christian Examines Planned Parenthood," 17.

13. Cabell, 17.

14. Private Rights and Rising Birth Rates," 30.

15. Irvine, "Population Growth in the United States," 8.

16. Tentler, Catholics and Contraception, 34.

17. American Jewish Committee, "News."

18. Roberts, *Killing the Black Body*.

19. Cater, "Church and the 'Reliefers,'" 232–235.

20. The Northern Baptists' early but unofficial support for contraception seems to have landed them halfway between the ultimate sexual progressiveness of the early liberalizers and the staunch sexual conservativism of the other groups. However, because their promotion of birth control through the 1960s was much closer to the religious promoters than to the reluctant endorsers examined in the next chapter and they would have been quite lonely in a chapter on their own, I have included them here.

21. The Society of Friends reunified with the Hicksite Friends (to become the Friends General Conference) in 1955.

22. The Evangelical and Reformed Church formed as a merger between the Evangelical Synod of North America and the Reformed Church in the United States in 1934, just after the first wave of birth control liberalization. The Evangelical Synod had been an unofficial supporter of birth control, whereas the Reformed Church in the United States had been one of the most outspoken critics of eugenic beliefs among religious leaders. I found no evidence that the Reformed Church in the United States' minority skepticism about eugenics affected the attitudes of the new denomination. The UCC was an outspoken promoter of birth control and as racialized as any of the other groups examined here. The UCC published four articles on birth control in 1965, which is among the most of any early liberalizer. The tone of its articles is very similar to the others, with a focus on the "crisis" in India, China, and Latin America and weaker, but still present, concern about the inner cities in the United States.

23. Those two groups merged with the Presbyterian Church in the United States, the Southern wing of the denomination that was initially quite critical of reform and maintained its identity as a sexual conservative.

24. United States v. One Package of Japanese Pessaries (1936), 11–13.

25. Black, *War against the Weak*; Larson, *Sex, Race, and Science*; Pickens, *Eugenics and the Progressive*.

26. Lopez, "Hijacking Immigration?," 50; Baker, "Christianity and Eugenics," 301; Allen, "Eugenics and Modern Biology," 324.

27. Allen, "Eugenics and Modern Biology"; Barkan, *Retreat of Scientific Racism*; Black, *War against the Weak*; Hansen and King, *Sterilized by the State*; Larson, *Sex, Race, and Science*; Pickens, *Eugenics and the Progressive*.

28. Bruinius, *Better for all the World*; Burch and Pendell, *Human Breeding and Survival*; Franks, *Margaret Sanger's Eugenic Legacy*; Hansen and King, *Sterilized by the State*, 186–187; Larson, *Sex, Race, and Science*; Pickens, *Eugenics and the Progressive*.

29. Baker, "Christianity and Eugenics," 299; Franks, *Margaret Sanger's Eugenic Legacy*, 186–187.

30. Franks, 83; Burch and Pendell, *Human Breeding and Survival*, 153.

31. Bruinius, *Better for all the World*; Burch and Pendell, *Human Breeding and Survival*, 153.

32. It was published under that name until 1969, when it changed its name to *Social Biology*.

33. Osborn, "Population Problems and the American Eugenics Society," 3a.

34. Van Cleave, "Letters to the Editor," 26.

35. Montagu, "Too Many People," 20.

36. "Encourage Medical Missions to Promote Family Planning," 22.

37. Bailey, "Crisis Demands Leadership," 24.

38. "Coping with Illiteracy," 11.

39. Other areas of the world with large Catholic presences were also mentioned in relation to Vatican II. Take, for example, the following summary of Bishop Simmons of India's statements in *Friends Journal* in 1965:

> Bishop Simmons of India linked [concerns about peace] to the problem of controlling the population increase and made it clear that he sees no ground for withholding birth control, on the ground that interfering with nature, in a world where the very process of modern technology and medicine have uplifted man by precisely the method of "interfering with nature" and directing it to the service of man's needs. This kind of voice from India is of high significance here. Steere, "Extracts from a Roman Journal," 585–586.

40. Crook, "Hope for Birth Control," 16.

41. The first indication that the Roman Catholic Church was not going to liberalize on contraception was suggested by Paul VI in his speech to the United Nations in late 1965. In that speech the pope emphasized that world leaders should focus on feeding the hungry, not limiting their presence at the "banquet of life": "Your task is so to act that there will be enough bread at the table of mankind and not to support an artificial birth control that would be irrational, with the aim of reducing the number of those sharing in the banquet of life." http://w2.vatican.va/content/paul-vi/en/speeches/1965/documents/hf_p-vi_spe_19651004_united-nations.html. However, at this time even the pope's speech was not seen as the final word on the matter, as the following quote from *Presbyterian Life* indicates: "The Pontiff has spoken before against 'artificial' control of birth. It remains to be seen whether the final Roman Catholic position on the subject will be that the new birth control pills are 'artificial' in this sense. (The matter is now in the hands of a papal commission.)." Fiske, "Prospects for Peace Following Papal Visit," 22–23.

42. In 1940, the *Christian Century* published the following strong article still focused on the fertility of poor whites in Appalachia:

> In one of his addresses dealing with the social effects of the new racialism in the American scene, Dr. Haynes pointed out that some of the fundamental problems involved are not so much racial as economic. He made the astonishing statement that "in the depleted and eroded lands from Virginia to Mississippi the largest families in America are being born today, both among whites and blacks. They are the sharecroppers of both races, the migrant, landless people who are called upon to till the peopleless land—land owned by absentees who are interested only in what they take out and are not concerned about putting anything back into the soil." These people, he went on to point out, are the sources of industrial labor today, crowding the cities ready to work at starvation wages and flooding the relief agencies. And for every Negro among them, he said, there are at least two poverty-stricken whites. "Haynes Calls Race Issue Economic," 358.

43. "Private Rights and Rising Birth Rates," 30.

44. "Birth Control Statute to Go to High Court," 26 (emphasis added; see also 55).

45. "Simple Justice," 8.

46. "Private Rights and Rising Birth Rates," 29–31.

47. Cabell, "Christian Examines Planned Parenthood," 16.

48. Emko Company, "You Were Mentioned in a Discussion on Birth Control," 56–57.

49. Emko Company, 56–57.

50. Emko Company, 56–57.

51. "Population Problem," 141.

52. Cater, 232–235.

53. Cater, 232–235.

54. Cater, 232–235.

55. Cater, 232–235.

56. Cater, 232–235.

57. Cater, 232–235.

58. "Simple Justice," 8.

59. Vaughn, "California's Disgrace," 8–9.

60. Thorkelson, "Biological Engineering," 188–189.

61. Thorkelson, 188–189.

62. Guttmacher, "Church, State, and Babies," 3–4.

63. "Promoting Family Planning," 980 (emphasis mine).

64. Costales, "Letter from Pakistan," 108.

65. "Private Rights and Rising Birth Rates," 30 (emphasis added).

66. Guttmacher, "Church, State, and Babies," 3.

67. Emko Company, 56–57.

68. "Better Ministry Needed in Parenthood Population Field," 23.

69. Cabell, "Christian Examines Planned Parenthood."

CHAPTER EIGHT. THE FORGOTTEN HALF

1. The sole exception to this statement is the Norwegian Lutheran Church in America, which was a very eugenicist, but unofficial, supporter of birth control in the first wave. By the second wave, this denomination and its eugenicist beliefs had virtually disappeared in a series of mergers that are difficult to disentangle. In 1946 it changed its name to the Evangelical Lutheran Church. In 1960, it merged with a few other denominations to become the American Lutheran Church of America. The American Lutheran Church published only two brief articles on birth control in its periodical the *Lutheran Standard* during the years searched. Both of them appeared in 1965, and both affirmed its place only within the confines of Christian marriage—arguing, for example:

> To enable them more thankfully to fully receive God's blessing and reward, a married couple may so plan and govern their sexual relations that any child born to their union will be desired both for itself and in relation to the time of its birth. In God's

providence, and as a result of the power He gave man to subdue the earth and have dominion over it (Gen 1:28), man has developed various means by which a married couple may control the number and the spacing of the births of their children. The means which the married pair uses to determine the number and spacing of the births of their children are a matter for them to decide with their own consciences, on the basis of competent medical advice, and in a sense of accountability to God. Schneider, "Question Box," 28.

The American Lutheran Church merged with the Lutheran Church of America (formerly the United Lutheran Church of America, which had been critical of eugenics and silent on birth control during the first wave) to form the Evangelical Lutheran Church of America in 1988 but began making joint statements as early as 1966. Although these Lutheran denominations went through too many mergers to justify any serious claims about them, the 1966 joint statement makes no reference to world population and focuses entirely on whether and when married couples might want or need to use contraception. This is consistent with my argument that the groups that were either silent or critical of birth control during the first wave liberalized in a much more circumscribed fashion.

2. In 1965, the *Lutheran* reported that the Lutheran Church in America's Executive Council had decided that contraceptive information should be made available to all people, in a statement that was much more focused on responsible parenthood than the other denominations chronicled in this chapter:

> Information on responsible parenthood and family planning should be made available to all people. . . . "To deprive large segments of the world's population at home and abroad of the learning essential to *responsible* family planning . . . is a cruel complement to the life-saving outreach of Christian charity," the statement continued. "*Irresponsible conception of children* . . . and selfish limitation of offspring" are both violations of Christian precepts, it noted. "Share Information about Family Planning, LCA Advises," 29.

3. Given the global and more hierarchical nature of the Roman Catholic Church, where doctrinal decisions about things such as contraception are made at the Vatican and apply to the entire world, the issue of Roman Catholic decisions about birth control needs much more attention than I have the space to give in this chapter. Please see my book on Vatican II and particularly my chapter on birth control reform (or the reasons for the lack thereof) at the council for an in-depth look at how and why the council ultimately did not reform the Roman Catholic stance on contraception. Wilde, *Vatican II*.

4. Of course, it is possible that the silent groups mentioned contraception on an off year for which I did not conduct key word searches. However, the point here is that whereas the religious promoters of contraception discussed it actively, usually in both 1955 and 1965, these groups remained much more circumspect.

5. "Sixth World Order Study Conference," 242.

6. Because this was a focus of almost all of the religious groups in my sample in 1965, I excluded these discussions from the analysis in both this and the previous chapter.

7. Maasen, "More Children, Please!," 10.

8. General Synod of the Reformed Church in America, 1960, 181–182.

9. General Synod of the Reformed Church in America, 1960, 181–182.

10. General Synod of the Reformed Church in America, 1960, 181–182.

11. General Synod of the Reformed Church in America, 1960, 181–182 (emphasis added).

12. One article by Klein in *Conservative Judaism* mentioned overpopulation. The article, titled "Science and Some Ethical Issues," was a review of a paper by neuroendocrinologist Hudson Hoaglang, leader of the foundation that helped invent the birth control pill. It dispassionately discussed issues as varied as eugenic sterilization, nuclear testing, artificial insemination, and lobotomies and was thus very different in tone from the strong concern about overpopulation (although concern was certainly present) articulated in the articles published by the religious promoters of contraception.

13. Lasker, "Rabbi and the Pre-Marital Interview," 30.

14. Bokser, "Committee on Jewish Laws and Standards," 1452.

15. Disciples of Christ, "Reports of the Church," 167–168.

16. Disciples of Christ, 168.

17. Disciples of Christ, 168.

18. Southern Baptist Convention, *Annual of the Southern Baptist Convention.*

19. Schuller, "God Is Calling Us to Take Part in a Revolution," 7–8.

20. Lutheran Church–Missouri Synod, *Human Sexuality*, 19–20.

21. Lutheran Church–Missouri Synod, 19–20.

22. Church of Jesus Christ of Latter-day Saints, "Birth Control."

23. Booth-Clibborn, "Pulse of a Dying World: New Birth Control," 13.

24. Booth-Clibborn, "Pulse of a Dying World: Sterilization or Regeneration," 12.

25. "Birth Control by Pills," 2.

26. https://ag.org/Beliefs/Topics-Index/Medical-Birth-Control.

27. "Watchman Answers," 27.

28. Seton, "Christian Ideals for Modern Marriage"; *Review and Herald*, 2.

29. Seventh-day Adventists, for whom a focus on religious freedom was always paramount, did spend a great deal of time on the Roman Catholic Church and industrialized countries like the United States, Canada, Spain ("Spanish Catholics Are Polled on Religious Freedom," 32), and Italy ("Birth Control in the News," 27), where the Roman Catholic Church had so far successfully prevented birth control from being legalized. For example, an article titled "Cardinal Will Not Oppose Amendment of Birth Control Law" reported that Roman Catholic

authorities in Boston said they would not oppose an amendment to the Massachusetts birth control laws allowing greater access (31).

30. Winn, "Birth Control; Pro or Con?," 46.

31. Maxwell, "Is the White Domination of the World about to End?," 5.

32. "News in Review," 12.

33. Seventh-day Adventist Church, "Ironically, Early Adventists Were Reluctant Missionaries," www.adventist.org/en/information/history/article/go/-/ironically-early-adventists-were-reluctant-missionaries/.

34. Seventh-day Adventist Church, "United for Mission: One Hundred and Fifty Years," www.adventist.org/en/information/history/article/go/-/united-for-mission-one-hundred-and-fifty-years/.

35. *Wikipedia*, "History of Jehovah's Witnesses, https://en.wikipedia.org/wiki/History_of_Jehovah%27s_Witnesses.

36. Roper, "Items on Birth Control," 629.

37. Ancketill, "On Birth Control," 114.

38. "Will Spend $51,000,000 Studying Man," 559.

39. The Witnesses did not exactly paint a flattering portrait of immigrants, particularly Roman Catholics. One article titled "Distribution of Insane" in their periodical *Golden Age* implied that Roman Catholics made up the bulk of the insane:

> The distribution of the insane is interesting. Of course, the location of the sanest of the country must be the capital city, but the District of Columbia leads in the number of insane with a percentage of 0.8406 per cent., over twice that of the next competitor, which is Roman Catholic Massachusetts with 0.3761 per cent. The Federal Hospital for the insane is at Washington, but no such excuse can be offered for Massachusetts. What foreign birth and religion may have to do with this may appear from the fact that the percentage of insane in Wyoming is 0.1207 percent. Massachusetts has between three and four times the best of Wyoming both in insane and in foreign born (56).

Likewise, in another article, the Witnesses criticized Catholic education:

> The percentage of illiteracy in the various classes in the United States show that the nation takes care of its own, but neglects the immigrant. Among the foreign-born whites, illiteracy is highest among those who come to our shores from countries where the Roman Catholic religion predominates. Much education is carried on in the United States in sectarian parochial schools; but it is reported that when students are transferred from parochial schools to good public schools they often have to be dropped one or two grades, suggesting that education under Roman Catholic auspices, as far as efficiency is concerned, is a mere camouflage, and that ecclesiasticism has no intention of giving its young people any better education than it is compelled to give. "Educational Failure at Home," 495.

40. "Questions from Readers," 766.

41. "Questions from Readers," 766.

42. "Birth Control—Who Should Decide?," 23–24.

CONCLUSION

1. "Prizes for Sermons on Eugenics," 48.

2. "Prizes for Sermons on Eugenics," 48.

3. "Prizes for Sermons on Eugenics," 48.

4. Harless, "New Morality," 741–742; Van Oostenburg, "Report on the State of Religion," 8–13, 29.

5. As Marie Griffiths argues in *Moral Combat*, these divergent paths on birth control are clearly connected to divergent views on other issues of sex and sexuality—issues that deeply divide American politics today. A comparative-historical study of these issues, which include sex education, feminism, abortion, and homosexuality, would require the same amount of data to be gathered over the sixty years since the pill was invented.

6. The four contraceptives were two emergency contraceptive pills called Plan B (levonorgestrel) and Ella (ulipristal acetate) and two intrauterine devices (IUDs) called ParaGard (copper IUD) and Mirena and Skyla (levonorgestrel-releasing IUDs).

7. https://penews.org/features/the-battle-for-religious-liberty and https://penews.org/news/return-on-investment.

8. Of course, the sides went far beyond religious divisions. Political conservatives, eager to critique Obama and his health-care plan, leaped to the defense of the plaintiffs. One article in the *New York Times* reported that Rick Santorum described the health-care policy as "a direct assault on the First Amendment, not only a direct assault on freedom of religion, by forcing people specifically to do things that are against their religious teachings" on Fox News. (Mr. Santorum also accused Mr. Obama of having argued that the Catholic Church should be forced to ordain women, which of course is not true.) The same article also reported: "In a floor speech, House Speaker John Boehner called the contraception rule an 'unambiguous attack on religious freedom' and said the federal government was 'violating a First Amendment right that has stood for more than two centuries.' Mr. Boehner also floated the idea that he would take legislative action. Mitch McConnell, the minority leader in the Senate, noted that he and other Republican senators had already put forward bills to override the rule." Cited in Rosenthal, "It's Not about Religious Freedom."

9. Today these groups are joined by the ever-growing segment of the population that has no religious affiliation, the *nones*, or the *seculars*, who are often pitted against the religious Right. For example, see Margolis, *From Politics to the Pews.*

10. Walton, "Hobby Lobby Supreme Court Case."

11. Walton.

12. Of course, this is at its very core gendered—in the way that "reproducing the race" became the sole responsibility of women. See Beisel and Kay, "Abortion,

Race, and Gender in Nineteenth-Century America"; Roberts, *Killing the Black Body.*

13. Unfortunately, despite theoretical advances like "doing religion" that argue that one cannot "do religion" (Avishai, "'Doing Religion' in a Secular World") without "doing gender" (West and Zimmerman, "Doing Gender"), the study of gender is often marginalized in "the subfield of sociology of religion" and there is a "lackluster interest in religion among sociologists of gender" (Avishai, Jafar, and Rinaldo, "Gender Lens on Religion").

14. Banks, "Southern Baptists Pray for 'Favorable' Hobby Lobby Ruling"; it is worth noting that the more moderate religious groups, the reluctant converts, have been largely left out of the debate.

15. United Church of Christ, "Health Equity and the Supreme Court Decision on Contraception."

16. United Church of Christ, "Statement of Mission," www.ucc.org/beliefs _statement-of-mission.

17. Crosby, "Experiment in Colored Work," 567–568; Woodruff, "New American Policy Regarding Immigration, 468."

18. Hinman, "'Self-Cure of Race Prejudice,'" 267; Clinchy, "Up from Patronage," 170–171; Bishop, "Eugenics and the Church."

References

"Aids to a Better Race." *Christian Register* 109, no. 28 (1930): 586.

Alba, Richard. *Italian Americans: Into the Twilight of Ethnicity.* Englewood Cliffs, NJ: Prentice-Hall, 1985.

Alba, Richard, Albert J. Raboteau, and Josh DeWind. *Immigration and Religion in America: Comparative and Historical Perspectives.* New York: New York University Press, 2008.

"Aliens." *Reformed Church Messenger* 94, no. 43 (1925): 5.

Allen, Garland E. "Eugenics and Modern Biology: Critiques of Eugenics, 1910–1945." *Annals of Human Genetics* 75, no. 3 (2011): 314–325.

Alvis, Joel L. *Religion and Race: Southern Presbyterians, 1946–1983.* Tuscaloosa: University of Alabama Press, 1994.

Amenta, Edwin. "What We Know about the Development of Social Policy." In *Comparative Historical Analysis in the Social Sciences,* edited by James Mahoney and Dietrich Rueschemeyer, 91–130. Cambridge: Cambridge University Press, 2003.

American Baptist Convention. *Year Book of the American Baptist Convention, 1959, Containing Historical Documents and Tables; Minutes of and Reports Submitted at the Fifty-Second Meeting of the Convention Held at Des Moines, Iowa June 4–9, 1959.* Des Moines: American Baptist Publication Society, 1959, 170.

———. *Year Book of the American Baptist Convention, 1960, Containing Historical Documents and Tables; Minutes of and Reports Submitted at the*

Fifty-Third Meeting of the Convention Held at Rochester, New York June 2–7, 1960. Philadelphia: American Baptist Publication Society, 1960.

American Jewish Committee. "News." 1964. http://ajcarchives.org/main.php.

Ancketill, Henry. "On Birth Control." *Golden Age* 5, no. 100 (1932): 114.

Anderson, L. O. "In the Slums of a City." *Lutheran Church Herald* 14, no. 29 (1930): 988.

Atwood, Craig D., Frank S. Mead, and Samuel S. Hill. *Handbook of Denominations in the United States*. 12th ed. Nashville: Abingdon, 2005.

Avishai, Orit. "'Doing Religion' in a Secular World: Women in Conservative Religions and the Question of Agency." *Gender and Society* 22, no. 4 (2008): 409–433.

Avishai, Orit, Afshan Jafar, and Rachel Rinaldo. "A Gender Lens on Religion." *Gender and Society* 29, no. 1 (2015): 5–25.

Ayres, Richard Flagg. "Lambeth and Moral Enlightenment." *Living Church* 84, no. 9 (1930): 307–308.

Bailey, J. "Crisis Demands Leadership." *United Church Herald* 8, no. 18 (1965): 24.

Baker, G. J. "Christianity and Eugenics: The Place of Religion in the British Eugenics Education Society and the American Eugenics Society, C. 1907–1940." *Social History of Medicine* 27, no. 2 (2014): 281–302.

Baker, Gordon H. "How to Play the Game." *Baptist* 10, no. 47 (1929): 1435.

Baker, Ray Sannard. "The Godlessness of New York." *American Magazine* 68, no. 2 (1909): 117–127.

Baltzell, E. Digby. *The Protestant Establishment: Aristocracy and Caste in America*. New York: Random House, 1964.

Banks, Adelle M. "Southern Baptists Pray for 'Favorable' Hobby Lobby Ruling." *Christian Century*, June 12, 2014. www.christiancentury.org /article/2014-06/southern-baptists-pray-favorable-hobby-lobby-ruling.

Barkan, Elazar. *The Retreat of Scientific Racism: Changing Concepts of Race in Britain and the United States between the World Wars*. Cambridge: Cambridge University Press, 2000.

Barnett, Carl. "The Responsibility of the Church toward the Problem of Crime." *Reformed Church Messenger* 93, no. 43 (1924): 9.

Barrett, Deborah, and Charles Kurzman. "Globalizing Social Movement Theory: The Case of Eugenics." *Theory and Society* 33, no. 5 (2004): 487–527.

Beacon Press Book Ad. "The Silent Explosion." *Unitarian Universalist Register-Leader* 147, no. 2 (1965): 12.

"Before We Vote." *Christian Register* 107, no. 42 (1928): 840–841.

Beisel, Nicola, and Tamara Kay. "Abortion, Race, and Gender in Nineteenth-Century America." *American Sociological Review* 69, no. 4 (2004): 498–518.

Benedik, Anthony M. "What Causes Crime?" *America* 32, no. 8 (1924): 173–174.

Benjamin, P. S. "The Philadelphia Quakers in the Industrial Age, 1865–1920." PhD diss., Columbia University, New York, 1967.

"Better Ministry Needed in Parenthood Population Field." *Christian Advocate* 9, no. 8 (1965): 23.

Bevans, George E. "The Problems of Marriage." *Presbyterian Magazine* 35, no. 12 (1929): 631–632.

Beyl, John L. "The Religious Implications of Modern Psychology." *Baptist* 10, no. 44 (1929): 1342–1344.

Binns, W. P. Moultrie "Book Reviews: Five Present-Day Controversies." *Christian Index* 104, no. 25 (1924): 31.

"Birth Control and Prosperity." *America* 42, no. 7 (1929): 151.

"Birth Control by Pills." *Pentecostal Evangel*, no. 2136 (1955): 2.

"Birth Control in the News." *Liberty* 60, no. 2 (1965): 27.

"Birth Control." *Lutheran Church Herald* 15, no. 15 (1931): 451.

"Birth Control Out as Issue of Presbyterians." *New Era and Presbyterian Magazine*. Philadelphia: 1998 Society, 1931.

"Birth Control Statute to go to High Court." *Presbyterian Life* 18, no. 2 (1965): 25–26.

"Birth Control—Who Should Decide? You or the Church?" *Awake!* (September 1989): 22–24.

Bishop, Edwin. "Eugenics and the Church." *Congregationalist* 114, no. 37 (1929): 342–344.

"Bishop Stewart on Birth Control." *Baptist* 12, no. 16 (1931): 484.

Black, Edwin. *War against the Weak: Eugenics and America's Campaign to Create a Master Race.* New York: Four Walls Eight Windows, 2004.

Blanchard, Ferdinand Q. "Birth Control." *Congregationalist and Herald of Gospel Liberty* 117, no. 15 (1932): 474–475.

Blemker, R. W. "Atmosphere." *Reformed Church Messenger* 93, no. 22 (1924): 9.

"Board of Temperance and Social Welfare." *World Call* 11, no. 10 (1929): 45.

Bolzendahl, Catherine, and Clem Brooks. "Polarization, Secularization, or Differences as Usual? The Denominational Cleavage in U.S. Social Attitudes since the 1970s." *Sociological Quarterly*, no. 46 (2005): 47–79.

"The Bookshelf: Eugenics and Marriage." Review of *Incompatibility in Marriage*, by Felix Adler; *What Is Eugenics?*, by Major Leonard Darwin; *The Christian and Birth Control*, by Edward Lyttelton. *Congregationalist and Herald of Gospel Liberty* 115, no. 38 (1930): 389.

Booth-Clibborn, William E. "The Pulse of a Dying World: Birth Control to the Rescue!" *Latter Rain Evangel* 22, no. 9 (1930): 17.

———. "The Pulse of a Dying World: New Birth Control." *Latter Rain Evangel* 26, no. 1 (1934): 13.

———. "The Pulse of a Dying World: Sterilization or Regeneration." *Latter Rain Evangel* 25, no. 12 (1933): 12.

Bokser, Ben Zion. "Statement on Birth Control." *Proceedings of the Committee on Jewish Law and the Standards of the Conservative Movement, 1927-1970*, edited by David Golinkin, 1451-1457. Jerusalem: Rabbinical Assembly and Institute of Applied Halakhah, 1960.

Bose, Christine E. *Women in 1900: Gateway to the Political Economy of the 20th Century*. Philadelphia: Temple University Press, 2001.

Boyer, Claire S. "Sustaining the Glory of Motherhood." *Improvement Era* 32, no. 7 (1929): 575-578.

Brewer, Rose M. "Theorizing Race, Class and Gender: The New Scholarship of Black Feminist Intellectuals and Black Women's Labor." In *Theorizing Black Feminisms: The Visionary Pragmatism of Black Women*, edited by Stanlie M. James and Abena P.A. Busia, 13-30. New York: Routledge, 1993.

Brodkin, Karen. *How Jews Became White Folks and What That Says about Race in America*. New Brunswick, NJ: Rutgers University Press, 1998.

Brooks, Clem. "Religious Influence and the Politics of Family Decline Concern: Trends, Sources, and U.S. Political Behavior." *American Sociological Review* 67, no. 2 (2002): 191-211.

Bruinius, Harry. *Better for All the World: The Secret History of Forced Sterilization and America's Quest for Racial Purity*. New York: Alfred A. Knopf, 2006.

Burch, Guy Irving, Elmer Pendell, and Walter B. Pitkin. *Human Breeding and Survival: Population Roads to Peace or War*. New York: Penguin, 1947.

Burkett, Phillip H. "Sociology: The New Criminal Science." *America* 32, no. 14 (1925): 334.

Burnham, F.W. "Unredeemed America." *World Call* 2, no. 5 (1920): 11-16.

Burstein, Abraham. "Race Prejudice." *Jewish Forum* 7, no. 12 (1924): 784-785.

Butchart, Mary B. "The Reinterpretation of the Immigrant." *World Call* 6, no. 5 (1924): 24.

Cabell, Kathleen. "Christian Examines Planned Parenthood." *Presbyterian Survey* 25, no 1 (1965): 15-17.

Cadge, Wendy. *Heartwood: The First Generation of Theravada Buddhism in America*. Chicago: University of Chicago Press, 2005.

Cadge, Wendy, and Elaine Howard Ecklund. "Immigration and Religion." *Annual Review of Sociology* 33 (2007): 359-379.

Cadge, Wendy, Laura R. Olson, and Christopher Wildeman. "How Denominational Resources Influence Debate about Homosexuality in Mainline Protestant Congregation." *Sociology of Religion* 69, no. 2 (2008): 187-207.

"Canada's Gain Is America's Loss." *Lutheran Church Herald* 8, no. 7 (1924): 197.

Canaday, Elizabeth. "New York City Mission and Cooperation in Immigrant Work." *Living Church* 72, no. 2 (1924): 49-50.

Cantril, Hadley. "Educational and Economic Composition of Religious Groups." *American Journal of Sociology* 48, no. 5 (1943): 574-579.

"Cardinal Will Not Oppose Amendment of Birth Control Law." *Liberty* 60, no. 1 (1965): 31.

Carter, Paul A. *The Decline and Revival of the Social Gospel*. Ithaca, NY: Cornell University Press, 1956.

Cartledge, Samuel J. "A Timeless Question." *Presbyterian Survey* 21, no. 9 (1931): 554.

Cater, Douglas G. "The Church and the 'Reliefers.'" *Christian Century* 82, no. 8 (1965): 232–235.

"Catholic Losses." *Christian Register* 110, no. 26 (1931): 514.

"A Catholic Woman's Opinion." *Birth Control Review* 13, no. 10 (1929): 300.

"Certain Areas Breed Crime." *Congregationalist and Herald of Gospel Liberty* 115, no. 8 (1930): 239.

Chalmers, Allan Knight. "It Is Not Enough." *Congregationalist and Herald of Gospel Liberty* 116, no. 29 (1931): 959.

Chambers, John Whiteclay II. *The Tyranny of Change: America in the Progressive Era, 1890–1920*. New Brunswick, NJ: Rutgers University Press, 1992.

Chang, Derek. *Citizens of a Christian Nation: Evangelical Missions and the Problem of Race in the Nineteenth Century*. Philadelphia: University of Pennsylvania Press, 2010.

Chaves, Mark. *Ordaining Women: Culture and Conflict in Religious Organizations*. Cambridge, MA: Harvard University Press, 1997.

Chen, Carolyn. "The Religious Varieties of Ethnic Presence: A Comparison between a Taiwanese Immigrant Buddhist Temple and an Evangelical Christian Church." *Sociology of Religion* 63 (2002): 215–238.

"Chicago Clergy Comment Favorably on Report of Lambeth Conference." *Living Church* 83, no. 17 (1930): 580.

"Christian Social Action: Report of the Committee: Future Program: The Family." *Acts and Proceedings of the Seventh Meeting of the General Synod of the Evangelical and Reformed Church* (1947): 252–256.

"A Christian View of Exclusion." *World Call* 6, no. 10 (1924): 65.

Chronbach, Abraham. "Social Studies at the Hebrew Union College." *Union Tidings* 10, no. 5 (1930): 3–4.

"The Church Cannot Be a Political Agency." *Lutheran Church Herald* 15, no. 12 (1931): 357–358.

Church of Jesus Christ of Latter-day Saints. "Birth Control." *Church Handbook of Instructions*. Salt Lake City: Church of Jesus Christ of Latter-day Saints, 1998, 158.

Clausen, Bernard C. "The First Fundamentalist." *Baptist* 5, no. 21 (1924): 496–498.

———. "The First Liberal." *Baptist* 5, no. 22 (1924): 521–522.

———. "Why Quarrel?" *Baptist* 5, no. 23 (1924): 546, 548–549.

Clinchy, Russell J. "Up from Patronage." *Congregationalist and Herald of Gospel Liberty* 115, no. 6 (1930): 170–171.

Coffman, Elesha. *The Christian Century and the Rise of the Protestant Mainline.* New York: Oxford University Press, 2013.

Collins, Patricia Hill. *Black Feminist Thought: Knowledge, Consciousness, and the Politics of Empowerment.* Boston: Unwin Hyman, 1990.

"A Compelling Home Missions Task." *Presbyterian Survey* 15, no. 6 (1925): 354.

"Concerning Infant Damnation." *Herald of Gospel Liberty* 116, no. 44 (1924): 1036.

"Concerning World Population Growth." *Yearbook and Directory of the Christian Church Disciples of Christ.* Indianapolis: General Office of the Christian Church Disciples of Christ, 1972, 167–168.

"Conference Discusses Wellesley Girls' Views." *Living Church* 91, no. 4 (1934): 72.

Cook, Howard J. "The Contribution of Science to Missionary Work." *Presbyterian Survey* 15, no. 8 (1925): 458–460.

Cooper, James F. "Birth Control and the New Morality." *Christian Register* 108, no. 27 (1929): 567–568.

"Coping with Illiteracy." *Living Church* 150, no. 14 (1965): 11.

"The Corporate Application of Christianity." *Methodist Quarterly Review* 74, no. 4 (1925): 719, 721–724.

Costales, V. "Letter from Pakistan." *Friends Journal* 11, no. 5 (1965): 107–108.

Cott, Nancy F. *The Grounding of Modern Feminism.* New Haven, CT: Yale University Press, 1987.

"The Council Findings and Resolutions." *Congregationalist and Herald of Gospel Liberty* 116, no. 31 (1931): 1031–1034.

County Shapefile—United States. 1930. National Historical Geographic Information System: Pre-Release Version 0.1. [MRDF]. Minneapolis: Minnesota Population Center at the University of Minnesota [distributor]. www.nhgis.org.

Crenshaw, Kimberle. "Mapping the Margins: Intersectionality, Identity Politics, and Violence against Women of Color." *Stanford Law Review* 43 (1991): 1241–1299.

"Criticizing the Federal Council." *Reformed Church Messenger* 104, no. 28 (1931): 3–4.

Crook, Margaret B. "A Hope for Birth Control." *Register-Leader* 147, no. 8 (1965): 16.

Crosby, John. "An Experiment in Colored Work." *Living Church* 86, no. 18 (1932): 567–568.

"Darwinian Law Given Unique Interpretation." *National Baptist Union Review* 37, no. 1 (1931): 2.

Davidson, James D., and Ralph E. Pyle. *Ranking Faiths: Religious Stratification in American Society.* Lanham: Rowman and Littlefield, 2011.

Davis, Angela Y. *Women, Race and Class.* New York: Vintage Books, 1981.

Davis, James J. "Old-Fashioned Religion." *Baptist* 5, no. 4 (1924): 81.

Davis, Nancy J., and Robert V. Robinson. "Are the Rumors of War Exaggerated? Religious Orthodoxy and Moral Progressivism in America." *American Journal of Sociology* 102, no. 3 (1996): 756–787.

Davis, Tom. *Sacred Work: Planned Parenthood and Its Clergy Alliances.* New Brunswick, NJ: Rutgers University Press, 2005.

Deer, Irvin E. "Consequences of Neglect of American Childhood." *Reformed Church Messenger* 94, no. 6 (1924): 10.

———. "Consequences of the Neglect of Childhood." *Herald of Gospel Liberty* 116, no. 3 (1924): 56–57.

Demarest, William T. "Interpretations." *Christian Intelligencer and Mission Field* 95, no. 23 (1924): 358.

Demerath, N. J. *Social Class in American Protestantism.* Chicago: Rand McNally, 1965.

De St. Denis, R. "Reformation or Short Cuts." *America* 32, no 1 (1924): 10.

DiMaggio, Paul J., John Evans, and Bethany Bryson. "Have American's Social Attitudes Become More Polarized?" *American Journal of Sociology* 102, no. 3 (1996): 690–755.

DiMaggio, Paul J., and Walter W. Powell. "The Iron Cage Revisited: Institutional Isomorphism and Collective Rationality in Organizational Fields." *American Sociological Review* 48, no. 2 (1983): 147–160.

Disciples of Christ. "Reports of the Church," 1972, 167–168.

"Distribution of Insane." *Golden Age* 1, no. 6 (1919): 56.

"Divorce and Birth Control." *Christian Index* 111, no. 19 (1931): 5.

"Dr. Fosdick Freed of Heresy Charge." *United Presbyterian* 82, no. 4 (1924): 8–9.

"Dr. Speer on Divisions among Christians." *Evangelical Herald* 23, no. 6 (1924): 81–82.

Edgell, Penny. *Religion and Family in a Changing Society.* Princeton, NJ: Princeton University Press, 2006.

"Editorials: Flag-Waving Patriots." *America* 32, no. 6 (1924): 135.

"Editorials: The Screen of Prejudice." *America* 32, no. 6 (1924): 135.

"Editorials: Victims of Persecution." *America* 32, no. 10 (1924): 231.

"Editorial: White Baptists." *National Baptist Union Review* 31, no. 23 (1926): 4.

"Editorial: Women at the Polls." *Congregationalist* 105, no. 44 (1920): 527–528.

"Educational Failure at Home." *Golden Age* 3, no. 69 (1922): 495.

Eleazar, Robert B. "Popular Fallacies about Race Relations." *World Call* 8, no. 7 (1926): 30–31.

Ellis, Rachel. "Marketing to Whom? Desired Members and Jewish Denominational Niches, 1913–1920." Paper presented at the Annual Meeting of the
Society for the Scientific Study of Religion, Phoenix, AZ, 2012.

Elmore, Carl H. "America's Back Yard." *Congregationalist and Herald of Gospel
Liberty* 116, no. 27 (1931): 894–895.

Emerson, Michael O., and Christian Smith. *Divided by Faith: Evangelical
Religion and the Problem of Race in America.* New York: Oxford University
Press, 2000.

Emko Company. "You Were Mentioned in a Discussion on Birth Control."
Presbyterian Survey 55, no. 1 (1965): 56–57.

"Encourage Medical Missions to Promote Family Planning." *Christian Advocate*
9, no. 13 (1965): 22.

Enders, Chas. "Is Catholicism Losing Ground in the United States?: I." *Evangelical Herald* 21, no. 8 (1922): 6, 8.

———. "Is Catholicism Losing Ground in the United States?: II." *Evangelical
Herald* 21, no. 9 (1922): 6, 8.

Erie, Steven P. *Rainbow's End: Irish-Americans and the Dilemmas of Urban
Machine Politics, 1840–1985.* Berkeley: University of California Press, 1988.

———. "Two Faces of Ethnic Power: Comparing the Irish & Black Experiences."
Polity 13, no. 2 (1980): 263.

Espiritu, Yen L. *Asian American Women and Men.* Walnut Creek, CA: Altamira
Press, 2000.

"Eugenics." *Journal of the General Convention of the Protestant Episcopal
Church in the United States of America,* 1934, 292.

Evans, Daniel. "The Conflict of Science and Ethics." *Christian Leader* 32, no. 2
(1929): 36–37.

Evans, John Henry. "The Heritage and Promise." *Improvement Era* 28, no. 2
(1924): 131–132.

Evans, John H. *Playing God? Human Genetic Engineering and the Rationali-
zation of Public Bioethical Debate.* Chicago: University of Chicago Press,
2002.

Evans, W.W. "Evolution and the Bible." *A.M.E. Zion Quarterly Review* 36, no. 2
(1925): 10–11.

Ewers, John R. "This Things of Prejudice." *World Call* 8, no. 7 (1926): 27–29.

"Expecting Too Much of Prohibition." *Lutheran* 1, no. 4. (1919): 71.

"Factors in Eminence." *Christian Register* 104, no. 3 (1925): 50–51.

"The Family a Divine and Holy Institution." *Lutheran Church Herald* 15, no. 15
(1931): 453.

Farmer, J.S. "Current Topics: Birth Control." *Biblical Recorder* 101, no. 26
(1935): 7, 11.

"The Federal Council Message on Evangelism." *United Presbyterian* 89
(1931): 6.

Finke, Roger, and Rodney Stark. *The Churching of America, 1776–2005: Winners and Losers in Our Religious Economy.* New Brunswick, NJ: Rutgers University Press, 1992.

Finn, Albert H. "Anent the Problems of the Great Cities." *Baptist* 5, no. 47 (1924): 1128.

Fiske, Ted. "Prospects for Peace Following Papal Visit." *Presbyterian Life* 18, no. 21 (1965): 22–23.

FitzGerald, David Scott, and David Cook-Martin. *Culling the Masses: The Democratic Origins of Racist Immigration Policy in the Americas.* Cambridge, MA: Harvard University Press, 2014.

Fletcher, Norman D. "Social Issues." Review of *What Is Eugenics?*, by Major Leonard Darwin. *Christian Leader* 33, no. 21 (1930): 663.

———. "The Suppression Which Results in Expression." *Christian Leader* 32, no. 22 (1929): 692.

"Folks, Facts and Opinion: Another Protestant Organization." *Baptist* 6, no. 20 (1925): 611.

"Folks, Facts and Opinion: Authorities of the Roman Catholic." *Baptist* 6, no. 7 (1925): 219.

"Folks, Facts and Opinion: Down in Kentucky." *Baptist* 10, no. 7 (1929): 214.

"Folks, Facts and Opinion: The Eugenics Society." *Baptist* 6, no. 24 (1925): 738.

"Folks, Facts and Opinion: The Following Story." *Baptist* 5, no. 7 (1924): 167.

"Folks, Facts and Opinion: The Jewish Attitude toward Birth Control." *Baptist* 12, no. 15 (1931): 475.

"Folks, Facts and Opinion: Louisiana Baptists." *Baptist* 6, no. 46 (1925): 1395.

"Folks, Facts and Opinion: Ministers' Homes Were Given." *Baptist* 11, no. 5 (1930): 183.

"Folks, Facts and Opinion: A Resolution Favoring Legalization." *Baptist* 10, no. 48 (1929): 1474.

"Folks, Facts and Opinion: A Severe Criticism." *Baptist* 5, no. 12 (1924): 286.

"The Foreigner." *Herald of Gospel Liberty* 116, no. 36 (1924): 844.

Franklin, Leo M. "Message of the President." *Yearbook of Central Conference of American Rabbis*, no. 31 (1921): 99–119.

Franks, Angela. *Margaret Sanger's Eugenic Legacy: The Control of Female Fertility.* Jefferson, NC: McFarland, 2005.

Freas, William. "Port Work for Immigrants." *Lutheran* 12, no. 36 (1930): 8.

Freeman, Fred W. "Statement Concerning Our Relation to the Federal Council of Churches of Christ in America." *Baptist* 10, no. 35 (1929): 1088.

Frisch, Ephraim. "Commission on Social Justice: Birth Control." *Yearbook of the Central Conference of American Rabbis*, no. 37 (1927): 144–146.

———. "Report of the Commission on Social Justice." *Yearbook of the Central Conference of American Rabbis*, no. 36 (1926): 102–109.

Furnas, Elizabeth A. W. "Report of Women's Problems Group." *Friend* 103, no. 48 (1930): 571.

Gassmann, Gunther. "Slavery." *Historical Dictionary of Lutheranism*. Lanham, MD: Scarecrow Press, 2001.

"Georgia Baptist Orphans Home Has Fine Dairy." *Christian Index* 104, no. 1 (1924): 9.

Ginzberg, Louis. "A Response to the Question Whether Unfermented Wine May Be Used in Jewish Ceremonies." *American Jewish Yearbook* 25 (1922): 400–425.

Glass, Bentley. "Geneticists Embattled: Their Stand against Rampant Eugenics and Racism in America during the 1920s and 1930s." *Proceedings of the American Philosophical Society* 130, no. 1 (1986): 130–155.

Gleiss, H. C. "Can Our Large Cities Be Reached by Present Evangelistic Methods?" *Baptist* 5, no. 3 (1924): 57.

Glenn, Evelyn N. *Unequal Freedom: How Race and Gender Shaped American Citizenship and Labor*. Cambridge, MA: Harvard University Press, 2002.

Golding, Louis. "Klintolerance." *Jewish Forum* 13, no. 3 (1930): 110.

Goldstein, Adam, and Heather A. Haveman. "Pulpit and Press Denominational Dynamics and the Growth of Religious Magazines in Antebellum America." *American Sociological Review* 78, no. 5 (2013): 797–827.

Gordon, Linda. *Woman's Body, Woman's Right: The History of Birth Control in America*. New York: Penguin, 1990.

Gordon, Robert A., and Franklin D. Elmer Jr. "The Northern Baptist Convention: Engirdling the Globe." *Baptist* 11, no. 24 (1930): 782–783.

Gordon, William. "The Nature and Method of Religion." *A.M.E. Zion Quarterly Review* 35, no. 3 (1924): 8.

"Gospel in Italian for One Cent." *Presbyterian Survey* 15, no. 5 (1925): 264.

Graebner, Theodore. "Birth Control—and a Fair Jesuit." *Lutheran Witness* 43, no. 11 (1924): 199.

———. "Birth-Control Bill before Congress." *Lutheran Witness* 53, no. 4 (1934): 60.

———. "Birth Control." *Lutheran Witness* 50, no. 7 (1931): 120.

Grammer, Carl E. "The Lambeth Conference and Church Unity." *Presbyterian Magazine* 36, no. 11 (1930): 645–646, 658.

Granade, W. T. "Nibbles." Quoted in Dawson, J. M. "The Light That Grows." *Christian Index* 104, no. 2 (1924): 30.

Greeley, Andrew M. *The American Catholic: A Social Portrait*. New York: Basic Books, 1977.

Griffith, Ruth Marie. *Moral Combat: How Sex Divided American Christians and Fractured American Politics*. New York: Basic Books, 2017.

"Growing into Our Full Selves." *Christian Advocate* 79, no 31 (1931): 754.

"Guidance for the Common Man." *Baptist* 11, no. 48 (1930): 1467.

Guttmacher, A. "Church, State, and Babies." *Register-Leader* 147, no. 7 (1965): 3–4.

Hall, Prescott F. "Immigration Restriction and World Eugenics." *Journal of Heredity* 10 (March 1919): 125.

Haller, Mark H. *Eugenics: Hereditarian Attitudes in American Thought.* New Brunswick, NJ: Rutgers University Press, 1963.

Hammond, L. H. "Human Races and the Race of Man." *Methodist Quarterly Review* 73, no. 4 (1924): 624.

Hansen, Randall, and Desmond S. King. *Sterilized by the State: Eugenics, Race, and the Population Scare in Twentieth-Century North America.* Cambridge: Cambridge University Press, 2013.

Harkness, Georgia E. "The Stranger within Our Gates." *Presbyterian Survey* 15, no. 7 (1925): 390.

Harless, L. D. "The New Morality." *Gospel Advocate* 107, no. 46 (1965): 741–742.

Harper, Roland M. "Some Neglected Aspects of the Immigration Problem." *Eugenics* 2, no. 11 (1929): 22–30.

Harris, Mark W. "Abolition of Slavery." *Historical Dictionary of Unitarian Universalism.* Lanham, MD: Scarecrow Press, 2004.

Hart, D. G., ed. *Dictionary of the Presbyterian and Reformed Tradition in America.* Downers Grove, IL: InterVarsity Press, 1999.

"Haynes Calls Race Issue Economic." *Christian Century* 57, no. 11 (1940): 358.

Hein, David, and Gardiner H. Shattuck Jr. *The Episcopalians.* Westport, CT: Praeger, 2004.

Heller, James G. *Isaac M. Wise: His Life, Work and Thought.* New York: The Union of American Hebrew Congregations, 1965.

Herberg, Will. *Protestant, Catholic, Jew: An Essay in American Religious Sociology.* Chicago: University of Chicago Press, 1955.

Herbster, B. "The State of the Church." *United Church Herald* 8, no. 14 (1965): 7–9, 30.

"The Heredity Fiasco." *Lutheran.* 9, no. 33 (1927): 13.

"Heredity and Individual Responsibility." *United Presbyterian* 87, no. 25 (1929): 10.

Hering, Ambrose. "What about Illegitimate Parents." *Lutheran Church Herald* 15, no. 4 (1931): 104–105.

Herring, Hubert. "This Little Room of Ours: From the Adult Bible Class Magazine." *Christian Index* 104, no. 50 (1924): 20.

Hillerbrand, Hans J., ed. "Abolition of Slavery." *The Encyclopedia of Protestantism.* Vol 4. New York: Routledge, 2004.

Hinks, Peter, and John McKivigan. "Church of Jesus Christ of Latter-Day Saints and Antislavery." In *Encyclopedia of Antislavery and Abolition.* Vol. 1. Westport, CT: Greenwood Press.

———. "Congregationalists and Antislavery." In *Encyclopedia of Antislavery and Abolition.* Vol. 1. Westport, CT: Greenwood Press.

———. *Encyclopedia of Antislavery and Abolition.* Westport, CT: Greenwood Press, 2007.

———. "Methodists and Antislavery." In *Encyclopedia of Antislavery and Abolitionism.* Vol. 2. Westport, CT: Greenwood Press, 2007.

———. "Quakers and Antislavery." In *Encyclopedia of Antislavery and Abolition.* Vol. 2. Westport, CT: Greenwood Press, 2007.

———. "Unitarianism and Antislavery." In *Encyclopedia of Antislavery and Abolitionism.* Vol. 2. Westport, CT: Greenwood Press, 2007.

Hinman, George Warren. "'The Self-Cure of Race Prejudice': A Review of *Blind Spots.*" Review of *Blind Spots: Experiments in the Self-Cure of Race Prejudice,* by Henry Smith Leiper. *Congregationalist* 114, no. 35 (1929): 267.

Hoffmann, John P., and Alan S. Miller. "Social and Political Attitudes among Religious Groups: Convergence and Divergence over Time." *Journal for the Scientific Study of Religion* 36, no. 1 (1997): 52–70.

Holmes, Joseph. "Our Newspapers and Criminals." *Presbyterian Magazine* 36, no. 4 (1930): 220–222.

"Home and Family Life: Being the Report of a Joint Commission to General Convention." *Living Church* 74, no. 2 (1925): 55–56.

"Home Mission Board Departments: Foreigners, Indians, Negroes." *Christian Index* 105, no. 6 (1925): 17.

Hooks, Bell. *Ain't I a Woman: Black Women and Feminism.* Boston: South End Press, 1981.

———. *Feminist Theory: From Margin to Center.* Boston: South End Press, 1984.

Hopkins, C. Howard. *The Rise of the Social Gospel in American Protestantism, 1865–1915.* New Haven, CT: Yale University Press, 1967.

Hout, Michael, Andrew M. Greeley, and Melissa J. Wilde. "The Demographic Imperative in Religious Change." *American Journal of Sociology* 107, no. 2 (2001): 468–500.

Howard, R. E. "Sociology: Welfare and Birth Control." *America* 32, no. 23 (1930): 552–554.

Hoyt, Donald G. "The Genesis of the Social Gospel." *Christian Leader* 33, no. 12 (1930): 370.

Hoyt, Margaret. "Christian Americans." *Presbyterian Survey* 21, no. 9 (1931): 523.

Hulburt, D. W. "Foreign Missions in Milwaukee." *Baptist* 5, no. 17 (1924): 413.

Hunt, Harrison R. "Why Birth Control?" *Eugenics* 3, no. 4 (1930): 128–129.

Hunter, James Davison. *Culture Wars: The Struggle to Define America.* New York: Basic Books, 2001.

Hutchinson, William R. *The Modernist Impulse in American Protestantism.* Durham, NC: Duke University Press, 1992.

Hutchison, R. A. "The Fitness of the Anglo-Saxon." *United Presbyterian* 88, no. 3 (1930): 4.

———. "Why the Anglo-Saxon." *United Presbyterian* 88, no. 2 (1930): 4.

Ignatiev, Noel. *How the Irish Became White.* New York: Routledge, 2009.

"The Illusion of the Horizon." *Presbyterian Survey* 24, no. 6 (1934): 329.

"In Darkest Boston." *Congregationalist* 114, no. 22 (1929): 729.

"Individual Responsibility." *Presbyterian Magazine* 37, no. 10 (1931): 544–545.

"Industry Adrift." *Living Church* 85, no. 19 (1931): 611–612.

Inge, W. R. "Some Moral Aspects of Eugenics." *Birth Control Review* 10, no. 6 (1920): 9–10. Previously published in *Eugenics Review* 1 (April 1909).

"Instinct and Promiscuity." *Christian Register* 110, no. 4 (1931): 66.

"Is Birth Control Hostile to Race Culture?" *Evangelical Herald* 28, no. 35 (1929): 683.

"Is National Temperance a Cure for All Human Ills?" *Lutheran Witness* 38, no. 9 (1919): 137.

"Is Protestantism Middle Class?" *Congregationalist* 109, no. 3 (1925): 68.

Irvine, S. "Population Growth in the United States." *United Presbyterian* 113, no. 12 (1955): 8.

Israel, Edward L. "Report of the Commission of Social Justice." *Yearbook of the Central Conference of American Rabbis*, no. 39 (1929): 80–86.

Jacobson, Matthew Frye. *Whiteness of a Different Color: European Immigrants and the Alchemy of Race.* Cambridge, MA: Harvard University Press, 1998.

Jacobson, Moses P., Harry H. Mayer, G. Deutsch, William S. Freidman, Harry Weiss, and Isaac Rypins. *Yearbook of Central Conference of American Rabbis* 23 (1913): 120.

Jensen, C. C. A. "Home Missions a Real Problem." *Lutheran Church Herald* 14, no. 33 (1930): 1161–1162.

Johnson, J. K. "The Immigration Problem in the United States." *Herald of Gospel Liberty* 116, no. 49 (1924): 1159–1160.

Johnson, Roswell H. "Marriage and Birth Rates at Bryn Mawr." *Eugenics* 2, no. 9 (1929): 30.

"The Johnson Immigration Bill." *Lutheran Church Herald* 8, no. 15 (1924): 452–453.

Jones, Rufus M. "The Nursery of Spiritual Life." *Friends' Intelligencer* 82, no. 18 (1925): 344.

K., J. W. "Reviews: Christianity and the Race Problem." Review of *Christianity and the Race Problem*, by J. H. Oldham. *America* 32, no. 13 (1925): 306.

K. K. "Communications: Immigration and Prosperity." *America* 62, no.11 (1929): 268.

Kane, William T. "The Row over Evolution." *America* 32, no. 6 (1924): 125–126.

Kaplan, Mordecai M. "Why It Is Hard to Be a Jew." *S.A.J. Review* 8, no. 22 (1929): 4–12.

Kaulfuss, Harold P. "The Problem of the Underprivileged and Unadjusted Girl." *Living Church* 84, no. 11 (1931): 367–369.

Keeler, Floyd. "A New Anglo-Eastern Entente." *America* 32, no. 9 (1924): 199–200.

Keister, Lisa A. "Religion and Wealth: The Role of Religious Affiliation and Participation in Early Adult Asset Accumulation." *Social Forces* 82, no. 1 (2003): 175–207.

Kennedy, David M. *Birth Control in America: The Career of Margaret Sanger.* New Haven, CT: Yale University Press, 1970.

Kern, Robert. "The Proper Starting Point—Religion in the Home." *Reformed Church Messenger* 93, no. 22 (1924): 12–13.

Keyles, Daniel J. *In the Name of Eugenics: Genetics and the Uses of Heredity.* New York: Random House, 1995.

Kincheloe, Samuel C. "Changing Chicago: Will Unity Emerge from Chaos?" *Congregationalist and Herald of Gospel Liberty* 116, no. 45 (1931): 1479, 1507.

King, Deborah K. "Multiple Jeopardy, Multiple Consciousness: The Context of a Black Feminist Ideology." *Signs* 14, no. 1(1988): 42–72.

King, Miriam, and Steven Ruggles. "American Immigration, Fertility Differentials, and the Ideology of Race Suicide at the Turn of the Century." *Journal of Interdisciplinary History* 20, no. 3 (1990): 347–369.

Klaw, Spencer. *Without Sin: The Life and Death of the Oneida Community.* New York: Penguin, 1994.

Klein, Isaac. "Science and Some Ethical Issues—The Jewish View." *Conservative Judaism* 13, no. 4 (1959): 35–47.

Kline, Wendy. *Building a Better Race: Gender, Sexuality and Eugenics from the Turn of the Century to the Baby Boom.* Berkeley: University of California Press, 2001.

Kohler, Max J. "Discussion of Dr. David Philipson's Address on the Union and Kindred Organizations." *Annual Report of the Union of American Hebrew Congregations*, no. 41 (1915): 7722–7734.

Kurien, Prema. "Multiculturalism, Immigrant Religion, and Diasporic Nationalism: The Development of an American Hindusim." *Social Problems* 51, no. 3 (2004): 362–385.

"The Lambeth Conference." *United Presbyterian* 88, no. 38 (1930): 6.

"The Lambeth Resolutions." *Lutheran Church Herald* 15, no. 15 (1931): 451.

Landesman, Alter F. "Lessons We Can Learn from the Economic Crisis: Its Effects on the Spiritual Life of American Jewry." *Proceedings of the Rabbinical Assembly of the Jewish Theological Seminary of America*, no. 4 (1931): 192.

Larson, Edward J. *Sex, Race, and Science: Eugenics in the Deep South*. Baltimore: Johns Hopkins University Press, 1995.

Lasker, Arnold A. "The Rabbi and the Pre-marital Interview." *Conservative Judaism* 6, nos. 2–3 (1949): 30.

"Law of Birth Control." *Christian Register* 110, no. 30 (1931): 582.

Lehmann, Titus. "General Home Mission News: New Americans." *Evangelical Herald* 23, no. 29 (1924): 463.

———. "General Home Mission News: Will Immigrants Overthrow the Civilization of This Country?" *Evangelical Herald* 23, no. 3 (1924): 41.

Leiper, Henry Smith. "Finds Booze, Incipient Crime, and Primitive Religion." *Congregationalist* 114, no. 11 (1929): 336.

Leitch, A. "Take It from Here . . ." *United Presbyterian* 113, no. 45 (1955): 2.

Leon, Sharon M. "'Hopelessly Entangled in Nordic Pre-suppositions': Catholic Participation in the American Eugenics Society in the 1920s." *Journal of the History of Medicine and Allied Sciences* 59, no. 1 (2004): 3–49.

Lewis, Alfred Baker. "A More Adequate Social Gospel." *Christian Register* 112, no. 28 (1933): 455.

Lilien, Ernest. "Birth Control among Polish-American Women." *Birth Control Review* 13, no. 4 (1929): 103–104.

Lingle, Walter L. "Religious Liberty." *Christian Index* 104, no. 30 (1924): 30.

Lopez, Mario H. 2012. "Hijacking Immigration?" *Human Life Review* 38, no. 4 (2012): 49.

Lovett, W. P. "Detroit Baptist Doings." *Baptist* 10, no. 47 (1929): 1448.

Ludmerer, Kenneth M. *Genetics and American Society*. Baltimore: Johns Hopkins Press, 1972.

Lutheran Church–Missouri Synod, Commission on Theology and Church Relations, Social Concerns Committee. *Human Sexuality: A Theological Perspective*. St. Louis: Concordia, 1981, 19–20.

Lutz, Ronald. "The Jew at Our Door: Practical Ways of Solving a Difficult Religious Racial Problem." *Presbyterian Magazine* 30, no. 12 (1924): 596–597.

Maasen, Pierce. "More Children, Please!" *Church Herald*, January 1955, 10.

MacArthur, Kenneth C. "Eugenics and the Church: The Church and Courtin'." *Eugenics*, no. 7 (1930): 278.

———. "Eugenics and the Church." *Eugenics* 1, no. 3 (1928): 6–9.

Macht, David I. "Torah and Science Twenty-Seven Years Ago and Now." *Jewish Forum* 14, no. 10 (1931): 380.

Mahoney, James, and Dietrich Rueschemeyer. "Comparative Historical Analysis." In *Comparative Historical Analysis in the Social Sciences*, edited by James Mahoney and Dietrich Rueschemeyer, 3–38. Cambridge: Cambridge University Press, 2003.

"Make America Catholic." *Christian Register* 104, no. 12 (1925): 267.

Margaret Sanger Papers. Sophia Smith Collection. Smith College, Northampton, MA.

Margolis, Michele, F. *From Politics to the Pews: How Partisanship and the Political Environment Shape Religious Identity*. Chicago: University of Chicago Press, 2018.

Marion, Kitty. "What Catholics Say." Birth Control Review 13, no. 11 (1929): 333.

Marlin, H. H. "Emigration Exceeding Immigration in the United States." *United Presbyterian* 90, no. 35 (1932): 2.

———. "Health Tests before Marriage." *United Presbyterian* 89, no. 12 (1931): 3.

———. "Presbyterian Commission Approves Birth Control." *United Presbyterian* 89, no. 19 (1931): 2–3.

———. "Startling Increase in Negro Population." *United Presbyterian* 89, no. 34 (1931): 3.

Marquis, John. "National Missions and the World: The Tremendous New Problems of Our Day and What We Must Do to Meet Them." *Presbyterian Magazine* 31, no. 11 (1925): 542–544.

Marsden, George M. *Fundamentalism and American Culture*. 2nd ed. New York: Oxford University Press, 2006.

Marti, Gerardo. "Affinity, Identity, and Transcendence: The Experience of Religious Racial Integration in Diverse Congregations." *Journal for the Scientific Study of Religion* 48, no. 1 (2009): 53–68.

Martin, John Levi. "What Is Field Theory?" *American Journal of Sociology* 109, no. 1 (2003): 1–49.

Maxwell, Arthur S. "Is the White Domination of the World about to End?" *Signs of the Times* 54, no. 50 (1927): 5.

May, Henry. *Protestant Churches and Industrial America*. New York: Harper, 1949.

McAllister, F. B. "The Church Saw It First." *Baptist* 10, no. 3 (1929): 72–73.

McCall, Leslie. *Complex Inequality: Gender, Class, and Race in the New Economy*. New York: Routledge, 2001.

———. "The Complexity of Intersectionality." *Signs* 30, no. 3 (2005): 1771–1800.

McCammon, Holly J., and Karen E. Campbell. "Allies on the Road to Victory: Coalition Formation between the Suffragists and the Woman's Christian Temperance Union." *Mobilization* 7, no. 3 (2002): 231–251.

McConkey, Dale. "Whither Hunter's Culture War? Shifts in Evangelical Morality, 1988–1998." *Sociology of Religion* 62, no. 2 (2001): 149–174.

McCracken, Elizabeth. "The General Convention: Action the Last Two Days." *Living Church* 91, no. 23 (1934): 551–552.

McDowell, John. "Applied Christianity." *Presbyterian Magazine* 37, no. 6 (1931): 335–336.

McGuire, U. M. "The World in Transit: Would Scrape the Scum from the American Melting Pot." *Baptist* 6, no. 30 (1925): 895.

McRoberts, Omar M. *Streets of Glory: Church and Community in a Black Urban Neighborhood.* Chicago: University of Chicago Press, 2003.

Mehler, Barry Alan. *A History of the American Eugenics Society, 1921–1940.* PhD diss., University of Illinois at Urbana-Champaign, 1988.

Melton, J. Gordon. *Melton's Encyclopedia of American Religions.* 8th ed. Detroit: Gale Cengage Learning, 2009.

"A Message to the Churches of America." *Christian Advocate* 100, no. 1 (1925): 14.

Miller, Kenneth. "Among the Czech Farmers in Texas: The Making of Bohemian Immigrants into Good American Presbyterians." *Presbyterian Magazine* 30, no. 11 (1924): 549–551.

Miller, Robert S. "Religion and Eugenics: Does the Church Have Any Responsibility for Improving the Human Stock?" *Christian Register* 111, no. 37 (1932): 515–517.

"Minutes of the Universalist General Convention at Washington, DC." In *Universalist Yearbook for 1930.* Boston: Universalist General Convention, 1930.

"Modernism and Fundamentalism." *Lutheran Church Herald* 16, no. 33 (1932): 949.

Montagu, A. "Too Many People." *Register-Leader* 147, no. 5 (1965): 20.

Mooney, Margarita A. *Faith Makes Us Live: Surviving and Thriving in the Haitian Diaspora.* Berkeley: University of California Press, 2009.

Moore, Walter W. "Religion in the Home." *Presbyterian Survey* 24, no. 2 (1934): 70–73.

Moraga, Cherrie, and Gloria Anzaldua. *This Bridge Called My Back: Writings by Radical Women of Color.* Latham, NY: Kitchen Table: Women of Color Press, 1983.

"More than a Bad Dream." *Christian Century* 82, no. 27 (1965): 861.

Morgan, Walter Amos. "Facing the Down and Outs." *Congregationalist* 114, no. 41 (1929): 476–477.

Morse, Hermann. "The Question Mark in National Missions: One Measure and Limitation of Our Mission Work." *Presbyterian Magazine* 31, no. 3 (1925): 122–124.

"Mother's Day—a New Angle." *Evangelical Herald* 30, no. 19 (1931): 363–364.

Mullins, E. Y. "Christianity at the Cross Roads: A Clear Statement of the Present Status of the Debate between Evangelical Christianity and Its Opponents in the Light of Scientific Scholarship." *Christian Index* 104, no. 15 (1924): 7.

Murphy, Joseph P. "Communications: Slow Catholic Growth." *America* 32, no. 16 (1925): 373.

"National Prohibition." *Evangelical Herald* 18, no. 6 (1919): 1.

"National Prohibition a Reality." *Christian Index* 99, no 5 (1919): 3.

"A New Classification of Baptists." *Baptist* 6, no. 44 (1925): 1333–1334.

"News and Notes." *Eugenics* 2, no. 4 (1929): 34.

"The News in Review: Race Decadence." *Signs of the Times* 54, no. 22 (1927): 12.

Niebuhr, H. Richard. *The Social Sources of Denominationalism*. New York: World, 1929.

"No Longer Evolution's Pawns." *Christian Register* 109, no. 39 (1930): 758.

Northern Baptist Convention. *Annual of the Northern Baptist Convention, 1933, Containing the Proceedings of the Twenty-Sixth Meeting Held at Washington, D.C. May 23-28, 1933*. Philadelphia: American Baptist Publication Society, 1933.

Olgers, Bertha. "What the Reformed Church Is Doing to Bring the Spirit of Christ in Race Relations." *Presbyterian Survey* 15, no. 11 (1925): 668.

Omi, Michael, and Howard Winant. *Racial Formation in the United States: From the 1960s to the 1980s*. New York: Routledge, 1986.

"One Month of Prohibition." *Lutheran Church Herald* 3, no. 32 (1919): 498.

Osborn, F. "Population Problems and the American Eugenics Society." *Science* 119, no. 3098 (1954): 3a.

Oshatz, Molly. *Slavery and Sin: The Fight against Slavery and the Rise of Liberal Protestantism*. New York: Oxford University Press, 2012.

"The Other Side of the Immigration Question." *United Presbyterian* 83, no. 37 (1925): 4.

"Our Foreign Religious Groups." *Living Church* 71, no. 18 (1924): 555-556.

"Parents—Stop, Look and Listen!" *Reformed Church Messenger* 93, no. 11 (1924): 3-4.

Park, Jerry Z., and Samuel H. Reimer. "Revisiting the Social Sources of American Christianity 1972-1998." *Journal for the Scientific Study of Religion* 41, no. 4 (2002): 733-746.

Patten, Arthur Bardwell. "Eugenics Again." *Congregationalist* 114, no. 42 (1929): 511.

Patterson, Orlando. *Rituals of Blood: Consequences of Slavery in Two American Centuries*. New York: Basic Civitas, 1998.

Pattillo-McCoy, Mary. "Church Culture as a Strategy of Action in the Black Community." *American Sociological Review* 63, no. 6 (1998): 767-784.

Paxon, Frederic J. "Forecast of Business Conditions." *Christian Index* 104, no 13 (1924): 19.

Perry, Joseph S. "Be Fruitful and Multiply." *Improvement Era* 33, no. 10 (1930): 679.

Phillips, Paul T. *A Kingdom on Earth: Anglo-American Social Christianity, 1880-1940*. University Park: Pennsylvania State University Press, 1996.

Pickens, Donald K. *Eugenics and the Progressives*. Nashville: Vanderbilt University Press, 1969.

Pope, Liston. "Religion and the Class Structure." *Annals of the American Academy of Political and Social Science* 256 (March 1948): 84-91.

"The Population Problem." *Friends Journal* 11, no. 6 (1965): 141.

Porter, Henry Alford. "The Virgin Birth of Jesus." *Christian Index* 105, no. 19 (1925): 8.

"Prejudices." *Christian Register* 110, no. 30 (1931): 582.

"Presbyterian Birth Control Report." *Baptist* 12, no. 20 (1931): 634.

Presbyterian Church in the US General Assembly. *Minutes of the PCUS General Assembly*. Augusta, GA: Constitutionalist Job Office, 1934.

"Present Day Foes of Christianity." *Christian Intelligencer and Mission Field* 100, no. 34 (1929): 532.

"The Present 'Flare Up' of the Old Controversy . . ." *Evangelical Herald* 24, no. 31 (1925): 481.

"Private Rights and Rising Birth Rates." *Presbyterian Life* 18, no. 14 (1965): 29–31.

"Prizes for Sermons on Eugenics." *Eugenical News* 11 (1926): 48.

"Prize Winners in the Sermon Contest." *Eugenical News* X1 (March 1925): 48.

"Professor Skinner on Censorship." *Christian Leader* 32, no. 42 (1929): 1314, 1340.

"Promoting Family Planning." *Christian Century* 82, no. 32 (August 11, 1965): 980.

"Prosperity of the American People." *United Presbyterian* 82, no. 4 (1924): 8.

"Protestant Catholics." *United Presbyterian* 87, no. 31 (1929): 6–7.

"Protestantism Falling Behind through Unproductive Marriages." *Current Opinion* 5, no. 1 (1915): 40.

"Protests from Catholic Organizations." *Lutheran Church Herald* 15, no. 15 (1931): 453.

"Psychic Expert Finds Child Is 'Born Criminal.'" *Lutheran Church Herald* 14, no. 23 (1930): 888.

"The Puritan's Detractor." *Christian Advocate* 100, no. 39 (1925): 1155–1156.

"Put the Accent on Evangelism." *Reformed Church Messenger* 93, no. 1 (1924): 5.

Pyle, Ralph E. *Persistence and Change in the Protestant Establishment*. Westport, CT: Praeger, 1996.

Pyle, Ralph E., and James D. Davidson. "The Origins of Religious Stratification in Colonial America." *Journal for the Scientific Study of Religion* 42, no. 1 (2003): 57–76.

———. "Questions from Readers." *Watchtower*, December 1969, 766–767.

———. "Social Reproduction and Religious Stratification." In *Religion and Inequality*, edited by Darren Sherkat and Lisa Keister. Cambridge: Cambridge University Press, 2014.

Rafter, Nicole H. "Claims-Making and Socio-Cultural Context in the First U.S. Eugenics Campaign." *Social Problems* 39, no. 1 (1992): 17–34.

———. *Creating Born Criminals: Biological Theories of Crime and Eugenics*. Urbana: University of Illinois Press, 1997.

———. *White Trash: The Eugenic Family Studies, 1877–1919*. Boston: Northeastern University Press, 1998.

Ramsden, Edmund. "Carving Up Population Science: Eugenics, Demography and the Controversy over the 'Biological Law' of Population Growth." *Social Studies of Science* 32, nos. 5–6 (2002): 857–899.

———. "Social Demography and Eugenics in the Interwar United States." *Population and Development Review* 29, no. 4 (2003): 547–593.

Raynale, E. M. "Michigan State Convention." *Christian Leader* 34, no. 46 (1931): 1459.

Reed, James. *From Private Vice to Public Virtue: The Birth Control Movement and American Society since 1830.* New York: Basic Books, 1978.

"Regulating Marriage." *Herald of Gospel Liberty* 116, no. 19 (1924): 436.

Reilly, Phillip R. *The Surgical Solution: A History of Involuntary Sterilization in the United States.* Baltimore: Johns Hopkins University Press, 1991.

"Religion in the Home." *Reformed Church Messenger* 93, no. 22 (1924): 4.

"Religion in the News." *Church Herald*, January 1965, 3.

"The Report on Birth Control." *Baptist* 12, no. 14 (1931): 425.

"Report on the Joint Commission on a World Conference on Faith and Order." *Living Church* 73, no.1 (1925): 14–15.

"Resolutions by Federal Council of Churches." *Lutheran Church Herald* 15, no. 15 (1931): 451–452.

Rev. P. Olin Stockwell of Methodist Episcopal Church in Lamont, OK. "Methodist Sermon on Eugenics (Third Prize)." AES Papers. Box 20. Folder "Stockwell, F. Olin." American Philosophical Society (APS).

Rev. Rufus C. Baker to First Methodist Episcopal Church in Albuquerque, NM, 1926. "Methodist Sermon on Eugenics." AES Papers. Box 13. Folder "Baker, Rufus C. 1926." APS.

Roberts, Dorothy E. *Killing the Black Body.* New York: Pantheon, 1997.

Robinson, Caroline H. "Recent Statistics on Differential Birth Rates." *Eugenics* 3, no. 11 (1930): 413–418.

Robnett, Belinda. *How Long? How Long? African-American Women in the Struggle for Civil Rights.* New York: Oxford University Press, 1997.

Roehner, Henry C. "The United Lutheran Church and the Immigrant." *Lutheran* 9, no. 11 (1926): 19.

Roper, Myrtle H. "Items on Birth Control." *Golden Age* 4, no. 99 (1923): 629.

Rose, William Wallace. "Notes on a Papal Encyclical." *Christian Leader* 34, no. 6 (1931): 170–172.

Rosen, Christine. *Preaching Eugenics: Religious Leaders and the American Eugenics Movement.* New York: Oxford University Press, 2004.

Rosenthal, Andrew. "It's Not about Religious Freedom." *New York Times*, February 8, 2012.

Sanford, Elias B. *Federal Council of the Churches of Christ in America: Report of the First Meeting of the Federal Council, Philadelphia, 1908.* London: Forgotten Books, 2018.

Schaeffer, Charles. "The Christian Endeavor Topic: January 27. —How Can Christian Endeavor Help Our Church and Denomination?" *Reformed Church Messenger* 93, no. 3 (1924): 30–31.

Schneider, C. E. "Where Do We Stand." *Evangelical Herald* 24, no. 46 (1925): 741–743.

Schneider, Stanley D. "Question Box." *Lutheran Standard* 5, no. 12 (1965): 28.

Schuller, David. "God Is Calling Us to Take Part in a Revolution." *Lutheran Witness* 84, no. 9 (1965): 7–8.

Scotford, John. "Birth Control Seems to Be Working." *Congregationalist and Herald of Gospel Liberty* 116, no. 32 (1931): 1069.

"A Serious Danger." *Evangelical Herald* 23, no. 31 (1924): 497–498.

Seton, Bernard E. "Christian Ideals for Modern Marriage." *Review and Herald: Official Organ of the Seventh-Day Adventist Church* 146, no. 2 (1969): 2.

"Share Information about Family Planning, LCA Advises." *Lutheran* 3, no 22 (1965): 29.

Shaw, Robert W. "Milwaukee Baptists." *Baptist* 5, no. 15 (1924): 353.

Sherbon, Florence Brown. "The Preacher's Part." *Eugenics* 1, no. 3 (1928): 3–5.

"Should Women Be Included." *National Baptist Union Review* 9, no. 10 (1919): 3.

Sieck, Louis J. "Attitude Lutherans Should Take towards Women's Suffrage." *Lutheran Witness* 38, no. 12 (1919): 162.

"Simple Justice." *Living Church* 150, no. 10 (1965): 7.

"Sixth World Order Study Conference." *A.M.E. Zion Quarterly Review* 77, no. 4 (1965): 241–247.

Skiff, Thelma. "Fecundity of Mothers in Dependent Families in Relation to Their Ages and Birthplaces." *Eugenics* 3, no. 8 (1930): 305–310.

Skocpol, Theda. "Doubly Engaged Social Science." In *Comparative Historical Analysis in the Social Sciences*, edited by James Mahoney and Dietrich Rueschemeyer, 407–428. Cambridge: Cambridge University Press, 2003.

Smith, A. Lapthorn. "Higher Education of Women and Race Suicide." *Popular Science Monthly*, March 1905, 466–473.

Smith, Christian, and Robert Faris. "Socioeconomic Inequality in the American Religious System: An Update and Assessment." *Journal for the Scientific Study of Religion* 44, no. 1 (2005): 95–104.

Smith, Eva Lewis. "Parent-Child Relationships." *Presbyterian Magazine* 37, no. 3 (1931): 165–166, 174.

———. "Parent-Child Relationships: Part II." *Presbyterian Magazine* 37, no. 4 (1931): 217–218, 223.

"The Social Gospel and the Community Church." *Christian Intelligencer and Mission Field* 95, no. 44 (1924): 689, 696.

"The Social Obligation of the Church." *Reformed Church Messenger* 94, no. 8 (1925): 4.

Sommer, Martin S. "Birth Control." *Lutheran Witness* 57, no. 18 (1935): 299.

------. "Blind Leaders." *Lutheran Witness* 52, no. 3 (1934): 37.

------. "Dr. Howard A. Kelly on Birth Control." *Lutheran Witness* 54, no. 7 (1935): 114.

------. "Federal Council under Fire." *Lutheran Witness* 50, no. 11 (1931): 185.

------. "Is the Lutheran Church a Foreign Church?" *Lutheran Witness* 43, no. 11 (1924): 197.

Southern Baptist Convention. *Annual of the Southern Baptist Convention.* Fort Worth, TX: Southern Baptist Convention, 1934.

------. "Resolution on Population Explosion." In *Annual of the Southern Baptist Convention.* Miami Beach, FL: Southern Baptist Convention, 1967.

"Southern Baptists Avoid the Federal Council of Churches." *Baptist* 10, no. 15 (1929): 471–472.

"Spanish Catholics Are Polled on Religious Freedom, Birth Control." *Liberty* 60, no. 4 (1965): 32.

Sparthey, S. S. "The Contribution of the Foreign-Born to the United States, by One of Them." *Presbyterian Survey* 15, no. 12 (1925): 715.

A Special Committee of the Women's Problems Group of Philadelphia Yearly Meeting of Friends. *A Statement on Birth Control.* Philadelphia: Philadelphia Yearly Meeting of the Religious Society of Friends, 1933.

Spinka, Matthew. "Race Prejudice and the Immigrant." *Reformed Church Messenger* 94, no. 38 (1925): 7–8.

Spitz, C. Thomas. "Motherhood." *Lutheran Witness* 42, no. 11 (1923): 161.

Spoolman, Jacob. "The Other Side of the Birth Control Question." *Congregationalist and Herald of Gospel Liberty* 117, no. 41 (1932): 1336–1337.

Spottswood, Stephen. "The State of the Church." *A.M.E. Zion Quarterly Review* 36, no. 3 (1925): 23.

Spurr, Frederic C. "The Old Faith and the New Knowledge: IV—the Relation between Religion and Science in General." *Baptist* 6, no. 27 (1925): 824–827.

Steadman, J. M. "Male and Female." *Methodist Quarterly Review* 78, no. 3 (1929): 450–457.

Steensland, Brian, Jerry Z. Park, Mark D. Regnerus, Lynn D. Robinson, W. Bradford Wilcox, and Robert D. Woodberry. "The Measure of American Religion: Toward Improving the State of the Art." *Social Forces* 79, no. 1 (2000): 291–318.

Steere, Douglas V. "Extracts from a Roman Journal." *Friends Journal* 11, no. 23 (1965): 585–586.

Stelzle, Charles. "The Challenge of the Modern City." *Presbyterian Magazine* 36, no. 5 (1930): 273–274.

Stern, Alexandra Minna. *Eugenic Nation: Faults and Frontiers of Better Breeding in Modern America.* Berkeley: University of California Press, 2005.

Stockdale, F. H. "The Lesson Exposition." *Christian Advocate* 106, no. 4 (1931): 122–123.

"Stop Alien Representation." *United Presbyterian* 90, no. 51 (1932): 6.

Strong, "America's Church Women Look South." *Presbyterian Survey* 32 (1965).

"Strong Protests by Minorities." *Lutheran Church Herald* 15, no. 15 (1931): 452.

Stub, H. A. "The City Church." *Lutheran Church Herald* 15, no. 2 (1931): 39.

Studens. "The Point of View: Mass Production." *Christian Intelligencer* 101, no. 27 (1930): 440.

———. "The Point of View: An Obfuscated Modern Rip Van Winkle. II." *Christian Intelligencer* 101, no. 4 (1930): 56.

"The Suffrage Victory." *National Baptist Union Review* 20, no. 34 (1919): 15.

Szasz, Ferenc Morton. *The Divided Mind of Protestant America: 1880–1930.* Tuscaloosa: University of Alabama Press, 1982.

Taylor, Alva W. "Why We Are Where We Are." *World Call* 11, no. 1 (1929): 27–28.

———. "Work of the Board of Temperance and Social Welfare." *World Call* 7, no. 7 (1925): 31–55.

Tentler, Leslie Woodcock. *Catholics and Contraception: An American History.* Ithaca, NY: Cornell University Press, 2004.

"They Were Desirable Because They Were Healthy and Strong . . ." *Lutheran Church Herald* 8, no. 23 (1924): 708.

"This Compact World." *World Call* 13, no. 10 (1931): 4.

Thompson, John Beauchamp. "Rural Arguments for Birth Control." *Congregationalist and Herald of Gospel Liberty* 117, no. 32 (1932): 1036–1037.

Thompson, Uldrick. "Mrs. Sanger and Birth Control in Our Country." *Christian Leader* 32, no. 17 (1929): 531–532.

Thorkelson, William L. "Biological Engineering." *Christian Century* 82, no. 6 (1965): 188–189.

Tobin, Kathleen A. *The American Religious Debate over Birth Control, 1907–1937.* Jefferson, NC: McFarland and Company, 2001.

Trager, Hannah. "The Jewish Women in Palestine." *Jewish Forum* 2, no. 11 (1919): 1300–1308.

"The Trend of Events: More Evidence That Low Wages Mean a High Death Rate." *Herald of Gospel Liberty* 116, no. 10 (1924): 221.

"The Trend of Events: Our Immigration Regulations Should Be Humane." *Herald of Gospel Liberty* 116, no. 5 (1924): 101–102.

"The Trend of Events: The Census." *Herald of Gospel Liberty* 121, no. 39 (1929): 744.

Treudley, Mary. B. "Scaling the Tower of Babel." *World Call* 3, no. 12 (1921): 8–11.

Underwood, Kenneth. *Protestant and Catholic: Religious and Social Interactions in an Industrial Community.* Boston: Beacon Press, 1957.

"The Unifying Fundamental." *Baptist* 6, no. 35 (1925): 1045.

"Unitarians Back Birth Control." *Christian Leader* 33, no. 22 (1930): 677.

United Church of Christ. "Health Equity and the Supreme Court Decision on Contraception." 2017. www.ucc.org/justice_health_health -equity_health-equity-and-the-supreme.

Universalist General Convention. *Universalist Yearbook for 1929*. Boston: Universalist General Convention, 1929.

US Bureau of the Census. *Census of Religious Bodies, 1916, Part I: Summary and General Tables*. Washington, DC: Government Printing Office, 1920.

———. *Census of Religious Bodies, 1926, Part I: Summary and Detailed Tables*. Washington, DC: Government Printing Office, 1930.

Van Cleave, B. "Letters to the Editor." *Advance* 147, no. 9 (1955): 26.

Vatican. "Visit to the United Nations: Speech to the United Nations Organization (October 4, 1965): Paul VI." Accessed July 03, 2019. http://w2.vatican .va/content/paul-vi/en/speeches/1965/documents/hf_p-vi_spe_19651004 _united-nations.html.

Vaughn, Joseph A. "California's Disgrace." *America* 74, no. 1 (1945): 8–9.

Vidich, Arthur J., and Joseph Bensman. *Small Town in Mass Society: Class, Power, and Religion in a Rural Community*. Princeton, NJ: Princeton University Press, 1958.

Vigness, L. A. "Educational Notes: Objects to Evolution." *Lutheran Church Herald* 8, no. 30 (1924): 934.

"Vision of Social Gospel." *Lutheran* 8, no. 4 (1925): 4.

Voss, Carl Hermann. "Where the Streams of Immigration Meet: How Our Churches Have Ministered to the Workers in the City of Steel." *Congregationalist and Herald of Gospel Liberty* 117, no. 44 (1932): 1419–1420.

Walsh, James J. "The Value of Later Children in Families." *America* 32, no. 1 (1924): 5–6.

Walton, Jeff. "Hobby Lobby Supreme Court Case: Kudos to Church Officials Defending Liberty." *Layman*, March 26, 2014. www.layman.org/hobby -lobby-supreme-court-case-kudos-church-officials-defending-liberty/.

Wang, Walter L. "What Does the Bible Say about Divorce?" *Lutheran Church Herald* 14, no. 2 (1930): 56–59.

Warner, R. Stephen, and Judith G. Wittner, eds. *Gatherings in Diaspora: Religious Communities and the New Immigration*. Philadelphia: Temple University Press, 1998.

Warnshuis, Paul. "Mexican Man-Power and Manhood: Mexican Mission Work in the Garden of the Southland." *Presbyterian Magazine* 30, no. 5 (1924): 220–222.

"The Watchman Answers." *Watchman* 40, no. 5 (1931): 27.

"Watch the Wets." *Baptist* 1, no. 13 (1920) 440–441.

Waters, Mary. *Ethnic Options: Choosing Identities in America*. Berkeley: University of California Press, 1990.

Watson, J. L. "Notes from St. Louis." *Baptist* 5, no. 10 (1924): 232.

"We and Our Children." *Reformed Church Messenger* 105, no. 4 (1931): 4.

Weber, Max. *The Protestant Ethic and the Spirit of Capitalism*. New translation and introduction by Stephen Kalberg. 1905; repr., New York: Routledge, 2001.

Welch, Herbert. "Some Considerations on the Immigration Question." *Christian Advocate* 100, no. 17 (1925): 527.

"A Well-Earned Victory." *Baptist* 1, no. 32 (1920): 1097.

Wells, J. M. "A New Fashion in Evangelism." *Baptist* 11, no. 14 (1930): 451–452.

West, Candace, and Zimmerman, Don H. "Doing Gender." *Gender and Society* 1, no. 2 (1987): 125–151.

"What Is Your Attitude toward the Foreigner?" *Christian Intelligence* 101, no. 15 (1930): 245.

"When Laws Prohibit." *Birth Control Review* 3, no. 1 (1919): 13.

White, Ronald C., and C. Howard Hopkins. *The Social Gospel: Religion and Reform in Changing America*. Philadelphia: Temple University Press, 1976.

"Whither Are We Drifting?" *Presbyterian Magazine* 37, no. 3 (1931): 257.

Whitney, Leon F. "The American Eugenics Society: A Survey of Its Work." *Eugenics* 3, no. 7 (1930): 252–258.

Wiggam, Albert Edward. "Progress and Prospects in the United States." *Birth Control Review* 2, no. 7 (1935): 5–6.

Wilbur, Ray Lyman. "The Intelligent Control of Our Human Stock." *Christian Register* 109, no. 50 (1930): 975–976.

Wilde, Melissa J. "Complex Religion: Interrogating Assumptions of Independence in the Study of Religion." *Sociology of Religion*, 2017, 1–12. Preprint, published in November 2017.

———. *Vatican II: A Sociological Analysis of Religious Change*. Princeton, NJ: Princeton University Press, 2007.

Wilde, Melissa J., and Hajer Al-Faham. 2018. "Believing in Women? Examining Early Views of Women among America's Most Progressive Religious Groups." *Religions* 9, no. 321 (2018): 1–19.

Wilde, Melissa J., and Lindsay Glassman. "How Complex Religion Can Improve Our Understanding of American Politics." *Annual Review of Sociology* 42, no. 1 (2016): 407–425.

Wilde, Melissa J., and Tessa Huttenlocher. "Who Were the Social Gospelers? Being Religious and Wealthy in the City on the Eve of the Depression." Paper presented at the annual meeting of the Association for the Sociology of Religion, New York, 2019.

Wilde, Melissa J., and Patricia Tevington. "Complex Religion: Toward a Better Understanding of the Ways in Which Religion Intersects with Inequality." In *Emerging Trends in the Social Sciences*, edited by Robert Scott and Marlis Buchmann, with Stephen Kosslyn. Hoboken, NJ: John Wiley and Sons, 2017, 1–13.

Wilde, Melissa J., Patricia Tevington, and Wensong Shen. "Religious Inequality in America." *Social Inclusion* 6, no. 2 (2018): 107–126.

Wilder, E. "Planned Parenthood in India." *Advance* 147, no. 7 (1955): 11–12.

"Will Spend $51,000,000 Studying Man." *Golden Age* 15, no. 384 (1934): 559.

Wilson, Frank E. "What Will We Do with It? The Episcopal Church and Non-Anglo-Saxon Elements in the United States." *Living Church* 88, no. 3 (1932): 71–75.

Winant, H. "Racism Today: Continuity and Change in the Post-civil Rights Era." *Ethnic and Racial Studies* 21, no. 4 (1998): 755–766.

Winn, Dick. "Birth Control; Pro or Con?" *Signs of the Times* 101, no. 1 (1974): 46.

Withoft, Mrs. Frank W. "W. M. S. and Y. W. A. Program for March." *Christian Index* 104, no. 6 (1924): 16–17.

"With the Hospital Family." *Christian Index* 104, no. 5 (1924): 28.

Wolf, Horace J. "Commission on Social Justice." *Yearbook of Central Conference of American Rabbis* 30 (1920): 87–90.

———. "Commission on Social Justice." *Yearbook of the Central Conference of American Rabbis* 32 (1922): 64–69.

"Woman's Best." *Christian Intelligencer* 90, no. 3 (1919): 51.

"Woman Suffrage to Date." *Baptist* 1, no. 8 (1920): 260.

"Women and the New Day." *Evangelical Herald* 18, no. 26 (1919): 1.

Wonderley, Anthony. *Oneida Utopia: A Community Searching for Human Happiness and Prosperity.* Ithaca, NY: Cornell University Press, 2017.

Wood, Rich. *Faith in Action: Religion, Race, and Democratic Organizing in America.* Chicago: University of Chicago Press, 2002.

Woodruff, Clinton Rogers. "A New American Policy Regarding Immigration." *Living Church* 71, no. 14 (1924): 465, 468.

———. "Social Programs: II. Man and Society." *Living Church* 84, no. 26 (1931): 906–908.

———. "The Social Trend." *Living Church* 70, no. 14 (1924): 467–468.

———. "What Is Prosperity?" *Living Church* 85, no. 12 (1931): 396–397.

Woolever, Harry Earl. "Is Congress Representative?" *Christian Advocate* 106, no. 35 (1931): 1062–1063.

———. "Parochial School Controversy Carried to Washington." *Christian Advocate* 100, no. 16 (1925): 496–497.

———. "President Hoover Checks Immigration." *Christian Advocate* 106, no. 19 (1931): 589–590.

———. "Prohibition, Crime and Criminals." *Christian Advocate* 100, no. 36 (1925): 1078.

Wuthnow, Robert. *The Restructuring of American Religion.* Princeton, NJ: Princeton University Press, 1998.

Yang, Fenggang, and Helen Rose Ebaugh. "Transformations in New Immigrant Religions and Their Global Implications." *American Sociological Review* 66, no. 2 (2001): 269–288.

Yarros, Rachele. "Objection Disproved by Clinical Findings." *Birth Control Review* 15, no. 1 (1931): 15–16.

Yearbook of the Central Conference of American Rabbis. Rochester, NY: Central Conference of American Rabbis, 1920.

Young, Michael. *Bearing Witness against Sin: The Evangelical Birth of the American Social Movement.* Chicago: University of Chicago Press, 2006.

Youngs, J. William T. *The Congregationalists.* Westport, CT: Greenwood Press, 1990.

Zorn, H. M. "Courtship and Marriage: Qualifications of a Future Helpmate." *Lutheran Witness* 43, no. 13 (1924): 226.

Zuberi, Tukufu. *Thicker than Blood: An Essay on How Racial Statistics Lie.* Minneapolis: University of Minnesota Press, 2001.

Index

Founded in 1893,
UNIVERSITY OF CALIFORNIA PRESS
publishes bold, progressive books and journals
on topics in the arts, humanities, social sciences,
and natural sciences—with a focus on social
justice issues—that inspire thought and action
among readers worldwide.

The UC PRESS FOUNDATION
raises funds to uphold the press's vital role
as an independent, nonprofit publisher, and
receives philanthropic support from a wide
range of individuals and institutions—and from
committed readers like you. To learn more, visit
ucpress.edu/supportus.